GROUNDBREAKING **FOOD GARDENS**

Groundbreaking
FOOD GARDENS

73 Plans That Will Change the Way You Grow Your Garden

 Niki Jabbour

Storey Publishing

The mission of Storey Publishing is to serve our customers by publishing practical information that encourages personal independence in harmony with the environment.

Edited by Sarah Guare and Carleen Madigan
Art direction by Cynthia N. McFarland
Book design by Alethea Morrison

Cover illustrations by © Anne Smith
Cover background texture by © wragg/iStockphoto.com
Author photo by Raylene Sampson

Interior illustrations by © Anne Smith, iii, iv, vii, viii, 1, 4, 17, 21, 29, 34, 37, 39 (bottom), 40, 47, 50, 53, 57, 62, 64, 74, 75, 79, 81, 82, 93, 97, 99, 103, 108, 109 (right), 110, 115, 120, 130, 138, 146, 151 (right), 158, 164, 168–169, 172, 175, 184, 186 (bottom), 197, 211, 213, 214, 217 (bottom), 218 (top), 220–221, 222, 225, 226, 233, 236, 238–239, 240, 244, 245, 264; © **Elayne Sears**, 15, 18, 22, 24 (top), 27, 32, 38, 41, 44, 51, 58, 65, 72–73, 91, 105, 111, 118, 128, 129, 135, 139, 140, 153, 157, 160, 180, 182–183, 189, 192, 194, 207 (top), 228–229, 242, 243; © **Mary Ellen Carsley**, 24 (bottom), 33, 35, 39 (top), 45, 55, 63, 78, 85, 87, 89, 95, 101, 109 (left), 113, 119, 121, 122, 125, 130–131, 137, 141, 143, 147, 149, 150, 151 (left), 159, 162–163, 165, 171, 173, 177, 179, 186–187, 195, 198, 199, 203, 207 (bottom), 209, 212, 215, 216, 217 (top), 218 (bottom), 223, 227, 231, 234
Illustrations edited by Ilona Sherratt

Indexed by Christine R. Lindemer, Boston Road Communications

© 2014 by Niki Jabbour

Storey Publishing
210 MASS MoCA Way
North Adams, MA 01247
www.storey.com

Printed in Canada by Transcontinental Printing
10 9 8 7 6 5 4 3 2 1

Library of Congress Cataloging-in-Publication Data on file

Storey Publishing is committed to making environmentally responsible manufacturing decisions. This book was printed on paper made from sustainably harvested fiber.

contents

As always, thank you to my cold-frame-building, manure-shoveling, kale-eating husband, Dany, who never asks why we need another garden bed.

And to Alex and Isabelle, who remind me to look closely at the garden to see the amazing world of butterflies, toads, hummingbirds, ladybugs, and, unfortunately, the occasional slug.

Acknowledgments

With a book like *Groundbreaking Food Gardens*, which includes 73 garden plans, it's obvious that this wasn't a solo effort. I would therefore like to extend a heartfelt thank you to each and every one of the 72 contributors who took time out of their busy schedules and lives to come up with an edible garden design for this book. I have been incredibly inspired by their passion for growing food and the innovative designs they created. I also appreciate their patience and willingness to answer my many (many!) pesky questions about their experiences and garden plans.

As always, I am very grateful to the fine folks at Storey Publishing for their hard work and continued support — art director Cynthia McFarland; creative director Alethea Morrison; illustration coordinator Ilona Sherratt; and artists Anne Smith, Elayne Sears, and Mary Ellen Carsley, who brought the gardens to life.

This book would not have happened if not for the vision and encouragement of editor extraordinaire Carleen Madigan. And Sarah Guare, my blue-ribbon editor, who took my piles of plans and descriptions and skillfully turned them into this book.

Finally, thank you to my mother, Joyce; parents-in-law, Kamal and Noha; sisters and brothers, Lisa and Jason, Jean-Louise and Nick, Leah, and Tony; and my nieces and nephews, Ryan and Lucy, Sophia and Mya, and Brayden and Jackson, who are always happy to play in the garden.

Introduction

There are many reasons to grow your own food, or at least a portion of it. Like many gardeners, I was hooked at an early age. Working beside my mother in the garden, I was enchanted by the simple act of planting a seed. In my young eyes, seeds seemed little more than lifeless kernels, but once tucked into the earth they quickly sprouted, and before long the harvest followed. When we picked our vegetables — typically just before we intended to eat them — they were packed with flavor and tasted nothing like the limp grocery store veggies we ate the other nine months of the year.

Today I grow much of my family's food, producing an organic bounty from our 2,000-square-foot garden. Over the years I've learned to stretch my harvest season to 365 days, which reduces our dependence on the "long-distance" vegetables found at our local supermarket. The ability to harvest from our winter cold frames and mini hoop tunnels from December through March — in Canada — is incredibly rewarding. Even if my children won't eat all of the vegetables and herbs (c'mon, Swiss chard is delicious!), they know where their food comes from and how it grows.

Because edible gardening is such a large part of my life, I am always looking for new techniques, designs, and ideas to grow more food. With this in mind, I dedicated 18 months of my life to tracking (stalking?) avid gardeners, garden writers, professional horticulturists, television and radio hosts, garden bloggers, managers of botanical gardens, university staff, and community gardeners across North America and the United Kingdom to find out how and why they grow their own food. The result of that research is this book, which spotlights the rapidly growing trend of food gardening, offering 73 plans for edibles that I hope will inspire you to think differently about where and how you can grow food.

Gardens by Theme

As you flip through this book, you'll find that the garden plans are all extremely varied in size, shape, style, and location. Some are even placed in the front yard, an area traditionally reserved for grass. In today's increasingly eco-conscious world, more and more gardens are sneaking from the back to the front yard. Although I don't expect *everyone* to dig up the entire front property to grow food (like Shawna Coronado), you may decide to incorporate food plants that are both beautiful and productive into your front garden beds (like Kenny Point). Who knows, you may even inspire the neighbors!

Those whose only garden space is a windy rooftop or a concrete balcony can produce a bumper crop of organic food using plans that focus on "difficult" sites, such as the ornamental edible balcony garden by Andrea Bellamy, the author of *Sugar Snaps and Strawberries* and the blogger behind the popular site *Heavy Petal*. Or perhaps you'll find inspiration from Jean Ann Van Krevelen, co-author of *Grocery Gardening* and the blogger at *Gardener to Farmer*. Jean Ann shows us how to jazz up a large deck or patio with delicious homegrown veggies, herbs, and fruits. Renee Shepherd

created her seed company, Renee's Garden, to provide gourmet, flavorful vegetables and herbs to home gardeners; here she has teamed up with Beth Benjamin to demonstrate how easy it is to grow good food in containers with their plan for a gourmet container garden. If a rooftop is the only sunny site you can find, check out the design by Colin McCrate and Hilary Dahl of the Seattle Urban Farm Company, which details growing techniques and edibles that do best in such an exposed site.

Common garden challenges like excess shade, tiny lots, or short seasons can quickly deflate a would-be gardener. Don't worry, we've got you covered. Marjorie Harris, author of 15 garden books, including *Thrifty Gardening* (her latest), tackles less-than-ideal light conditions in her

GARDENER VS. THE WILD

Gardeners living in deer, rabbit, or groundhog country may want to consider installing a fence around their food gardens. "Fencing a vegetable garden avoids so much heartache," says Master Gardener, author, and blogger Marie Iannotti. "You can't fault the animals for lusting after your tomatoes and cucumbers, but they don't like to share." She recommends an 8-foot-tall fence to exclude deer, while rabbits and groundhogs can be kept out with a 4-foot fence buried 18 inches below ground.

"Partially Shaded Vegetables" plan. Theresa Loe, co-executive producer of the PBS television show *Growing a Greener World*, carves out an urban homestead in her small Los Angeles lot. Steven Biggs, the author of *Grow Figs Where You Think You Can't*, has figured out how to enjoy bushels of Mediterranean figs in his Canadian backyard.

Those who aren't limited by space restrictions may wish for the traditional style of the formal kitchen garden designed by famed food and garden writer Ellen Ecker Ogden. Jennifer Bartley, founder and principal of the design firm American Potager, inspires us with her plan for an ornamental kitchen garden that is both bountiful and beautiful. Prolific food and garden writer and *New York Times* columnist Leslie Land shows us how to grow what we can't buy with her "Modern Truck Garden" plan.

Amanda Thomsen — the sassy author and blogger behind *Kiss My Aster* — is in a class by herself with her funky design for an authentic "Chicago Hot-Dog Garden." (Add ketchup at your own risk!) And while you're enjoying your hot dog, peruse the "Cocktail Garden" plan by Amy Stewart and Susan Morrison; their garden will help you explore the age-old connection between good food and drink. Or read what Stephen Westcott-Gratton, the senior horticultural editor of *Canadian Gardening* magazine, has to say about some of the unique vegetables of history with his "Elizabethan Garden."

Following the theme of unconventional gardens, take a peek at the plan by Ellen Zachos, author of *Backyard Foraging*, who shares the design of her own New York garden where she grows wild edibles.

Jessi Bloom, author of *Free-Range Chicken Gardens*, combines chickens and food plants in her plan for a chicken garden. Chickens also play a key role in the plan designed by Emma Cooper, a U.K. author, blogger, and Master Composter. Her "Circle of Life" plot is visually stunning but also incredibly practical, allowing plenty of space for vegetables, herbs, fruits, chickens, and waste recycling.

Several contributors designed edible gardens that not only produce food, but also encourage and support populations of bees, beneficial bugs, and other important pollinators. Jessica Walliser, the author of *Attracting Beneficial Bugs to Your Garden* and *Good Bug, Bad Bug*, shares her plan for a "good bug" garden, which includes a tempting mix of veggies, herbs, and flowers. Paul Zammit, the Nancy Eaton Director of Horticulture at the Toronto Botanical Garden, has designed a smaller pollinator-friendly edible raised bed, as well as a portable pollinator pot that will sustain pollinators wherever it is placed.

Many experts created edible gardens that also serve as landscape features. Debra Prinzing, author of *The 50 Mile Bouquet* and the recently released *Slow Flowers*, designed an edible cutting garden that will add much beauty to a backyard with her appealing — and delicious

— combination of herbs, vegetables, berries, and fruits. Charlie Nardozzi is the author of *Northeast Fruit & Vegetable Gardening* and host of *In the Garden* on WCAX Channel 3 in Vermont. He's a strong advocate of edible landscaping and has designed an edible hedge that is both productive and ornamental.

Children can — and should — be taught to grow food, and what better way to introduce them to a garden than by capturing their imagination as well as their taste buds? The "Garden Squares for Kids" design by Karen Liebreich and Jutta Wagner is a childhood delight that mixes fun and food in four charming mini-gardens. Lure children in with their favorite food — pizza! — by breaking ground on a pizza garden, inspired by the OTTO Pizza Garden at the New York Botanical Garden.

Smaller-scale plans make great weekend projects. Try Jayme Jenkins's "Hanging Gutters" or the "Pallet Garden" provided by Joe Lamp'l, host of *Growing a Greener World* on PBS. Even the edible edging described by Helen Yoest ("An Easy Way to Expand Your Existing Garden," page 200) can be installed in mere hours for years of juicy gourmet strawberries.

At the end of the day, if you get no more out of this book than the message that food can be grown anywhere — especially with some creative thinking — then I will feel that I've done my job. Of course, I also hope to reinforce the idea that edible plants can be just as beautiful, if not more so, than ornamental plants. Think dinosaur or 'Redbor' kale, purple cabbage, curly parsley, architectural leeks, and the many colors and textures of lettuce, for example. An unexpected consequence of writing this book is that I've begun to seriously rethink my own garden. I've started to sketch out a new plan, adapting elements from many of the designs in this book for my "new and improved" kitchen plot.

I am so grateful to the many contributors of this project, who have inspired me with their creativity and expertise. I hope you enjoy peeking into their gardens as much as I have.

HOW TO SELECT WHICH PLANTS TO GROW

As I talked to the many contributors of this book, I heard the same advice, time and again: "Grow what you like to eat." Many of the designers balked at the thought of suggesting individual varieties to accompany their garden plans because they wanted to encourage gardeners to experiment in their own plots, and to grow vegetables, herbs, and fruits that would do well in their individual regions. Therefore, don't feel tied down to the plant lists; rather, take them as they are — suggestions. One of the greatest pleasures of being a food gardener is exploring the diverse range of crops and varieties available through seed companies, so have fun trying a handful of new vegetables and herbs each season.

Need some more guidance? Avid blogger, gardener, and author Daniel Gasteiger provides these questions you can ask yourself to help narrow your search:

1. What do you like to eat that you can grow in your climate and space?

2. Of those foods, which taste most noticeably better when you grow them yourself?

3. Of those foods, which provide the highest value? (For example, at a farmers' market, beans are cheap and raspberries expensive.)

4. Will you preserve any of your homegrown produce, and if so, how much time do you have for preserving?

5. Most importantly: What will make you happiest, even if it doesn't rank among the other criteria?

GETTING THE MOST OUT OF YOUR GARDEN

All gardeners want to reap maximum yield from their plots, and cultivating healthy plants is the best way to ensure a bountiful harvest. For healthy plants, follow these steps:

1. Feed your soil. Healthy, high-producing plants grow in rich, organic soil. Feed your soil with compost, aged manure, and other soil amendments before planting and between successive crops.

2. Check the soil. If productivity declines, have a soil test done to see what is going on. A basic soil test will tell you the pH level (aim for 5.5 to 7.0) and the percentage of organic matter (5 percent is ideal). It will also tell you the levels of the three primary nutrients (nitrogen, phosphorous, and potassium), as well as what you need to add to your soil to bring these nutrients up to optimum amounts.

3. Try a cover crop. There is no easier and less expensive way to boost soil than by sowing a cover crop like buckwheat, winter rye, oats, or cowpeas. The folks at Growing Places Indy suggest adding a cover crop into your seasonal rotation so that one portion of the garden is always planted with a cover crop. "It is much better to cover crop or mulch soil through the winter than to leave it barren and open to erosion and weed growth," they advise.

4. Rotate those crops. By growing vegetables of the same family together (for example, tomatoes, potatoes, and peppers), and then moving them from bed to bed each year, you will reduce disease and pest issues. Plus, different crops use different nutrients. By rotating your vegetables, you can reduce nutrient deficiencies. For example, corn is a nitrogen pig and should be followed with a nitrogen-fixing, soil-enriching crop such as beans or peas to support soil health.

About the Contributors

Toby Adams (p. 225)
New York Botanical Garden
www.nybg.org
Toby is director of the Edible Academy at the New York Botanical Garden. An enthusiastic green thumb and vocal advocate of garden-based education, Toby has spoken nationally on behalf of the Ruth Rea Howell Family Garden's pioneering gardening programs.

Susan Appleget Hurst (p. 17)
Applehurst
www.applehurst.com
Susan is the owner of Applehurst, a store that brings the garden, the table, and the soul together in a historic 1903 jailhouse in Iowa. A former garden magazine editor at the Meredith Corporation, she has produced, written, and edited for *Better Homes and Gardens*, *Country Gardens*, and *Garden Shed*. Always on the hunt for beautiful yards and gardens, she continues to produce and write for garden magazines and local media. Susan has made many guest appearances on radio and television stations in the Midwest, including *Living the Country Life* on RFD-TV, and she is a popular speaker at consumer garden shows and symposia.

Karen Atkins (p. 127)
Proper Gardens
www.propergardens.com
Karen owns Proper Gardens, a firm that designs and installs period-inspired gardens. She designed the Victorian gardens at the Merrick Art Gallery (on the National Register of Historic Places) and the Pioneer Entrance Garden for Pittsburgh Botanic Garden. Karen also writes for *Historic Gardens Review* and other garden magazines.

Donna Balzer (p. 31)
http://gardenguru.net
Donna is an award-winning media personality, blogger, and author of three books. Her urban gardening television show *Bugs and Blooms*, formerly aired on HGTV, had a devoted following, and her seasonal CBC garden phone-in show is popular across Alberta. You can read her seasonally in the *Calgary Herald* and affiliated Postmedia Network newspapers. Her latest book, co-authored with Steven Biggs, is *No Nonsense Vegetable Gardening* (St. Lynn's Press).

Jennifer R. Bartley (p. 34)
www.americanpotager.com
Jennifer, RLA (Registered Landscape Architect) and ASLA (American Society of Landscape Architects), is the founder and principal designer of the design firm American Potager LLC in Granville, Ohio. Jennifer is the author of *Designing the New Kitchen Garden* and *The Kitchen Gardener's Handbook*, both published by Timber Press. She has written for *Fine Gardening* magazine, *Organic Gardening* magazine, and *Birds & Blooms* magazine. She frequently lectures around the country on seasonal, sustainable, and edible garden design.

Andrea Bellamy (p. 25)
Heavy Petal
www.heavypetal.ca
Andrea is the creator of *Heavy Petal*, a blog devoted to urban organic gardening, and the author of *Sugar Snaps and Strawberries* (Timber Press), a book about creating small edible gardens. She has a certificate in garden design from the University of British Columbia and studied permaculture methods for food production at an urban microfarm. She is the garden columnist for *Edible Vancouver* magazine and is an active guerrilla gardener in Vancouver, Canada. She has grown food on rooftops, balconies, boulevards, and patios, as well as in community garden beds, window boxes, traffic circles, and front and backyards.

Beth Benjamin (p. 178)
Renee's Garden
www.reneesgarden.com
Beth, who studied under renowned English gardener Alan Chadwick, founded and developed Camp Joy Gardens, a nonprofit education center and 5-acre demonstration garden in Boulder Creek, California. She is also the co-founder of Renee's Garden and works as the horticultural adviser to the company.

Vikram Bhatt (p. 232)
McGill University Minimum Cost Housing Group
www.mcgill.ca/mchg
Vikram is a professor of architecture and urban design at McGill University and director of the Minimum Cost Housing Group (MCHG) of the McGill School of Architecture. The Edible Campus was awarded the 2008 National Urban Design Award by the Royal Architectural Institute of Canada, Canadian Institute of Planners, and the Canadian Society of Landscape Architects.

Steven Biggs (p. 40)
www.stevenbiggs.com
www.noguffvegetablegardening.com
Grow Figs
www.grow-figs.com
Steven is a horticulturist and an award-winning journalist and author specializing in gardening, farming, and food production. He has gardened wherever he's lived, creating allotment, container, and indoor gardens as well as gardens

in the overgrown backyards of rental houses. He favors a practical, no-nonsense — and fun — approach to gardening. Steven runs a how-to website, and is the co-author of *No-Nonsense Vegetable Gardening* (St. Lynn's Press) and the author of the award-winning *Grow Figs Where You Think You Can't* (No Guff Press). Steven gardens in Toronto, Canada, with his three young children.

Carolyn Binder (p. 28)
Cowlick Cottage Farm
www.cowlickcottagefarm.com
Carolyn is a lifelong gardener and foodie with a sense of humor and a passion for sharing her life experiences. Her popular blog has been featured in *GRIT* magazine, P. Allen Smith's newsletter, and *GrowWrite!* magazine. She is a contributing editor of *Tallahassee Woman* magazine.

Jessi Bloom (p. 37)
N.W. Bloom
http://nwbloom.com
Jessi is an award-winning landscape designer whose work emphasizes ecological systems, sustainability, and self-sufficiency. She is also the author of *Free-Range Chicken Gardens* and *Practical Permaculture Design* (both by Timber Press). Jessi is a certified professional horticulturalist and certified arborist, as well as a longtime chicken owner with a free-ranging flock in her home garden. Owner of the multiple award-winning landscape design-build firm N.W. Bloom EcoLogical Landscapes, based in the Pacific Northwest, Jessi has been praised as an innovator in sustainable landscape design.

Karen Chapman (p. 43)
Le Jardinet
www.lejardinetdesigns.com
Karen was born in England and grew up with an appreciation for the beauty of nature and the wonders of gardening. In 2006, Karen established Le Jardinet, a custom container garden design service in the Seattle area, in order to share her enthusiasm, artistry, and knowledge with others. Her work has been published in *Fine Gardening* magazine, and she has appeared regularly on television and radio. Along with Christina Salwitz, Karen co-wrote *Fine Foliage: Elegant Plant Combinations for Garden and Container* (St. Lynn's Press).

Michelle Chapman (p. 214)
Veg Plotting
http://vegplotting.blogspot.ca
Michelle is a freelance writer and author of the popular UK gardening blog *Veg Plotting*. Her writing credits include pieces for the BBC and the *Guardian*. Her 52-week salad challenge is being followed and tweeted (via #saladchat) across nine countries, from Australia to the United States.

Nan K. Chase (p. 46)
Eat Your Yard!
http://eatyouryardbook.com
Nan has been gardening in the mountains of western North Carolina for 30 years, specializing in perennial ornamentals and native Appalachian trees, shrubs, and wildflowers. She wrote *Eat Your Yard! Edible Trees, Shrubs, Vines, Herbs, and Flowers for Your Landscape*, and co-wrote *Drink the Harvest*. She also writes extensively for newspapers and magazines, including the *New York Times*, the *Washington Post*, the *Christian Science Monitor*, and *Southern Living*. She has lectured extensively about edible landscaping in the urban setting.

Chicago Botanic Garden (p. 53)
www.chicagobotanic.org
The Chicago Botanic Garden was founded in 1962 when the Chicago Horticultural Society agreed to create and manage a new public garden. It opened a decade later with the mission of promoting the enjoyment, understanding, and conservation of plants and the natural world. Within the Chicago Botanic Garden, the Regenstein Fruit and Vegetable Garden is a living demonstration of the best ways to grow the most ornamental and delicious plants for the Chicago region. There are more than 400 types of edible plants, a selection that includes vegetables, herbs, nut trees, berries, and fruits.

Emma Cooper (p. 56)
http://emmacooper.org
Emma is an author, blogger, podcaster, and Master Composter in Oxfordshire, England. She has written three books: *The Alternative Kitchen Garden: An A–Z* (Permanent Publications), *The Allotment Pocket Bible* (Pocket Bibles), and *Growing Vegetables Is Fun!* (Dennis Publishing). Outside of the United Kingdom, she is best known for her free gardening podcast, "The Alternative Kitchen Garden Show."

Kate Copsey (p. 62)
www.katecopsey.com
America's Web Radio
www.americaswebradio.com
Kate is a Master Gardener as well as a popular garden writer and speaker. She has grown herbs commercially for 10 years. Kate is the host of *America's Home Grown Veggie Show*, a web radio program. She is a member of the Herb Society of America who has lived and gardened in many areas; currently she resides in New Jersey.

Shawna Coronado (p. 59)
www.shawnacoronado.com
Shawna is an author, on-camera spokes-person, professional writer, keynote speaker, and front-lawn vegetable gardener. She teaches about green lifestyle living, organic growing, and culinary arts, and she has dedicated her life to campaigning for social good. You can learn more about her and her gardening adventures on her website.

Mark Cullen (p. 208)
www.markcullen.com
Mark is one of Canada's most well-known gardeners. He reaches over 1 million Canadians every week through various media outlets. He is a best-selling author of 18 gardening titles, with more than 500,000 books in print.

He's also president of Mark's Choice Ltd, a horticultural communications and marketing company, and he's the national spokesperson for Home Hardware Canada and Premier Home and Garden. He is a recipient of the Queen Elizabeth II Diamond Jubilee Medal and volunteers extensively.

Hilary Dahl (p. 175)
Seattle Urban Farm Company
www.seatttleurbanfarmco.com
Hilary is a photographer with a background in design and landscape architecture. In 2007, Hilary received her BA in Community, Environment, and Planning (CEP) from the University of Washington. She is also the communications director and photographer for Seattle Urban Farm Company.

Dave DeWitt (p. 64)
Cross Country Nurseries
www.chileplants.com
Dave is a food historian and one of the foremost authorities in the world on chile peppers, spices, and spicy foods. He has authored more than 45 books, including *The Complete Chile Pepper Book* (Timber Press) and *Dishing Up New Mexico* (Storey Publishing). Dave is also the producer of the National Fiery Foods and Barbecue Show — the trade and consumer show for the multibillion-dollar fiery foods and barbecue industries, now in its 25th year.

Roger Doiron (p. 67)
Kitchen Gardeners International
http://kgi.org
Roger is founder and director of Kitchen Gardeners International (KGI), a Maine-based nonprofit network of more than 30,000 individuals from 100 countries who are taking a (dirty) hands-on approach to re-localizing the food supply. In addition to his kitchen garden advocacy work, Roger is a freelance writer and public speaker specializing in gardening and sustainable food systems. His successful proposal and petition campaign to replant a kitchen garden at the White House gathered more than 100,000 signatures and international media coverage.

Benjamin Eichorn (p. 219)
http://growyourlunch.com
Benjamin is an educator, farmer, and entrepreneur. He is also the founder of Grow Your Lunch, an organization that takes the edible school garden concept on the road to bring educational and high-yielding gardens to institutions such as schools, prisons, convalescent homes, and corporations. He worked for four years at the Edible Schoolyard in Berkeley, California, which was inspired by the philosophy and vision of chef Alice Waters of Chez Panisse Restaurant.

Colby Eierman (p. 77)
www.colbyeierman.com
Colby designs and manages diverse garden and farm projects, providing his clients with craft-grown produce of the highest quality. He has served as director of sustainable agriculture for Benziger Family Winery in Sonoma, California, and as director of gardens for the American Center for Wine, Food, and the Arts (COPIA) located in Napa, California. He is co-founder of the School Garden Project in Lane County, Oregon, and he has built many educational gardens for youth and adult audiences. He is the author of *Fruit Trees in Small Spaces* (Timber Press). For more information, please visit his website.

Sarah Elton (p. 80)
http://sarahelton.ca
Sarah is the bestselling author of *Locavore: From Farmers' Fields to Rooftop Gardens — How Canadians are Changing the Way We Eat* and *Consumed: Food for a Finite Planet* (both published by HarperCollins). She is also the food columnist for CBC Radio's *Here and Now* and writes for publications such as the *Globe and Mail* and *Maclean's*.

Jenks Farmer (p. 74)
www.jenksfarmer.com
Jenks is a plantsman and garden designer. He established and managed two major public gardens in South Carolina, including Riverbanks Botanical Garden, and he currently operates an organic bulb nursery. He has lectured for many organizations, including the Smithsonian, Wave Hill, and the Northwest Flower Show. Jenks writes for popular magazines. His book *Deep Rooted Wisdom: Skills and Stories from Generations of Gardeners* (Timber Press) tells stories of old-style gardeners and leads us to live more gently on the earth.

Daniel Gasteiger (p. 82)
Your Small Kitchen Garden
www.smallkitchengarden.net
Daniel is an avid blogger, gardener, and author of *Yes, You Can! And Freeze and Dry It, Too!* (Cool Springs Press). He and his family live on a third of an acre in rural Pennsylvania, where Daniel cultivates fruit trees, berry bushes, and dozens of types of vegetables in his kitchen garden. He's a self-proclaimed "obsessive canner," and he also preserves his food by freezing and dehydrating. Find him online at his website.

Marjorie Harris (p.49)
http://marjorieharris.com
Marjorie is the author of 15 books on gardening, including *Botanica North America: The Illustrated Guide to Our Native Plants* (Collins Reference). Her most recent book is *Thrifty Gardening: From the Ground Up* (House of Anansi Press). She also writes a garden column for the *Globe and Mail*, manages a website on which she occasionally blogs, and runs a garden design business in Toronto, Ontario.

Rhonda Massingham Hart (p. 130)
Rhonda is a Master Gardener and the author of *Vertical Vegetables & Fruit*, *The Dirt-Cheap Green Thumb*, *Deerproofing Your Yard & Garden*, *Squirrel Proofing Your Home & Garden* (all by Storey Publishing), and *North Coast Roses* (Sasquatch Books). She has written articles for a variety of magazines, including *Flower & Garden*, *Woman's Day*, and *Fine Gardening*. She has written extensively on organic gardening techniques and lives in Washington State.

Tammi Hartung (p. 96)

Desert Canyon Farm Green Thoughts Blog
http://desertcanyonfarm. wordpress.com

Tammi is an herbalist and organic grower with more than 31 years of experience. She and her husband, Chris, own Desert Canyon Farm in southern Colorado, a certified organic farm where they grow all types of herbs, heritage food plants, and perennial open-pollinated flower seeds. Tammi is the author of *Growing 101 Herbs That Heal* as well as *Homegrown Herbs* and *The Wildlife-Friendly Vegetable Gardener*, all by Storey Publishing. She lectures internationally and writes on her blog.

Mac Mead (p. 167)

The Pfeiffer Center
www.pfeiffercenter.org

Mac Mead is the director of the Pfeiffer Center. The mission of the Pfeiffer Center in Chestnut Ridge, New York, is to practice, teach, and spread awareness of the biodynamic method of agriculture and land care. Located at the site of the first biodynamic farm in North America, the Pfeiffer Center encompasses a variety of spaces that support teaching and research in biodynamic food production, adult education, children's programs, beekeeping, and draft horse work.

Laura Henderson (p. 86)

Growing Places Indy
www.growingplacesindy.org
Slow Food USA
www.slowfoodusa.org

Laura is the director of Growing Places Indy. She designed the Slow-Food Garden in collaboration with the 2012 summer apprentices: Megan Mirro, Muriel Page, Kafhii King, Marco Paliza-Carre, Tracy Cork, Kate Langdon, Sarah Robinson, Emma Engelhardt, and Ellen Mail. Growing Places Indy is a nonprofit organization of people committed to empowering individuals and communities to "grow well, eat well, live well, and be well." They cultivate this full-circle vision for sustainable health in communities through Slow-Food Gardens.

These programs provide food and education, as well as yoga and mindfulness-based training. The outreach programs cover a broad range of topics from gardening basics to sustainability, to how to make healthier food and life choices. For more information, please visit their website.

Marie Iannotti (p. 93)

Gardening, About.com
http://gardening.about.com
Practically Gardening
www.practicallygardening.com

Marie is a gardener who writes, photographs, and speaks irreverently about gardening. She is a Master Gardener emeritus as well as a former Cooperative Extension horticulture educator. Marie is currently the gardening expert for About.com and writes about the Hudson Valley and her own garden adventures at her blog *Practically Gardening*. Her first book, *The Beginner's Guide to Growing Heirloom Vegetables: The 100 Easiest-to-Grow, Tastiest Vegetables for Your Garden* allowed her to indulge in eating copious amounts of vegetables under the guise of research and led to her second book, *The Timber Press Guide To Vegetable Gardening in the Northeast* (both published by Timber Press).

Dan Jason (p. 90)

Salt Spring Seeds
www.saltspringseeds.com

Dan is dedicated to safe and sustainable agriculture. His company, Salt Spring Seeds, specializes in heritage and heirloom open-pollinated and non-GMO (genetically modified organism) seed varieties of dozens of edible plants, including a wide range of crops considered power foods. Dan is also the founder and head of the Seed and Plant Sanctuary for Canada and the author of many books, including the recent *Saving Seeds As If Our Lives Depended on It*.

Jayme Jenkins (p. 100)

Nest In Style
www.nestinstyle.com

Jayme is the former owner of aHa! Modern Living, an online store specializing in stylish, modern home décor and garden accessories. She co-authored the book *Garden Rules: The Snappy Synopsis for the Modern Gardener* (Cool Springs Press). Very active in social media, she has been a garden lifestyle blogger (*Nest In Style*) since December 2007, specializing in spreading excitement about gardening to new people.

LaManda Joy (p. 108)

www.theyarden.com
Peterson Garden Project
www.petersongarden.org

LaManda is the founder and president of the award-winning Peterson Garden Project. She is also a Master Gardener and square-foot gardening instructor whose vision and hard work have grown the Peterson Garden Project into an education and community garden organization dedicated to teaching the City of Chicago to grow their own food. For more information, please visit her website.

Wendy Kiang-Spray (p. 110)

Greenish Thumb
www.greenishthumb.net

Wendy is a freelance writer who is working on her first book about growing and cooking Chinese vegetables. She volunteers as a Master Gardener and works full-time as a school counselor. In her free time, she is always trying to figure out how to expand her backyard garden. Follow her family and garden blog for more information.

Rebecca Kneen (p. 222)

Crannóg Ales
www.crannogales.com

Rebecca has been farming since her first pair of rubber boots at age 3. She is currently a partner in Left Fields, a mixed organic farm and hopyard in Sorrento, British Columbia, as well as a brewer at Crannóg Ales with Brian MacIsaac. Crannóg Ales is Canada's first on-farm microbrewery, while Left Fields's hops manual has been the guide for the new hop farming industry in Canada. She is currently a director of the North

Okanagan Organic Association and serves as an executive of the Certified Organic Associations of British Columbia.

Joe Lamp'l (p. 191)

Growing a Greener World
www.growingagreenerworld.com
Joe is the host and executive producer of *Growing a Greener World* on PBS, former host of *Fresh from the Garden* on the DIY Network and *GardenSMART* on PBS. He is also the author of several books, including *The Green Gardener's Guide* and *Over the Fence* (both published by Cool Springs Press), as well as a contributor to many others. Joe is also a nationally syndicated columnist.

Leslie Land (p. 103)

In Kitchen and Garden
http://leslieland.com
Leslie spent more than 35 years writing garden articles, including 8 years of weekly garden columns in the *New York Times*. Her syndicated column, "Good Food," ran for 20 years in newspapers from Philadelphia to San Francisco. She co-authored *The 3,000 Mile Garden* (Viking) and co-starred in the television series based on the book. She was also the garden editor and lead writer for *The New York Times 1000 Gardening Questions and Answers* (Workman).

Craig LeHoullier (p. 240)

From The Vine
http://nctomatoman.com
Craig is known as the North Carolina Tomato Man because of his intense love of heirloom tomatoes. He joined the Seed Saver's Exchange in the mid-1980s, serves at the SSE tomato adviser, and was instrumental in introducing 'Cherokee Purple', 'Lillian's Yellow Heirloom', and 'Anna Russian' tomatoes to the wider gardening world. He is driven to grow, see, taste, and share with others the treasures of these and hundreds of other tomato varieties. He is the author of *Epic Tomatoes* (Storey Publishing).

Karen Liebreich (p. 114)

www.karenliebreich.com
Karen Liebreich is a fiction and nonfiction writer who also runs an educational/horticultural charity in London. She is part of the steering committee of the Chelsea Fringe, a festival of flowers, gardens, and gardening that takes place across London. Karen is also the recipient of a Member of the Order of the British Empire medal from the Queen for Services to Horticulture and Education. She is the co-author of *The Family Kitchen Garden* (Timber Press).

Theresa Loe (p. 117)

Living Homegrown
http://livinghomegrown.com
Theresa is the co-executive producer and the on-air canning/homesteading expert for the national PBS gardening series *Growing A Greener World*. She writes and blogs for several online publications about living local, growing her own food, and canning. Her work has also appeared in numerous print media, including *Natural Home, Hobby Farm Home, Herb Companion, Fine Gardening,* and others.

Jeff Lowenfels (p. 120)

Anchorage Daily News
http://adn.com/jeff-lowenfels
Teaming with Microbes
http://teamingwithmicrobes.com
Jeff is the author of the new book *Teaming with Nutrients: The Organic Gardener's Guide to Optimizing Plant Nutrition* (reveals how plants eat and what to feed them), and the best-selling book *Teaming with Microbes: The Organic Gardener's Guide to the Soil Food Web* (both by Timber Press). He is also the longest-running gardening columnist in America; Jeff's columns have been appearing in the *Anchorage Daily News* every week since November 13, 1976. He hosts the radio call-in show *Garden Party* in Alaska and is an extremely popular and humorous keynote speaker, appearing at all sorts of venues. He is passionate about organics and is a leading voice against the use of chemicals.

Kathy Martin (p. 124)

Skippy's Vegetable Garden
http://skippysgarden.blogspot.ca
Kathy is the blogger behind the popular blog *Skippy's Vegetable Garden*, named one of the best gardening blogs by *Horticulture* magazine in 2011. She gardens near Boston, in Zone 6a, and spends her days as a biochemist.

Laura Mathews (p. 138)

Punk Rock Gardens
http://punkrockgardens.com
Laura is a garden writer and photographer. She writes for gardening websites, publications, and blogs. Her interests are local food, organic gardening, backyard homesteading, and native plants. She assists gardening-related clients with social media, and, occasionally, she'll offer a solicited opinion as a garden coach.

Rachel Mathews (p. 134)

Successful Garden Design
www.successfulgardendesign.com
www.youtube.com/user/Successfulgardens
Rachel is an international garden designer and best-selling author. She has developed a technique that simplifies the design process, which she teaches in online garden design courses at her Successful Garden Design website. Rachel passionately believes the average garden can and should be so much more than average. She has written numerous landscape design books as part of a series called How to Plan Your Garden, available for Kindle on Amazon. Rachel also hosts a fortnightly garden design show which can be viewed as a video podcast on iTunes and also on her YouTube channel.

Colin McCrate (p. 175)

Seattle Urban Farm Company
www.seattleurbanfarmco.com
Colin is the founder and co-owner of Seattle Urban Farm Company. He has 12 years of experience working in sustainable agriculture, and his past projects include the design and construction of educational and residential gardens,

management of a 5-acre diversified vegetable farm, development of garden-based environmental education curriculum, and small-farm and garden consultation. His new book *Food Grown Right, In Your Backyard* (Mountaineers Books) is a step-by-step guide to small-scale food production for the beginning food gardener.

Chris McLaughlin (p. 142)

A Suburban Farmer
www.asuburbanfarmer.com
Vegetable Gardener
www.vegetablegardener.com
Chris is the author of six gardening books, including *Vertical Vegetable Gardening* (Alpha Books) and *A Garden to Dye For* (St.Lynn's Press). She's a staff columnist for the online gardening site Vegetable Gardener and is currently launching the Mother Lode Seed Library in Placerville, California. Between breaths, Chris attempts to keep up with her own website and practices home agriculture in Northern California's gold country.

Susan Morrison (p. 181)

Creative Exteriors Landscape Design
www.celandscapedesign.com
Susan Morrison is a Northern California landscape designer, Master Gardener, and the co-author of *Garden Up! Smart Vertical Gardening for Small and Large Spaces* (Cool Springs Press). Her designs have been featured in various publications, including the *San Francisco Chronicle, Cottages & Bungalows,* and *Fine Gardening,* where she also contributes articles on design and plant selection. Susan writes regularly on the topic of small-space garden design, and is the author of the garden app *Foolproof Plants for Small Gardens* (Sutro Media).

Charlie Nardozzi (p. 155)

www.gardeningwithcharlie.com
Charlie is a garden coach and consultant who enjoys teaching and inspiring home gardeners to grow the best vegetables, fruits, flowers, trees, and shrubs they can in their yards. He co-hosts *In the*

Garden on a local Vermont television station and hosts the *Vermont Garden Journal* on Vermont Public Radio. He writes for many national magazines and newspapers. He has written four books: *Urban Gardening for Dummies* (Wiley), *Vegetable Gardening for Dummies* (Wiley), *The Ultimate Gardener* (HCI), and *Northeast Fruit & Vegetable Gardening* (Cool Springs Press).

Dee Nash (p. 145)

Red Dirt Ramblings
http://reddirtramblings.com
Dee is a professional writer, speaker, and blogger from Oklahoma. Her blog *Red Dirt Ramblings* has won several awards, including Best Garden Blog in 2011 by *Horticulture* magazine and one of their Top Ten Favorite Garden Blogs in 2010. Dee is hooked on roses, daylilies, and many other heat-loving perennials that thrive in her Zone 7a garden. Recently, she installed a formal, four-square kitchen garden and greenhouse that have become the centerpiece of her property. Dee is the author of the *The 20–30 Something Garden Guide: A No-Fuss, Down and Dirty, Gardening 101 for Anyone Who Wants to Grow Stuff.* Dee contributes to many magazines, including *Oklahoma Gardener, Organic Gardening,* and *Fine Gardening,* and is a regular blogger for the Fiskars Corporation website.

Michael Nolan (p. 161)

The Garden Rockstar LLC
www.thegardenrockstar.com
Michael has been gardening for more than 30 years. He founded the Riverside Community Garden in Atlanta, Georgia, and has been featured in the *New York Times, Horticulture* magazine, and *Eye See* magazine, to name a few. He is co-author of *I Garden: Urban Style* (Betterway Books), founder and managing editor of *GrowWrite!* magazine, and currently serves as editor of The Home Depot Garden Club. His passionate and sometimes irreverent gardening style have earned him the nickname "The Garden Rockstar," a badge he wears proudly.

Annie Novak (p. 225)

Eagle Street Rooftop Farm
http://rooftopfarms.org
Annie is the manager of the Edible Academy. She is also the founder and director of the nonprofit food education program Growing Chefs, and cofounder and Head Farmer of the Eagle Street Rooftop Farm in Greenpoint, Brooklyn. Annie's work in agriculture has been widely published.

Teresa O'Connor (p.148)

Seasonal Wisdom
www.seasonalwisdom.com
Teresa is a national writer and speaker about gardening, food, and folklore. A trained Master Gardener in California and Idaho, she co-authored *Grocery Gardening* (Cool Springs Press) and her writing has been published in *Fine Gardening, Horticulture, Coastal Home,* and *Gardening How-To* magazines. Known to many as Seasonal Wisdom (the name of her popular blog, which television personality and tastemaker P. Allen Smith called one of "ten great garden blogs"), Teresa combines history with contemporary trends to deliver creative ideas for today's lifestyle via social media.

Ellen Ecker Ogden (p. 71)

www.ellenogden.com
Ellen is a Vermont food and garden writer, and the author of four books including *From the Cook's Garden* (Morrow Cookbooks) and *The Complete Kitchen Garden* (Stewart, Tabori & Chang), featuring themed kitchen garden designs with recipes to match, for cooks who love to garden. Her articles and designs have appeared in national magazines, and she lectures on the art of growing food to inspire gardeners with ideas for how to create beautiful kitchen gardens.

Doug Oster (p. 158)

www.dougoster.com
Doug Oster is the *Pittsburgh Post-Gazette's* Backyard Gardener and co-host of the popular radio show *The Organic Gardeners* on KDKA radio every Sunday morning. Oster also

appears every Thursday on KDKA-TV's *Pittsburgh Today Live*. Oster works as producer, writer, and on-air talent for WQED-TV. He hosted, produced, and wrote the one hour special *The Gardens of Pennsylvania* for PBS, which won the Emmy for Outstanding Documentary in 2009. His fifth book has just been released. *The Steel City Garden: Creating a One-of-a-Kind Garden in Black and Gold* demonstrates how to create a garden using Pittsburgh's favorite colors. Oster's most satisfying accomplishment, though, was founding Cultivating Success, a garden program for foster and adoptive children. The program operates in two counties near Pittsburgh.

Barbara Pleasant (p. 152)
www.barbarapleasant.com
Compost Gardening
www.compostgardening.com
Barbara is an award-winning garden writer who lives and gardens in Floyd, Virginia. She is the author of numerous books, including *The Complete Compost Gardening Guide* and *Starter Vegetable Gardens* (both by Storey Publishing). Barbara is a contributing garden editor for *Mother Earth News* magazine, for which she writes the top-rated "Garden Know How" column.

Kenny Point (p. 236)
Veggie Gardening Tips
www.veggiegardeningtips.com
Kenny shares his growing techniques and gardening adventures with like-minded gardeners on his popular website. He hails from Washington, D.C., but now lives outside Harrisburg, Pennsylvania, where he tends a large food garden.

Liz Primeau (p. 172)
Born to Garden
www.lizprimeau.com
Liz is the author of numerous books on gardening, including the best-selling *Front Yard Gardens* (Firefly Books) and *In Pursuit of Garlic* (Greystone Books). She is also the founding editor of *Canadian Gardening* magazine and

the former host of *Canadian Gardening Television* on HGTV. A speaker who is much in demand, she frequently gives talks at horticultural society meetings and garden shows across Canada and the United States. She lives in Mississauga, Ontario.

Debra Prinzing (p. 164)
www.debraprinzing.com
Slow Flowers
www.slowflowers.com
Debra is a Seattle-based outdoor-living expert who writes and lectures on gardens and home design. She is the leading advocate for a sustainable and local approach to floral design and is credited with creating the term 'slow flowers.' Debra recently launched the website Slow Flower, a free online directory of florists, shops, and studios who design with American-grown flowers. She is the author of seven books, including Garden Writers Association Gold Award winner *Stylish Sheds and Elegant Hideaways* (Clarkson-Potter/Random House), *Slow Flowers,* and *The 50 Mile Bouquet* (the last two by St. Lynn's Press).

Renee Shepherd (p. 178)
Renee's Garden
www.reneesgarden.com
Renee is widely regarded as a pioneering innovator in introducing international specialty vegetables and herbs to home gardeners and to diners at gourmet restaurants. In 1997 she founded Renee's Garden, which offers seeds of exciting new and time-tested heirloom gourmet vegetables, culinary herbs, and a wide range of fragrant and cutting flowers sourced from seed growers both large and small around the world.

Nan Sterman (p. 204)
Plant Soup, Inc.
www.plantsoup.com
A Growing Passion
www.agrowingpassion.com
Nan Sterman is an expert in low-water, climate-appropriate edible and ornamental plants and gardens. Nan's professional life is dedicated to the

transformation of planted landscapes from overly thirsty and resource-intensive to climate-appropriate and sustainable. Nan hosts and co-produces *A Growing Passion,* which airs on Public Television. She is the author of *California Gardener's Guide Volume II* and *Water-Wise Plants for the Southwest* (both by Cool Springs Press), as well as the upcoming *Hot Colors, Dry Garden* (Timber Press). Nan speaks and teaches about low-water gardening and leads international garden tours. She also writes award-winning articles for, among others, the *Los Angeles Times, U-T San Diego, Sunset* magazine, *Better Homes and Gardens,* and *Organic Gardening* magazine.

Amy Stewart (p. 181)
www.amystewart.com
Garden Rant
www.gardenrant.com
Amy is the author of seven books on the perils and pleasures of the natural world, including her latest volume, *The Drunken Botanist* (Algonquin Books). Previous titles include three *New York Times* best sellers: *Wicked Bugs, Wicked Plants,* and *Flower Confidential*, all published by Algonquin. She is also the recipient of a National Endowment for the Arts fellowship, the American Horticultural Society's Book Award, and a California Horticultural Society Writer's Award.

Rebecca Sweet (p. 228)
www.harmonyinthegarden.com
Gossip in the Garden
www.gossipinthegarden.com
Rebecca is a garden designer in Northern California and the owner of the design firm Harmony in the Garden. Her gardens have been featured in *Sunset, Fine Gardening, Horticulture, Woman's Day, Country Living*, and *American Gardener*, as well as on the critically acclaimed PBS series *Growing a Greener World*. Rebecca's latest book is *Refresh Your Garden Design with Color, Texture & Form* (F & W Media) and she is the co-author of the best-selling *Garden Up! Smart Vertical Gardening*

for Small and Large Spaces (Cool Springs Press). She also writes a column for *Horticulture* magazine.

Amanda Thomsen (p. 185)
Kiss My Aster!
  www.kissmyaster.co
Amanda is a Master Gardener, garden designer, and the zany writer behind the wildly popular blog *Kiss My Aster*. Her recent book *Kiss My Aster* (Storey Publishing) takes the fear out of home landscaping with many inspiring ideas in a unique graphic-novel format. She blogs for the website Proven Winners. Amanda lives in Chicago and does not *ever* put ketchup on hot dogs.

Patti Marie Travioli (p. 14)
My Urban Farmscape
  http://myurbanfarmscape.com
Patti is a freelance writer and photographer in Michigan who has always loved growing plants. She studied horticulture at Michigan State University and grew vegetables, fruits, herbs, and flowers at her USDA-certified organic farm. She blogs about organic gardening in small spaces and writes about growing veggies, fruits, and herbs for *Michigan Gardening* magazine.

Jean Ann Van Krevelen (p. 188)
Gardener to Farmer
  www.gardenertofarmer.net
Good Enough Gardening
  www.goodenoughgardening.com
Jean Ann is a (somewhat) lazy gardener, social media fanatic, and non-snooty foodie. She is the co-author of *Grocery Gardening* (Cool Springs Press). Her photography and writing have appeared in a variety of traditional and digital publications, including *Fine Gardening, Green Profit*, and the *Chicago Sun-Times*. She writes for her own blog and teams with Amanda Thomsen to produce the slightly off-kilter "Good Enough Gardening" podcasts.

Jutta Wagner (p. 114)
  www.juttawagner.eu
Jutta Wagner and Karen Liebreich worked together to create the Chiswick House Kitchen Garden, an innovative project maintained by local children; the project led to their book, *The Family Kitchen Garden* (Timber Press), which has been published in several languages. Jutta lives in Germany, where she works as a garden designer and garden writer.

Jessica Walliser (p. 194)
  www.jessicawalliser.com
Jessica co-hosts *The Organic Gardeners* on KDKA radio in Pittsburgh, is a weekly columnist for the *Pittsburgh Tribune-Review*, and a regular contributor to *Fine Gardening, Organic Gardening, Urban Farm, Popular Farming, Hobby Farms*, and *Hobby Farm Home* magazines. Jessica is also the author of *Good Bug, Bad Bug* (St. Lynn's Press) and *Attracting Beneficial Bugs to Your Garden* (Timber Press), and the co-author of *Grow Organic* (St. Lynn's Press).

Stephen Westcott-Gratton (p. 197)
Stephen is the former chief horticulturist at the Civic Garden Center of Toronto (now the Toronto Botanical Garden). For four years, he traveled to many of the world's great gardens as the host and creative consultant of *Flower Power* (HGTV). He is also the author of *Creating a Cottage Garden in North America* (Fulcrum Publishing) and *The Naturalized Garden* (Prentice Hall, Canada). Stephen is currently senior horticultural editor at *Canadian Gardening* magazine.

Ellen Zachos (p. 201)
Acme Plant Stuff
  www.acmeplant.com
Ellen is the proprietor of Acme Plant Stuff, a garden design, installation, and maintenance company in New York City. She's also a garden writer, photographer, and instructor at the New York Botanical Garden. She has authored five books, the most recent being *Backyard Foraging* (Storey Publishing). Ellen is a former Broadway performer. Her CD *Green Up Time* combines her two passions of gardening and music by taking a botanical look at Broadway.

Paul Zammit (p. 21)
  www.paulzammit.ca
Toronto Botanical Garden
  http://torontobotanicalgarden.ca
Paul is the Nancy Eaton Director of Horticulture at the Toronto Botanical Garden. Formerly, he was employed at Plant World, where he was in charge of the perennials for almost two decades. He is a regular speaker at garden clubs and horticultural trade shows across Canada and the United States, and he has appeared both on television and in print. In 2008, he won first place in the Scotts Miracle-Gro "Do Up the Doorstep" competition for his container entry at Canada Blooms.

THE GAR-DENS

Urban Farmscape

U rban farmscapers are gardeners who find ways to grow food productively in urban areas. Avid gardener Patti Marie Travioli doesn't have a large property, but she has managed to turn a sunny side yard into an urban farm that produces a steady supply of vegetables and herbs for her family 12 months of the year.

> An intensively planted, but compact garden for urban or small spaces

> The attractive design will work well in a side or front yard

> A wooden arch holds up vining crops and welcomes visitors to the garden

Patti Marie Travioli is an urban farmscaper, a phrase she coined to describe both her garden and her way of gardening. Her goal is to grow food in the city, in a productive and attractive way. "I can't think of anything more picturesque than an urban farmscape," she says. Her home garden is located in her side yard — the spot that receives the most sun.

Perfect for a small yard. Her plan for a summer-harvested 10- by 20-foot urban farmscape is ideal for a front, side, or backyard. Thanks to her plant suggestions, it packs plenty of production and curb appeal into a compact space. "This design will work very well in a small yard," she notes. "The key is that it has to have a southern exposure." Patti grows the crops in her own garden in raised beds framed with plain 2- by 12-foot pine boards, which are affordable and durable. "In my farmscape, I like to organize the garden, and I like the look of raised beds, which help me to keep plants where they need to be kept," she says. She also notes that her raised beds make it easy to extend the garden season with cold frames.

The perimeter bed is 2 feet wide, and the center beds are 3 feet wide. "There isn't much space for the 1½-foot-wide paths," she admits, "but it makes me feel as if I am walking between rows of edible delights!" An arbor marks the entrance to the plot; Patti suggests planting fast-growing annual hyacinth beans at the base so that by midsummer it will be smothered in pretty purple flowers followed by extremely ornamental burgundy-purple bean pods.

City plants. Patti's plant choices are well suited to a small space garden. "I have selected varieties based on my experience, or sizes that grow well in an urban setting," she says. "Tomatoes are one of my favorite vegetables, and I am becoming a master of pruning, caging, staking, and trellising." Her top cherry tomatoes are 'Gold Nugget' and 'Sungold' because of their earliness, incredible flavor, and brightly colored fruits. She also grows carrots year-round. "Once someone grows winter carrots, they will be amazed at how naturally sweet and delicious a carrot can be," she declares.

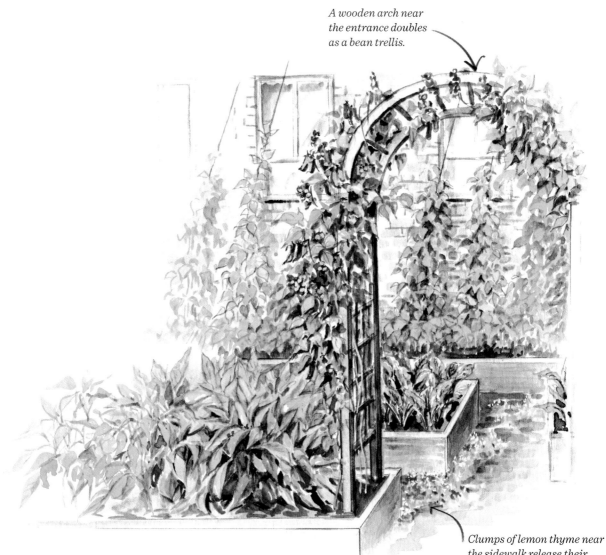

A wooden arch near the entrance doubles as a bean trellis.

Clumps of lemon thyme near the sidewalk release their perfume when trod upon.

Lemony edging. Like any avid cook, Patti appreciates a steady supply of homegrown herbs, used fresh during the growing season or dried for winter. Near her sidewalk she has even planted clumps of lemon thyme to release their sharp, fresh lemony fragrance each time someone treads on them. "Guests come over and ask: 'What do I smell? It smells so good!'" she laughs. And to attract beneficial insects, she interplants nasturtiums and calendulas (both have edible flowers), as well as cosmos, sweet alyssum, and 'Helen Mount' johnny jump ups.

To keep the harvest coming from early spring to late winter, Patti is a serious succession planter. "I start planting smaller quick-growing plants for fall once my summer crops are about to be harvested," she says.

"It takes a little practice, but once I got started, I began to look at the space in the garden differently." She also divides her year into three seasons — spring, summer, and fall — with a planting plan for each, so that she stays on track of what needs to be seeded and planted for a nonstop harvest.

Patti's Picks for City Gardens

VEGGIES

- **Beans:** 'Provider' bush and 'Fortex' pole
- **Peppers:** 'Ace' sweet and 'Early Jalapeño' hot
- **Cucumbers:** 'Diva'
- **Large tomatoes:** 'Big Beef', 'New Girl', 'Brandywine', and 'Amish Paste' (indeterminate; staked or trellised)
- **Cherry tomatoes:** 'Gold Nugget' (determinate; caged) or 'Sungold' cherry tomato (indeterminate; staked or trellised)
- **Spinach:** 'Tyee'
- **Radishes:** 'Cherriette'
- **Scallions:** 'Nebechan'
- **Eggplants:** 'Fairy Tale'
- **Swiss chard:** 'Bright Lights'
- **Beets:** 'Cylindra'
- **Cabbage:** 'Gonzales'
- **Carrots:** 'Caracas'
- **Broccoli:** 'Belstar'
- **Lettuce:** 'Allstar Gourmet' baby lettuce mix

HERBS

- **Sage:** 'Extracta'
- **Thyme:** 'German Winter' and lemon
- **Dill:** 'Fernleaf'
- **Oregano:** 'Greek'
- **Basil:** 'Genovese Compact, Improved'

Patti's Garden Plan

10' DEEP X 20' WIDE

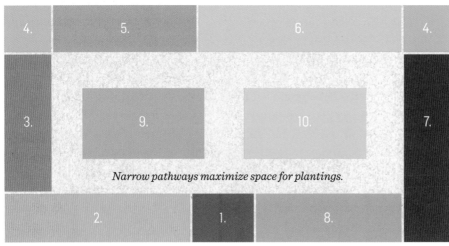

Narrow pathways maximize space for plantings.

1. Entryway arch with hyacinth beans
2. Sweet peppers and lemon thyme
3. Cucumbers, sage, thyme, and dill
4. Sunflowers
5. Bush and pole beans
6. Large and cherry tomatoes
7. Oregano, basil, and hot peppers
8. Spinach, lettuce, arugula, radishes, and scallions
9. Eggplants and Swiss chard
10. Beets, cabbage, carrots, and broccoli

Culinary Herbs for Beginners

I *s your food lacking flavor?* Consider growing some of your own culinary herbs, which can be enjoyed fresh from the garden or dried and frozen for winter use. And, as Susan notes, because most herbs are easy to grow they are also a great choice for those new to gardening.

> ❱ Versatile design is adaptable to sites of different sizes and shapes

> ❱ Features a gourmet selection of easy-to-grow, yet flavorful, herbs

> ❱ Allows you to flex your gardening skills by growing some of the herbs directly from seed

Susan Appleget Hurst has been an herb enthusiast for more than 20 years, but she recalls growing up in a household where the only herbs on her plate came from a jar. "It was a year in culinary school that introduced me to the flavor of fresh herbs," she admits. Her interest really took off when she realized she could have a thriving herb garden despite intense summer heat and pest pressure.

Choose the right spot. Susan defines herbs as useful plants, and culinary herbs are simply plants that are used primarily for seasoning food. Depending on the size and shape of the available site, Susan notes that the shape of the garden could be rectangular; bent or folded into a V- or U-shape; or split up into two or more smaller beds. Whatever shape garden you end up with, Susan emphasizes the importance of starting out with the right site. "Herbs are pretty tough plants, but they need full sun and good drainage," she advises. Some herbs, like spearmint, can tolerate less sun, but you can't get away with soggy soil.

At first glance, Susan admits that her plan might seem a little big for a beginner, though it includes some of the most commonly used herbs. "It also includes a few that are not so common, but should be!" she laughs.

Easy care. Once autumn arrives, most of the perennial herbs can be left in the ground to winter over and return the following spring. Tender herbs such as rosemary can be dug up and moved indoors to a sunny windowsill for winter seasoning.

In the waning days of autumn, many gardeners rush to clean up their plots in hopes of getting a jump on the following spring, but Susan recommends holding off. "The protection from the extra leaves and litter on top of the plants will help most perennials get through the winter better," she says. Plus, any seed heads left on the spent plants will provide a cold-weather snack for local birds.

Harvest before flowering. Once you've established an herb garden, it's time to learn how to cook with your garden-fresh bounty. Susan recommends harvesting herbs before they flower. "When a plant flowers, the flavor changes," she says. Often, herbs taste stronger after the plant has flowered; some become altogether unpalatable.

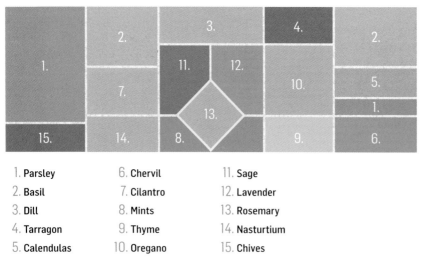

Most of the perennial herbs (like chives) can be left in the ground at the end of the season and will return the following spring.

Plant mint in pots so it won't overtake your garden.

Susan's Garden Plan

4' DEEP X 14' WIDE

1. Parsley
2. Basil
3. Dill
4. Tarragon
5. Calendulas
6. Chervil
7. Cilantro
8. Mints
9. Thyme
10. Oregano
11. Sage
12. Lavender
13. Rosemary
14. Nasturtium
15. Chives

Mix Tried and True with Brave and New

Susan encourages gardeners — even new gardeners — to be brave in their plant selection and not shy away from unfamiliar herbs. She suggests planting the following collection of herbs that offer a wide range of flavors.

ANNUALS

Basil. Start heat-loving basil indoors and move the seedlings to the garden once all risk of frost has passed. Even then, it'll sit and sulk until the hot weather begins. To keep a fresh supply going all summer long, put in new plants every few weeks.

Calendulas. This edible flower happily self-sows from year to year, and the young seedlings can be dug up and moved wherever you like. Sprinkle the bright yellow or orange petals into salads or over dinner plates for a hint of color (the leaves are also edible).

Chervil. Fresh chervil has a lot of flavor and tastes like a cross between parsley and anise. Try it in salads and in egg dishes.

Cilantro. Don't plant the entire seed package all at once. The plants bolt (go to seed) quickly, so you'll want to plant some every couple of weeks for a long season of harvest. Because it prefers cool weather, it'll do best in spring and autumn.

Dill. To get enough dill for both fresh eating and pickling, scratch a few seeds in the garden in spring for fresh leaves and sow again later to get the seeds for pickles.

Nasturtium. Heat-loving nasturtiums are very easy to grow and spill appealingly over garden beds and onto nearby footpaths. They also have edible seeds, flowers, and foliage. They're peppery, like radishes, and they're very striking with red, orange, yellow, and cream-colored blooms.

Parsley (biennial). Use curly parsley as a beautiful low border at the front of flower beds, because it stays bushy and green all season long. For culinary use however, flat-leaved (Italian) parsley is more robust in flavor. In addition to being easy to grow, parsley is also a host plant for swallowtail butterflies.

PERENNIALS

Chives (Zones 3 to 11). Most garden centers sell pots of chives, but because it's so common and prolific, consider getting a clump from a gardening friend or neighbor. Onion chives, those with tubular leaves and purple blossoms, seem to self-sow less aggressively than garlic chives (those with flat leaves and white blossoms).

Lavender (Zones 5 to 9). Neither gardeners nor bees can resist the fragrant purple flowers of lavender. Happy lavender plants need excellent drainage and full sun, but proper variety selection is also important. In colder climates, opt for 'Munstead' or 'Hidcote' English lavender, traditional and hardy varieties. Warm-climate gardeners can try French or Spanish lavender, both of which have silvery foliage and elongated purple bracts that are often compared to rabbit's ears.

Mints (Zones 3 to 11 depending on variety). Mints have a well-deserved reputation for being extremely invasive. Any plant with a square stem (the signature characteristic of the mint family) is likely to take over the garden. Keep an eye on it and don't put it in the ground; place it in a pot. To keep the plant healthy, repot it every few years, removing most of the rootball with a sharp knife and replanting just a quarter of the original plant.

HERBS FOR WINTER

During the summer, you can use fresh herbs for cooking and in teas, but you can also preserve some of the harvest for the cold season. "The only way to get good fresh flavor from preserved herbs is to freeze them," Susan says. To freeze, she adds 2 packed cups of clean, dry herbs to her food processor, pulsing lightly to chop. She then adds ¼ cup of oil and pulses a few more times to mix. She freezes the mixture in small containers or in freezer bags, flattening it into "herbal pancakes," so that you can easily break off a piece for winter soups, stews, and pastas.

Oregano (Zones 5 to 9). Common oregano is very hardy, but Greek oregano, which is the preferred type for culinary use, will only overwinter in Zones 5 and higher. In colder areas it may need to be replanted from year to year.

Rosemary (Zones 8 to 10). One of Susan's essential herbs, rosemary is a key ingredient in a well-stocked kitchen, where it is used to flavor potatoes, roast chicken, and homemade focaccia. It's very slow-growing, and you can save yourself time by picking up seedlings from your local garden center. To thrive, rosemary needs sun, plenty of air circulation, and good drainage. Clay soil gardeners beware — if planted in poorly drained soil, rosemary will sulk. Instead, consider planting it in a pot or window box.

Sage (Zones 5 to 9). Variegated and golden sages may be beautiful in pots and in the garden but aren't the best choice for your plate because they don't have a lot of flavor. Garden sage, also known as common sage, is the top pick for culinary use.

Tarragon (Zones 5 to 9). Look for plants at your local garden center. Culinary tarragon (sometimes called French tarragon) can only be grown from cuttings or division. Don't plant seeds, as they will be Russian tarragon, a less desirable species that is neither flavorful nor attractive.

Thyme (Zones 5 to 9). As a woody perennial herb, thyme is very slow-growing from seed, so for instant results pick up seedlings from your local garden center. The plants are extremely aromatic and compact, typically growing 6 to 10 inches tall, depending on the variety. Common (English) thyme is traditionally used for cooking, but don't be afraid to experiment and try different types like lemon thyme, which has a wonderful citrus fragrance!

START HERBS FROM SEEDS!

Herb lovers can flex their gardening skills by starting annual herbs — basil, calendulas, dill, cilantro, and nasturtiums — from seed. Perennials like sage, thyme, and oregano grow more slowly, and novice gardeners may wish to purchase plants from a local garden center.

To start herbs from seed, simply follow these steps.

1. Plant fresh seed at the right time. Read your seed packets carefully to learn how many weeks of growth your plants will need before they can be moved outdoors.

2. Fill clean containers with a high-quality potting soil. Pre-moisten the soil and loosely fill containers with the potting mix.

3. Provide ample light. Use a sunny window or grow-lights, left on for about 16 hours per day (use a timer to turn lights on and off). If using grow-lights, adjust the height of the fixture as the plants grow, so that the lightbulbs are always about 3 inches above the foliage.

4. Sow and cover the seeds. Sow your seeds at the proper depth (check seed packet for instructions) and cover with a plastic dome or plastic wrap. Don't forget to label each pot or flat. Remove covers as soon as seeds germinate.

5. Provide good air circulation. Keep a small fan near the seed starting area to keep air moving and reduce problems like damping off, a common fungal disease.

6. Harden off seedlings. About a week before transplanting, gradually acclimate your seedlings to outdoor conditions. Begin by putting them outside for a few hours on a warm day in a shady spot. Bring them indoors again at night. Over the next few days, gradually increase the amount of sunlight and time they spend outdoors. By the end of the week, they should be ready to be transplanted to the garden.

Pollinator-Friendly
Raised Bed

Paul Zammit knows the value of bees, butterflies, and other pollinators. He often chooses his garden plants — including edibles — based on the benefits they offer to pollinators. His design for a pollinator-friendly raised bed takes the guesswork out of planning for pollinators by including food for you *and* food for them. Gardeners will appreciate the pole beans and cherry tomatoes, while the bees and butterflies will gravitate toward the nasturtiums, borage, and catmint.

❯ Using little space, provides homegrown food for you *and* the pollinators

❯ Supports bees, butterflies, and beneficial insects

❯ Uses vertical structures to grow more in less space

❯ Includes a bonus design for a pollinator-friendly container for decks and patios

For a successful edible garden, Paul Zammit suggests you partner with pollinators by choosing pollinator-friendly plants, or by filling a container with some of his suggested plants and placing it near your garden. "These plants offer many benefits to an urban gardener, as well as the local insect populations," he says. "Plus, they are aesthetically pleasing, edible, and promote a more diverse ecosystem, which is critical for pollinators."

Picking for pollinators. Paul has long had an interest in how insects — particularly pollinators — are attracted to and use plants in the landscape. This has influenced how he selects and manages his plants. "When considering plants for the garden or for containers, I look very carefully at the values of each plant and I find myself asking how I can maximize the benefits," he says, noting that he seeks plants with more than just one purpose. They may be beautiful, but can they also be eaten? Do they support pollinators? Referring to his home garden, Paul says, "I was always a fan of pinching out flowering stems of basil and coleus to promote more vegetative growth and foliage, but more recently I have observed bees and hummingbirds feeding on the blooms." Now, when Paul finds himself in a "pinching mood," he questions his actions and typically leaves some or all of the flowers to support these populations.

Training to trellis. To take advantage of unused vertical space, Paul has placed an A-frame trellis at one end of the garden to support climbing peas and beans. Beneath the structure, Paul suggests planting edible flowers such as pansies and violas, as well hardy greens like pak choi. Typically, these plants thrive in the cooler temperatures of spring and fall, but they can often be grown well into summer if they are given some shading from the hot sun.

Fabulous flowers. The pansies, violas, nasturtiums, borage, and calendulas serve several purposes in Paul's design. First, they can be enjoyed for their bright flowers, which add cheer and color to the garden, but they also lure pollinating insects and birds to the neighboring edibles. Plus, the blooms are tasty and can be quickly tossed in mixed salads or used as a bed for fish or chicken.

In the center of the garden, two vining (indeterminate), small-fruited tomato plants grow up a trellis as espaliers, which keeps their rampant growth under control. Beside the trellis, an 'Early Girl' tomato produces larger fruits for summer sandwiches, homemade salsa, or bruschetta. A nearby row of spring greens is replaced in early summer with bush beans. Once the beans are harvested, the area can be planted with salad greens for autumn. There is also a row of curly parsley, which Paul likes to tuck into both his gardens and his containers. He likes parsley because it tastes and looks good, and because it's an important food source for swallowtail butterfly larvae.

Birdbath with perch. A birdbath filled with stones and branches sits near the tomatoes. "Fresh water is so important for creatures of all sizes," says Paul, adding that most of us only consider having water for the birds.

At the Toronto Botanical Garden, he enjoys watching the honeybees land on stones and twigs in the water bowls and crawl to the edge of the water for a drink. Of course, a birdbath will also attract insect-eating birds to your garden, helping to control garden pests.

Planting for pollinators in vegetable gardens, as well as creating gardens purely to attract and support various types of pollinators, is a new trend in gardening. "Ever since we added beehives to the Toronto Botanical Garden, and with all the more recent issues regarding the status of bees, I have found myself really refining my plant selections," reflects Paul. "More often than not, I catch myself questioning: Will this plant be a benefit to the bees, too? Really, who are we gardening for? We have such an amazing opportunity to do good through our passion for gardening."

Place twigs and stones in the birdbath to give honeybees a perch.

Allow some of your basil to flower to attract bees.

Paul's Top Picks for Pollinators

PLANTS FOR BEES

- **Basil.** A personal favorite is African Blue Basil (*Ocimum kilimandscharicum × basilicum* 'Dark Opal'), which has colorful, free-flowering edible blooms and is a magnet to all sorts of bees. It's also a great choice for an edible container plant.
- **Squash.** Its brilliant yellow edible flowers offer abundant nectar and are a favorite of bees.
- **Borage (*Borago officinalis*).** This plant has lovely eye-catching blue edible flowers that are much loved by the bees.
- **Jerusalem artichoke (*Helianthus tuberosus*).** This plant is always abuzz with activity when in bloom in late summer. Just remember it can be invasive, so consider the site before planting.

PLANTS FOR BUTTERFLIES

- **Alliums.** In particular, the butterflies love *Allium* 'Millenium' and *Allium* 'Blue Eddy'.
- **Daylilies.** Butterflies love their rich nectar.
- **Lavender.** Great for hot dry gardens, lavender provides fragrance and a rewarding nectar feast for the butterflies.
- **Parsley.** Swallowtail butterflies always seem to find the plants, whether planted in the ground or in pots, on which to lay their eggs.

PLANTS FOR OTHER BENEFICIALS

- **Pineapple sage (*Salvia elegans*).** The brilliant red tubular blossoms that appear in late summer are a magnet much loved by hummingbirds.

Paul's Garden Plan

5' DEEP X 15' WIDE

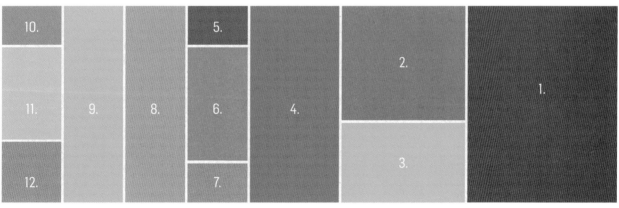

1. Trellis planted with spring-sown snow peas and pole beans; underneath, pak choi interplanted with violas and/or pansies
2. 1 'Juliet' grape tomato and 1 'White Currant' cherry tomato (espaliered)
3. 'Early Girl' tomato
4. Two rows of spring greens followed by bush beans
5. Nasturiums
6. Herb patch including rosemary, catmint, borage, basil, and calendulas
7. Birdbath with twigs and beach stones
8. Flat-leaved and curly parsley
9. Strawberries
10. Garlic chives
11. Thyme
12. Regular chives

"We have such an amazing opportunity to do good through our passion for gardening," says Paul Zammit.

An A-frame trellis supports climbing peas and beans. It should be positioned on the north end of the bed to avoid casting a shadow on the nearby plants.

Pansies and violas planted underneath the trellis attract pollinators.

POLLINATOR-FRIENDLY CONTAINER

No space for a full-sized pollinator-friendly garden bed? Consider potting up a large container (18 to 24 inches in diameter) and filling with plants that support pollinator populations and provide fresh herbs and fruits for your family. You can place the pot in a sunny spot on a deck or patio, or site it near your vegetable garden or fruit trees to help entice more pollinators to your in-ground edibles. Include the following:

- 1 African blue perennial basil standard

- 3 calendulas

- 2 curly parsley

- 3 'Fragoo Pink' everbearing strawberry (*Fragaria × ananassa*)

- 3 golden thyme ('Aureus')

Beautiful Balcony Edibles

iving in an apartment or condo can discourage even the most avid gardeners. If you're lucky enough to have a sunny balcony, Andrea Bellamy shows how you can grow a wide range of edibles that taste *and* look great. She suggests combining a mixture of small fruiting trees and shrubs, vegetables, strawberries, herbs, and edible flowers in large pots for maximum yield and visual effect.

> ❯ No space? No problem! Grow a bounty of vegetables, herbs, and fruits on a small deck or balcony

> ❯ Features edibles selected for productivity, flavor, and ornamental appearance

> ❯ Annual flowers not only attract good bugs, but also provide color, fragrance, and — in the case of nasturtiums — a tasty snack!

An avid gardener living in an urban environment, Andrea Bellamy has been growing food on a small balcony for the past 12 years. Gardening above ground level certainly offers its share of challenges (among them, gusty winds, lack of light, and the inconvenience of lugging soil, plants, and containers up elevators — or worse, several flights of stairs). For Andrea, a lush balcony filled with ripening fruits and tender salad greens is worth the small hassles. And there are other advantages to a balcony garden: there are no weeds and, aside from an occasional outbreak of aphids, pests are rarely a problem.

Wide-ranging possibilities. "Provided your containers are large enough, you can grow pretty much everything on a balcony," Andrea says. "I choose edibles based on what I want to eat and then I look at which are going to do well in containers, and in the conditions on my balcony." Once she has a list of possibilities, Andrea narrows it down further, selecting for productivity, flavor, decorative properties, and sometimes unique characteristics like color or shape (globe-shaped or purple carrots, for example).

Tomatoes and peas are among Andrea's top picks for container crops. "Homegrown tomatoes can't be beat," she says. "Peas help out the other things growing in the same container and will create a leafy screen." She uses tall climbing peas for screening and short-stemmed varieties on the edge of a container to spill over and create interest.

Edibles that make a splash. Andrea also loves combining blue-green dinosaur ('Lacinato') kale with orange nasturtiums or golden marjoram. She says she likes to pick edibles as she would ornamentals, considering color and form and using the "thriller, filler, and spiller" rule pioneered by Steve Silk.

While many balcony gardeners shy away from perennial crops or fruits, worried that they'll take up too much space or not overwinter when planted in containers, Andrea enjoys growing them on her balcony. She suggests growing a 'Brown Turkey' fig, strawberries, and two dwarf blueberry shrubs. Blueberries need to be cross-pollinated to yield a good supply of fruit, so Andrea says to make sure to select two different cultivars. Strawberries are self-fruitful, but still she suggests growing two types to ensure the longest season of harvest. The June-bearing plants will bear a heavy crop of sweet berries for three weeks in early summer, while the everbearing strawberries fruit intermittently through the spring, summer, and autumn. For winter, the figs can be brought indoors to a cool storage room or basement, and the blueberries and strawberries can be mulched with straw and wrapped in burlap.

A living screen. In the limited space of a balcony, there are many reasons to choose vertical crops like pole beans. Not only do vining vegetables produce more food in less space, but the 'Purple Peacock' pole beans, clambering up a teepee, help fill out that corner of the balcony and provide privacy from neighboring apartments or, if placed near the railing, the street.

Another technique that Andrea employs is underplanting, a method often used in traditional vegetable gardens to get more out of the available growing space. Underplanting involves choosing a tall plant for the center or back of a container and then filling up the lower space with compact or cascading vegetables, herbs, or edible flowers. Beneath the large 'Brown Turkey' fig, Andrea has planted common (English) thyme and trailing nasturtiums, whose edible flowers can be enjoyed for their bright colors or harvested and tossed into salads. The nasturtiums' rounded waterlily leaves and plump seeds add a radishlike heat to many dishes. Beneath the 'Fairy Tale' eggplant, she has tucked a clump of sweet alyssum. The tiny alyssum flowers add both fragrance and color to the balcony, and they attract beneficial and pollinating insects to the fruiting edibles.

"Provided your containers are large enough, you can grow pretty much everything on a balcony," Andrea Bellamy says.

STUNNING CONTAINER COMBINATIONS

- 'Brown Turkey' fig underplanted with common (English) thyme and trailing nasturtiums

- 'Top Hat' blueberry with June-bearing strawberries and pansies

- 'Purple Peacock' pole beans (grown on a teepee) underplanted with 'Red Sails' lettuce

- Dinosaur ('Lacinato') kale underplanted with golden marjoram and pansies

- 'Fairy Tale' eggplant underplanted with sweet alyssum

- 'Taxi' bush tomato (an extremely compact cultivar with bushy 2-foot-tall plants and flavorful yellow fruits) underplanted with Signet marigold (blossoms are edible) and basil

- 'Thai Dragon' chile pepper (both decorative and delicious, the 16-inch-tall plants bear clusters of slender red pointy peppers) underplanted with cilantro and trailing nasturtiums

- 'Northsky' blueberry with everbearing strawberries and pansies

A 'Brown Turkey' fig and a 'Purple Peacock' bean teepee provide a beautiful living screen.

Underplant the fig with thyme and nasturtiums to boost your harvest.

Southern-Style
Backyard Farm

Living in Florida allows Carolyn Binder to garden year-round, producing a bounty of homegrown organic food for her family. In her plan she re-creates her own Southern backyard garden in a stylish design with a central gazebo that provides a shaded perch for enjoying the — literal — fruits of one's labors. The surrounding raised beds are planted densely using the square-foot garden method (see box on page 163) and replanted often to keep production high.

> Intensively planted vegetables offer a higher-than-average yield

> The central gazebo is a welcoming space to dine and relax

> No-dig beds are planted in the square-foot-gardening method and mulched to withstand the Southern heat

> Supports pollinators and beneficial insects

Carolyn's plan for a Southern-style vegetable garden is based on her actual 40- by 42-foot garden at Cowlick Cottage Farm, the country homestead she shares with her husband, Eric, near Tallahassee, Florida. Carolyn's temperate climate allows her to garden year-round, but even cool-climate gardeners can apply her design and the majority of her crop choices to their own plots.

Year-round bounty and beauty. The goal of her design is twofold: to provide a long season of homegrown organic food for her family, and to create an inviting setting. "I want to cook with the best-tasting, highest-quality food possible, and I've always enjoyed gardening as well," says Carolyn. "One interest feeds the other, and the garden provides us with some of the most nutritious and delicious fruits and vegetables we have ever tasted."

The best of alfresco dining. A flagstone path leads the way into the garden from the main cottage,

traveling beneath a trellis covered with Malabar spinach to a square gazebo of stainless steel and aluminum that the couple built from a kit. The perfect focal point for their gardens, the gazebo is now where Carolyn and her family dine, entertain, and hang out.

Surrounding the gazebo are tidy raised beds separated by generous river rock pathways. Because she has found great success in the square-foot gardening method developed by Mel Bartholomew, Carolyn has also applied this intensive planting technique to her garden plan. "The square-foot method is a simplified version of intensive planting," she explains, whereby gardeners intensively plant crops in tidy 1-foot-square blocks in raised beds. (For more on square-foot gardening, see box on page 163).

Success with succession planting. Carolyn finds that succession planting, in which spent or declining edibles are replaced with fresh plants,

Carolyn's Garden Plan for Fall/Winter

River Rock pathway

Persimmon

Mixed herbs

Artichokes parsnips

Lettuce

Garlic bed

Carrots Swiss chard broccoli and Brussels Sprouts

Beets, Pak Choi and Collards

Malabar Spinach on trellis

Gazebo

Pineapple guava Soybeans, leeks, and fava beans

Cabbage and onions

Mustard greens and kale

Red onions and scallions

Kohlrabi and turnips

Fountain

Fig

Strawberry

Carolyn's Favorite Heat-Friendly Varieties

- **Artichokes:** 'Green Globe Improved'
- **Beans:** 'Envy' soybeans and 'Broad Windsor' fava beans
- **Beets:** 'Detroit Dark Red'
- **Broccoli:** 'Premium Crop'
- **Brussels sprouts:** 'Long Island Improved'

- **Cabbage:** 'Red Acre' and 'Late Flat Dutch'
- **Carrots:** 'Nantes Coreless' and 'Scarlet Nantes'
- **Collards:** 'Green Glaze'
- **Fig:** 'Alma'
- **Kale:** Dinosaur ('Lacinato')

- **Kohlrabi:** 'Gigant Winter'
- **Onions:** 'Yellow Multiplier'
- **Parsnips:** 'Hollow Crown'
- **Salad greens:** 'Red Giant' mustard greens and Malabar spinach
- **Strawberries:** 'Camarosa' June-bearing
- **Swiss chard:** 'Improved Rainbow Mix'

allows her to manage productivity so that she has the right amount of each vegetable for the longest possible time. She cites summer squash, a crop often used as the poster child for excess garden produce, as an example: "I may plant 4 square feet of summer squash, and then a few weeks later, another 4 square feet of summer squash," she says. "With succession planting, I can have just the right amount of squash for a longer period of time."

Feeding the soil. To keep production high and support her intensive gardening methods, Carolyn adds plenty of organic matter — compost, worm castings, and aged manures — to her beds between successive crops. "Intensive planting in properly enriched soil in raised beds results in higher yields, but it also helps keep garden chores manageable by significantly reducing the need for weeding and watering," Carolyn says. She explains that the foliage of the closely planted crops creates a living canopy above the soil, shading out any weeds and reducing soil moisture evaporation. Carolyn built her beds using the lasagna no-dig method, which involves smothering the existing grass with newspapers or cardboard and layers of organic matter (see page 70).

Along the back of the garden, Carolyn has placed narrow plantings of soybeans, leeks, fava beans, and pineapple guava between a persimmon and an 'Alma' fig. In colder climates, the pineapple guava could be replaced by a hedge of raspberries, and the warm-climate fig and persimmon with highbush blueberries or another type of fruiting tree or shrub.

Watering visitors too. The fountain is a gigantic resin vase fitted with fountain plumbing and placed over a 4-foot-wide pond. It provides ambiance as well as refreshment to visitors, including birds, bees, butterflies, and the occasional dog.

CAROLYN'S 4 STEPS TO A SUCCESSFUL SOUTHERN VEGETABLE GARDEN

1. Setting. One of the most critical elements of vegetable gardening is to select the right spot to site your garden. It should have the right amount of sun and shade to make you and your plants happy. Most vegetables require 6 to 8 hours of full sun a day, though Southern gardeners have a little more leeway — vegetable gardens won't mind a little late-afternoon shade.

2. Soil. If you feed your soil, the plants will thrive. I feed my soil with lots of organic matter such as composted yard matter, organic fertilizers, and worm castings. This helps to amend the heavy clay or sandy soil many Southerners face, as well as reduce heat stress during our long, hot summer. It's a good idea to sprinkle compost tea or liquid seaweed on your plants when they look a little tired or droopy.

3. Seeds or Seedlings. Southern gardeners have the advantage of being able to garden year-round, but it is important to plant fruits and vegetables that do well in your particular area and in the right season (you don't want to plant cool-season crops like kale too late, for instance). Visit your garden centers, farmers' markets, and roadside stands to learn about seasonal produce — if they can grow it, so can you!

4. Saturation. If your garden doesn't get watered regularly, it will not thrive, and Southern gardens require extra watering during our sizzling summers. An inexpensive micro-watering system that hooks directly to the outside faucet will help tremendously.

Edibles on a Patio

*D*onna Balzer uses every inch of space in her plan for both ornamental and edible plants, growing them in pots, raised garden beds, and a small greenhouse. Vining crops like squash are given room to roam, while compact vegetables and herbs are planted in containers and tidy beds in and around the outdoor sitting area.

> A productive combination of containers and garden beds

> Edible and ornamental plants are freely intermixed

> An 8- by 10-foot greenhouse extends the season and shelters warm-climate vegetables

> Self-watering pots and an automatic drip irrigation system reduce maintenance

When Donna Balzer's husband, Keith, took a two-week fishing trip to Canada's west coast, he ended up catching a really big one: a new home located 600 miles from their existing home in Calgary, Alberta. "He claimed he was doing it for me," says Donna with a laugh, "so I would be closer to my mother, and it would be great for gardening."

Their new coastal location is five gardening zones warmer than their Calgary home in the northern plains. Needless to say, Donna can now grow a much broader range of plants, but she also notes that "the new climate requires year-round weeding, pest patrol, and vigilance."

When the couple made the trek west, they brought with them their 8- by 10-foot greenhouse. To make a home for it, they took out their driveway and a 9-foot-wide laurel hedge. "Suddenly a place that could barely fit a single car was home to our greenhouse, a large sitting area, and a generous planting spot for additional herbs and vegetables." It just so happened that this area was also the only sunny spot with easy access to the kitchen, making it an ideal area for a patio garden of edibles.

Intermixing for fun and style. Donna's newly made-over patio is a compact but productive garden that demonstrates just how much can be grown in a small space. She freely intermixes edibles and ornamentals, combining zucchini with calla lilies, bush squash with ornamental vines, and rhubarb and herbs with roses and bulbs. "I include flowers in the vegetable beds for color and to attract beneficial bugs," she says. Inside the greenhouse she grows heat-loving crops such as tomatoes and peppers underplanted with cilantro and 'Golden Self Blanching' celery.

A combination of garden beds and pots surround the greenhouse. With such an extensive potted garden, Donna is always on the lookout for container-friendly edibles.

Best potted plants. Donna also has tuberous begonias "for color and the lemony zip they add to salads, romaine lettuce, watercress that I underseed beneath the begonias, arugula under a witch hazel shrub, and a lime tree in a pot," she says. Donna notes that she moves the lime into the greenhouse in the autumn. "I also have a pizza pot with a tomato plant, sage, rosemary, and basil," she adds.

In their second season at the house, Keith built the vegetable beds using cement blocks, and Donna quickly filled them with a handful of different squash and pumpkin varieties, including 'Galeux d'Eysines' pumpkin, 'Orangetti' spaghetti squash, and 'Early Butternut' winter squash. She trains the pumpkins to climb the deer-proof fence and wander into the lot beside their house, which they bought a few years ago.

(Almost) carefree gardening. Although they have settled on the West Coast, Keith and Donna still frequently commute back to Calgary for work, so they need to have a garden that is low-maintenance. To reduce watering and maintenance, Donna uses some pots with water reservoirs, and to other pots and her garden beds she has added an automatic drip irrigation system.

Take out your driveway and put up a greenhouse!

Flowers are intermixed with vegetables and herbs to add color and lure beneficial insects to the garden.

Donna's Garden Plan

25' DEEP X 25' WIDE

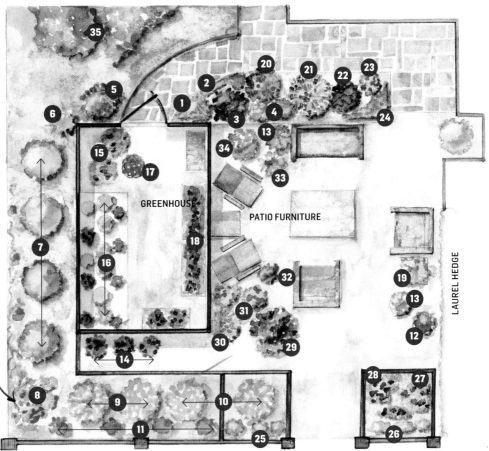

GREENHOUSE

PATIO FURNITURE

LAUREL HEDGE

The pumpkin, which spreads vigorously, was directed up a 2-foot rock wall and through a fence that bordered the property. This gave the vine room to grow without taking over Donna's garden.

Edibles

1. 'Bronze' fennel
2. Summer savory and oregano
3. Rhubarb
4. Flat-leaved (Italian) parsley and rosemary
5. Garden sage
6. Chives
7. Assorted cultivars of dwarf highbush blueberries
8. 'Galeux d'Eysines' pumpkin
9. 'Orangetti' hybrid spaghetti squash
10. Winter squash (a compact variety)
11. 'Capitola' Brussels sprouts
12. Arugula underplanted to witch hazel
13. 'Astia' zucchini
14. 'Mountain Spring' tomato
15. 'Sungold' and 'Isis Candy' tomatoes
16. 'Brandywine' tomato, 'Mini Apple' hybrid sweet pepper, 'Golden Self Blanching' celery, and cilantro
17. Potted dwarf Bearss seedless lime (goes into the greenhouse in the fall)
18. 'Juliet' tomatoes

Ornamentals Added for Color

19. Assorted flowering annuals
20. Miniature roses (orange)
21. Crocosmia
22. Dwarf hydrangea
23. 'Fabiana Princess Lilies' alstromeria
24. Echeveria (several)
25. Snail Vine
26. 'Unwin's Striped Butterfly Blend' and 'High Scent' sweet peas and 'Raspberry Sorbet' zinnias
27. 'Angel Wings' schizanthus
28. 'Ten Week Bouquet' stocks
29. 'Blushing Bride' hydrangea
30. Golden bamboo for year-round drama
31. Soft coral pink tuberous begonias, started from tubers in March, underplanted with watercress
32. Sedum telephium 'Lajos' ('Autumn Charm')
33. Calla lilies
34. Gardenia on a standard
35. Mock orange

American Potager

A potager is essentially a garden where you grow things to eat, but it's also a French philosophy of living that is connected to the seasons. In her American potager garden, Jennifer Bartley retains many of the basic elements of the French version, including growing fruits, vegetables, herbs, and flowers; picking a site near the kitchen; planning so that something can be picked every day of the year; and making the space beautiful and productive.

> ❯ French-inspired formal design spotlights the connection between the garden, the kitchen, and the seasons

> ❯ Food production takes place in four central beds, with drifts of colorful ornamentals surrounding the inner garden

> ❯ Gourmet plants were selected for outstanding flavor

Jennifer's company, American Potager, borrows the core concepts of a French vegetable garden, or *jardin potager*. "The French have always understood this connection between what is growing in the garden and what is being served at the table — the soup of the day changes throughout the year as the season changes," she says.

Jennifer explains that formal designs and vegetable gardens have gone hand-in-hand for centuries. "Rectangles and squares are easy to work with because they line up well with houses and garages," she says. "If you build raised beds out of wood, you find a way to combine rectangles and squares in a pleasing way, so formal designs for the structure of the garden make sense." When it comes to actually planting the beds, she says this is where creativity can run wild — plants can be laid out more randomly than in formal grids and rows and grown more closely together.

Choose sun and easy access. Gardens that produce food need at least 6 hours of direct sunlight, so look for a sunny location that is easily accessed from the house. She adds that the American potager is beautiful as well as useful, and she wants to be able to look at it every day.

POTAGER

Jennifer's Garden Plan

30' DEEP X 48' WIDE

Well-defined, symmetrical beds contrast with the looseness of the rambling flowers, vegetables, and herbs planted within them for a "yin and yang" design.

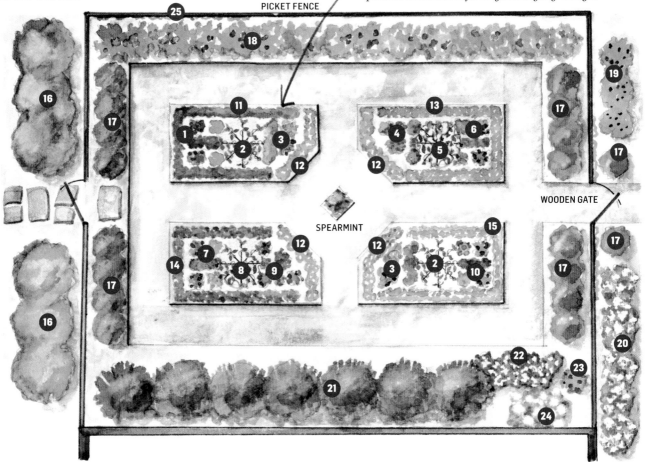

PICKET FENCE

WOODEN GATE

SPEARMINT

Vegetable Beds

1. Heirloom and hybrid tomatoes, lettuce, Thai basil, and ground cherries (Physalis)

2. Scarlet runner beans and pole beans

3. Okra, squash (bush variety), and eggplants

4. Brussels sprouts, 'Lemon Gem' marigolds, and tomatillos

5. Cucumbers (climbing) and Malabar spinach

6. Asian greens, rosemary, bulb fennel, and heirloom and hybrid tomatoes

7. Calendulas, heirloom and hybrid tomatoes, rosemary, and bulb fennel

8. Cucumbers (climbing) and pole beans

9. Sweet peppers, 'Lemon Gem' marigolds, and tomatillos

10. Calendula, heirloom and hybrid tomatoes, lettuce, and Thai basil

Edging Plants

11. 'Sweet Genovese' basil

12. 'Profusion White' zinnias (nonedible ornamental)

13. Marjoram

14. Flat-leaved (Italian) parsley

15. Sweet alyssum (nonedible ornamental) and garlic

Garden Border Plants

16. 'Little Lamb' hydrangea (nonedible ornamental)

17. 'Green Gem' boxwood (nonedible ornamental)

18. Mixed peony border (nonedible ornamental)

19. American cranberrybush viburnum (edible fruits)

20. 'Limelight' hydrangea (nonedible ornamental)

21. Yew hedge (nonedible ornamental)

22. 'Coronation Gold' yarrow (nonedible ornamental)

23. Borage

24. 'Annabelle' hydrangea (nonedible ornamental)

25. Hops

Structure and chaos. Her design follows a traditional style with four central beds, but Jennifer has surrounded these with flowering perennials (including generous clumps of peonies, yarrow, and 'Little Lamb' and 'Limelight' hydrangeas) as well as shrubs, evergreens, and a charming picket fence. "As a designer, I love the juxtaposition of rigid lines and sharp edges with the chaos and looseness of rambling flowers and plants," she says. "This yin and yang makes good design."

The four central beds are the main production areas of the garden. Each is edged with a low border of compact herbs — such as parsley, marjoram, and basil — and flowers such as sweet alyssum. Along the inside edge of each bed, a low hedge of 'Profusion White' zinnias supplies ample blooms for the vase and a convenient landing pad for busy pollinators. For the interior of each bed, Jennifer has chosen a selection of gourmet edibles. These include warm-season plants such as heirloom and hybrid tomatoes, eggplant, okra, Malabar spinach, and Thai basil; and cold-season crops such as lettuce, Asian greens, and Brussels sprouts. Certain plants, such as the tomatoes, have been repeated in each of the beds, lending further symmetry to the garden. A pot planted with spearmint sits at the heart of the garden.

Star edibles. Some of Jennifer's favorite edibles include Italian parsley, 'Sweet Genovese' basil, tomatoes, young squash, purple beans, and garlic. "The heirloom scarlet runner bean gets planted every year, to climb up bamboo poles or on metal trellises," she says. "We love watching the hummingbirds sip nectar from the bright red edible flowers."

Flowers also play an important role in Jennifer's plan, attracting insects, butterflies, and birds to the garden, and making beautiful centerpiece bouquets on a table. She likes to include ornamentals such as coneflowers, lavender, anise hyssop, yarrow, and peonies.

"The French have always understood this connection between what is growing in the garden and what is being served at the table — the soup of the day changes throughout the year as the season changes," Jennifer says.

Eggs & Everything

essi Bloom brings edible gardening and chickens together in her partitioned garden. The centrally located chicken coop provides a safe place for "the ladies" to roost and has three doors, each leading to a different part of the garden. The chickens offer a continuous supply of free-range eggs and ample manure that is composted and turned back into the garden to enrich the food plants.

❯ Sustainable design combines vegetable, fruit, and berry production with free-range chickens

❯ Features a central coop that opens into each of three sections for easy chicken rotation

❯ Conveniently placed composters turn chicken manure into a rich amendment for food crops

Jessi loves "her girls" and thinks that gardens and chickens make natural partners. "To a gardener, chickens are worth their weight in gold," says Jessi. "Not only do they produce a nitrogen-rich manure that can be composted and used to amend garden beds, but they also help to keep weeds down and grass clipped, and they gobble up a variety of insects and grubs." To get the most from her chickens' behaviors, she allows her birds to roam in her garden, rotating them to different areas.

Room to roam. Jessi has divided her garden plan into three distinct paddock sections using cross-fencing.

The chicken coop is the heart of the garden and is sited so that it borders each of the three sections. The three doors of the coop are cleverly hinged as ramps that open onto each paddock, so the chickens can be rotated quickly and efficiently. Before one section is decimated, the chickens are moved to another. To protect against predators, Jessi has surrounded the entire garden with a perimeter fence.

Collecting rainwater. A rain collection system near the coop captures water for the chickens, and any excess can be used to irrigate the garden crops. Jessi suggests using a rain barrel or cistern to collect the water; depending on the roof type and use of the water, she recommends installing a "first flush" device to capture the initial dirty water from the roof after a storm.

Section 1 is the largest part of the garden and contains a variety of plant materials, including perennial edible plants. "Fruit trees could be the uppermost layer of a 'food forest,' which contains several layers of useful plants that mimic nature," says Jessi, who suggests a combination of

trees, shrubs, perennials, vines, and ground covers to provide biodiversity. Section 1 also houses the three-bin composting system, which Jessi likes to site near the chicken coop to make coop chores like composting manure and bedding easier. Because of the size of this section and the types of plants located here — mostly woody trees and shrubs — this is where the chickens spend the majority of their time.

Section 2 is the smallest area of production in the garden. Hardy cane fruits — plants including raspberries, blackberries, and salmonberries that bear fruit on short woody stems — thrive here. "This section is a great place for chickens during the early spring months as the leaves are coming out," says Jessi, as the birds help to weed and raise soil fertility. In the late summer and fall they clean up fallen fruit that could harbor pests. The thorny, upright plants provide the chickens with shelter from both predators and inclement weather. They also provide abundant fruit for the gardener and ample flowers for pollinators.

To keep the rampant canes under control, consider training them on a simple T-bar trellis system that uses wooden crossbars at either end of the bed, connected with plant-supporting wires. A few fruiting shrubs such as highbush blueberries could also be planted in this area if space allows. (Remember that blueberries need at least two cultivars to ensure cross-pollination.)

Section 3 is for intensive annual vegetable production. During the growing season, the chickens are allowed here in a chicken "tractor" (a movable, floorless chicken coop), which prevents them from destroying the vegetables. At the end of the season, they are given free rein to "do some cleanup," Jessi says.

Eight raised beds hold vegetables, herbs, and edible flowers, and they are separated by generous pathways. Near the coop, Jessi has included cold frames to stretch the harvest season into winter and get a jump on spring seeding. A functional but decorative gated arbor separates this section of the garden from section 1 and can be used to support ornamental or edible vines.

Don't have a spacious-sized lot? Jessi's versatile plan can be tailored to fit virtually any size garden. In her book *Free-Range Chicken Gardens*, Jessi writes that a small urban lot that measures under 7,000 square feet should have no more than 3 to 5 chickens. Larger rural lots between 7,000 and 13,000 square feet, on the other hand, can support 5 to 8 chickens.

Hinged ramps make it easy for chickens to visit each section of the garden.

Chickens like their vegetables, too, so they are only allowed into this section when they are in a "chicken tractor."

Jessi's Garden Plan

40' DEEP X 35' WIDE

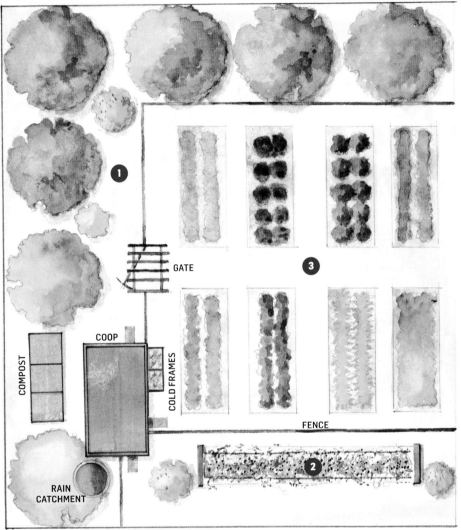

COMPOST

COOP

COLD FRAMES

GATE

RAIN CATCHMENT

FENCE

1. **Section One: Fruit and Nut Trees.** Jessi's top picks include almond, apple, apricot, cherry, chestnut, crab apple, filbert, mountain ash, oak, peach, pear, plum, and quince. She says that fruit and nut trees are a natural match for a chicken garden. The chickens will clean up fallen fruit, and the plants are sturdy enough to withstand the scratching of the flock.

2. **Section Two: Hardy cane fruits and shrubs.** Aronia, blueberry, red or black currant, elderberry, gooseberry, honeyberry, raspberry, and rugosa rose are among Jessi's favorites. Before adding fruiting shrubs to your garden, she recommends checking to see which ones will do best in your individual region.

3. **Section Three: Vegetables and edible flowers.** Chickens love their veggies too, which can work against the gardener if ripening crops are not protected from the flock. Use bird netting to prevent chickens from accessing your prized tomatoes or to keep the birds out of one zone altogether. Jessi says that chickens enjoy both greens and seeds, including dandelions, garlic, lettuce, mâche (corn salad), mustard, nasturtiums, sunflowers, and Swiss chard.

PLANTS TO AVOID WITH CHICKENS

In a chicken-friendly garden, avoid plants that are toxic to chickens. This includes castor bean (*Ricinus communis*), milkweed (*Asclepias* species), monkshood (*Aconitum* species), ornamental tobacco (*Nicotiana* species), and yew (*Taxus* species).

Fig-Pig Patio

Figs in the North? Why not? In his plan for a fig-pig patio, Canadian gardener Steven Biggs demonstrates that even tender Mediterranean plants like figs aren't off-limits to those living in cold climates. He trains his figs as small trees, rather than bushes, and he grows them in large pots so he can move them easily when it comes time to overwinter them in a shed.

> ❯ This super-compact design brings sweet, juicy figs to cold regions!
>
> ❯ Border a patio or deck, or add interest to a pathway
>
> ❯ Cardoon, lavender, and Swiss chard create a colorful and edible understory to the figs

Steven is a self-proclaimed fig-pig. In his yard, he can sit among the wide assortment of fig trees on his patio and pretend that he's in an Italian villa. "I love it. First, there's the fruit, which, when fresh and fully ripe — as you can only get straight from the tree — is sweet, juicy, and jamlike," he says. Then there is the Mediterranean atmosphere that the trees themselves provide. "The gray bark and lobed leaves offer Northerners the illusion of being somewhere other than the temperate North," he says with a laugh.

Steven started his first fig tree from a cutting when he was just a teenager. Twenty-five years later, he still has a descendant from that original tree, as well as several dozen other fig trees.

Selecting the right variety. There are a lot of different varieties of figs. Steven advises that you check in with a "fig fetishist" or a well-stocked nursery in your specific area when buying plants, so that you end up with the best varieties for your region. "Some have dark flesh, some light; and some have dark skin, some light. In addition, some give a good first (breba) crop in summer, while others give a better main crop in the autumn," he says. He recommends buying a variety that offers a good breba crop and another with a good main crop for the longest season of figs.

Creating a private spot. To increase privacy and provide a secluded feeling, Steven trains his fig plants to grow as trees instead of bushes. His goal is for the trees to reach a height of 6 feet, with side branches starting about 3 feet above the level of the pot. Because of this,

An artichoke cousin, cardoon's edible stalks are used in Mediterranean dishes.

Lavender, a perennial plant in many cold climates, hides the fig pots.

'Bright Lights' Swiss chard adds bold color and provides tasty greens all summer long.

Steven's design will work well along the border of a patio or sitting area.

The other advantage to growing the plants as trees is that you can grow more plants underneath them. In his design, Steven has chosen edible plants for his fig tree understory. The lavender and cardoon continue the Mediterranean theme of the figs, while the 'Bright Lights' Swiss chard adds bold color — and plenty of tasty salad greens!

Of cardoon, Steven says, "It's such a stunning plant with large, deeply cut leaves that add a Promethean quality to the garden." The edible stalks are used in a variety of Mediterranean dishes, but the plants themselves are highly architectural, and in late summer large purple thistlelike flowers emerge from the center of the foliage.

Steven likes that lavender has summer flowers and aromatic foliage with year-round structure. "The perennial lavender plants provide a 'placeholder' for the figs, and they also hide the buried fig pots," says Steven.

Easy overwintering. Gardeners in cold climates will need to overwinter their trees. That may sound intimidating, but Steven is quick to reassure prospective growers: "Over the winter, fig trees will need no more care than a potted houseplant — and probably less because they go dormant," he says. Fig growers in cold climates can overwinter their plants in several ways. "I overwinter most of my fig plants in an insulated shed that I keep near the freezing mark," he says, noting that an attached garage

Steven's Favorite Figs

Some fig varieties produce a good first (breba) crop in summer, while others produce a better main crop in autumn. Steven recommends mixing breba and main crops for the longest harvest, and planting varieties that work well in your region. "There are so many varieties of fig that, even with all my plants, I've grown only a fraction of what's out there," says Steven. In his own words, Steven describes some varieties that he has grown and particularly likes:

- **'Neveralla' (breba and main crop).** I like this variety because it consistently gives a breba crop. It has a light pulp inside and a brownish skin. If, like me, you garden someplace where it isn't guaranteed that your main crop will be ripen before the first frost, make sure you have at least one plant that consistently gives breba figs.

- **'Verte' (main crop).** This variety throws out the occasional breba, but it mostly produces main-crop figs. I love this one for the flavor, which I consider outstanding. These delicious figs have green skin and strawberry-colored flesh.

- **'Hardy Chicago' (main crop).** This cold-tolerant fig produces an abundant crop of small, dark main-crop figs that ripen earlier than many other varieties.

- **'Desert King' (breba crop).** A pollinating wasp is needed for the main-crop figs, so in my neck of the woods it only produces breba figs. The fruit is green-skinned, with a reddish pulp.

or even a cold room in a basement would work well too. "The ideal overwintering spot is a dark, cool (23 to 41°F or −5 to 5°C) storage area that keeps dormant trees snoozing until spring."

Because he grows his trees in pots that need to be moved in spring and autumn, Steven chooses containers of a manageable size. Though bigger pots will allow you to grow bigger trees, don't choose pots that are so big you can't carry them once they are filled with soil and the plant. This will make moving the trees inside for overwintering and outdoors for summer less of a chore.

Hiding pots. The containers can be buried completely in the soil, right down to the rim, but on paved patios or in areas with lots of rocks, tuck plants in between the fig trees to disguise the pots.

"A fig tree is easier to overwinter than a houseplant," says Steven Biggs.

Critter Control

Karen Chapman knows how frustrating it can be to try to grow food where animal pests are an issue. Her solution? A keeping-out-the-critters garden surrounded by two layers of fences to discourage deer, and a buried length of hardware cloth to bar burrowing animals like voles and rabbits. Good luck to any critter who dares to try to steal her veggies now!

› The fortified design keeps deer, rabbits, voles, and other veggie-stealing critters out of the garden

› The fence does double duty as a support for vining vegetables and espaliered fruits

› Raised beds provide plenty of space for raspberries, blueberries, vegetables, and herbs

› Two pergolas offer access and vertical space for ornamental or fruiting vines

After years of matching wits with the local vole population — and losing — the tipping point for Karen Chapman and her husband, Andy, came in 2011 when a parsnip-snatching vole foiled their plans for Thanksgiving dinner. "The vole ate all my parsnips, and I was furious," recalls Karen. "Having nurtured the parsnips all spring, summer, and fall, we were looking forward with great anticipation to our favorite Thanksgiving vegetable dish, Parmesan-coated roast parsnips. But when I went out to dig them up, only a few tops were left." With that, they decided to get serious about keeping the critters out of their garden.

Karen and Andy began to design a formal, but fortified, 45- by 40-foot plot that the voles, rabbits, and deer would not be allowed to access. They based the design on the gorgeous deer-proof plot of John and Lee Neff, avid gardeners in Kingston, Washington, but they tweaked it slightly to provide additional protection from smaller wildlife.

Blocking the burrowers. They used a Bobcat utility vehicle to dig trenches to lay drainage pipes, as the winter water table was only about 6 inches below the soil surface and they needed to drain water away from the garden. The water was directed to a nearby stream, and drainage pipes covered in landscape fabric were laid in the trench, as well as a 3-foot-deep swath of hardware cloth — $1/2$-inch galvanized metal mesh that keeps out burrowing animals (including the parsnip-stealing voles). This mesh barrier runs the perimeter of the garden and leans against the lower boards that form the base of the fence.

Twice the protection. Once the hardware cloth was in place, the fence, which Karen has nicknamed the "boing-boing fence," was erected. They installed two 5-foot-tall fences that were spaced 5 feet apart, on the principle that the deer wouldn't jump if they weren't assured of clearance. "In other words, they can't 'boing-boing' in or over a 5-foot span," Karen explains. The fence was constructed from galvanized panels of graduated hog wire, which has smaller holes at the bottom and larger ones at the top. "Rabbits can't get through the small holes, and deer can't get their muzzles through the bigger ones," notes Karen.

Support for espalier. The sturdy fence provides plenty of support for Karen's espaliered apples (see box on page 78), pole beans, and sweet peas (her preferred cultivars are 'Galaxy' and 'Mammoth'). "We already have two three-tiered espaliered apples, plus one dwarf that we transplanted from the old garden," says Karen. If espaliering sounds too intimidating (it's not, honest), you could also plant perennial fruiting vines such as hardy kiwi or grapes. Garden access is gained by passing beneath two gated 8-foot-tall pergolas. "The pergola adds the necessary additional height to the gate to prevent the deer from jumping," she says. At the base of each pergola grow grapevines and fragrant honeysuckle vines.

Inside the fences, Andy and Karen have built one large raised bed for trellised raspberries and ten smaller beds for vegetables, herbs, and annual flowers, which are rotated annually to ensure crop and soil health. The raised beds, framed with either cedar or untreated pine, are 12 inches high, 3 feet wide, and 10 feet long. To take advantage of all available growing space, they have also added raised beds to the 5-foot-wide area between the two perimeter fences. These beds vary in width from 18 inches to 3 feet, depending upon their intended use. "For example, 3-foot beds are wide enough for blueberries, but 18 inches

is plenty for leeks and onions," says Karen. The main garden pathways are a comfortable 4-foot width, with the side paths spanning 2 feet.

Money-saving tips. Building a critter-proof garden is no small task. Andy and Karen worked every weekend for three months to construct their new garden. Such a secure design also comes with a hefty price tag, but smart shopping and planning ahead can help keep you on budget.

"Andy built and dug everything himself," says Karen. "And we rescued our blueberry bushes, apple trees, and strawberry plants from the original garden." They also used inexpensive timber and saved excavated rocks to backfill drainage channels. As for the voles, Karen feels no guilt about denying them a taste of her homegrown parsnips. "The voles can go hungry!" she says with a laugh.

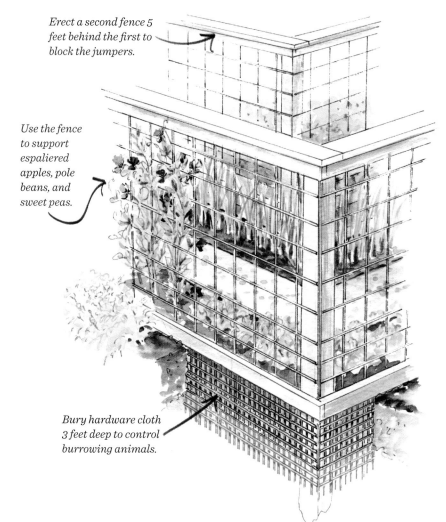

Erect a second fence 5 feet behind the first to block the jumpers.

Use the fence to support espaliered apples, pole beans, and sweet peas.

Bury hardware cloth 3 feet deep to control burrowing animals.

Karen's Garden Plan

40' DEEP X 45' WIDE

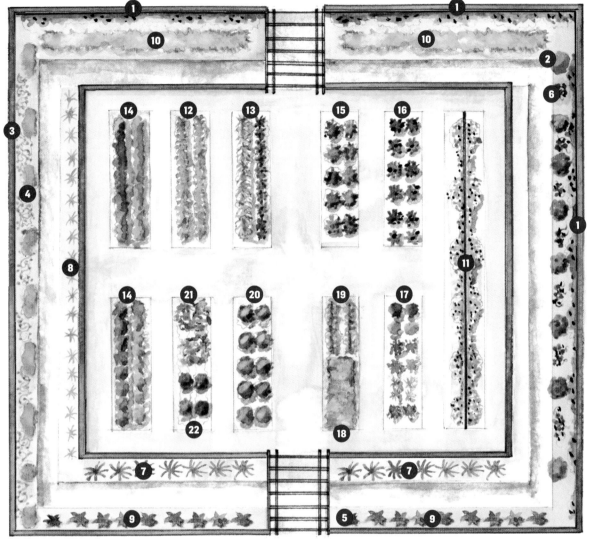

For Fence Edging

1. Espaliered apples
2. Blueberries
3. Sweet peas
4. Lettuce
5. Honeysuckle: Early Dutch 'Belgica' and Late Dutch 'Serotina' (nonedible ornamental)
6. Strawberries
7. Leeks: 'Giant Musselburgh'
8. Onions and garlic: 'Ailsa Craig' and 'Yellow Rock' onions, 'Silver Rose' garlic
9. Green beans
10. Lettuce and mesclun mix: 'Jericho' and 'Red Sails' lettuce

For Center Beds

11. Raspberries
12. Parsnips: 'Cobham Improved'
13. Carrots and beets: 'Little Finger' and 'Purple Dragon' carrots, 'Red Ace' and 'Chioggia' beets
14. Green beans
15. Potatoes: 'Yellow Finn' and 'German Butterball'
16. Tomatoes: 'Sungold' and 'Lemon Boy'
17. Hardy, biennial, and annual herbs: Includes parsley, chives, oregano, rosemary, thyme, and basil
18. Lettuce and mesclun mix
19. Radish: 'Cherry Belle'
20. Broccoli
21. Zucchini
22. Kale

Eat Your Yard

Traditionally, the front yard of a home is reserved for a lawn and maybe a foundation planting of trees and shrubs. Nan Chase upends conventional thought by growing fruiting trees, shrubs, and vines, as well as vegetables and herbs, alongside the ornamental plants in her landscape. The end result? Her small garden is able to supply much of her family's fruit and vegetable needs for the year and the majority of their fresh herbs.

> Combines fruit trees, shrubs, and vines, as well as vegetables and herbs for four seasons of homegrown food

> Clever vertical structures lend support to kiwi and grape vines

> Annual vegetables are planted in succession to ensure a non-stop harvest

WHAT NOT TO PLANT

Nan says to avoid planting these in your edible yard, due to their less-than-appealing appearance or pest and disease issues: zucchini, squash, cucumbers ("bugs and powdery mildew"), and tomatoes ("seriously homely, and everyone offers you their excess fresh ones").

Nan Chase has the good fortune to live in an ideal gardening climate near the Blue Ridge Parkway, a national park that runs through the Appalachian Mountains. Mild temperatures, lots of sunshine, and healthy biodiversity reign in this part of the world. The good climate, along with being a stay-at-home mom to three kids, gave her the opportunity to experiment with growing a wide range of edible plants. "I was encouraged to plant varieties that looked beautiful and produced a lot of food," she says. Her plan is based on her own garden, which is just under $\frac{1}{10}$ of an acre and includes a wide range of edible plants in informal beds.

Along with the vegetables, Nan has included trees, shrubs, vines, herbs, and wildflowers — plants she says are equally important. "To me, 'eat your yard' means gardening for landscape beauty that lasts through the four seasons," she says. "In some cases, I mix attractive edibles into ornamental plantings — Swiss chard, herbs, and roses, for example — but I also have a couple of all-vegetable spaces." She evaluates her plants from year to year to assess whether she has really used and liked them, and whether they are reliable.

She recommends that gardeners experiment with both common and unusual plants. For example, almond, peach, and pear trees are excellent landscape plants that are beautiful in full springtime bloom. For outstanding fall color, Nan suggests a sugar maple, pawpaws, serviceberries (also called Saskatoons or Juneberries), blueberries, and pomegranates.

Delicious and beautiful. Her best-tasting edibles include 'Callaway' crab apples ("the fruits are so sweet and juicy"), leeks, scallions (green onions), rugosa roses ("the hips!"), blueberries, and green beans ("they are incomparably tender and have such delicate flavor"). Of course, many of her favorite edibles are also extremely ornamental. "On the pretty side, some of the climbing or runner beans have lovely flowers and graceful habits," she notes. Then there are

Nan's Garden Plan

Mixed ornamentals and shrubs

Mixed vegetables, planted in succession

Persimmon

Climbing or bush rose

blueberries

Pawpaw

Ramps

Brush pile

Persimmon

Wildflowers

Oakleaf hydrangea (or similar)

Vegetables and Herbs

Rhubarb

Mixed ornamentals and shrubs

Lavender

ornamentals

Vegetables

Crab apple

ornamentals

Herbs

Grapes

HOUSE

Pears

Kiwi Vines

Stair garden

Herbs and vegetables

Apples

Pears

Birdbath

Rhubarb

Grapes

Herbs

Crab apple

Sidewalk

the "neutral" plants, which she says "disappear into the general look of an ornamental bed but provide lots of food." Among these are soybeans, which grow to be about 2 feet tall, and bush beans that can be broadcast in a small circle.

Certain areas of Nan's yard are dedicated to mixed vegetable and herb production, which allows the crops to be easily changed throughout the season as plants are harvested. Larger fruiting plants such as crab apples, apples, pawpaws, pears, and

blueberries are more permanent elements in the garden, but no less essential as they provide fruit and year-round interest and act as a screen against street traffic. Nan cautions that the trees and shrubs will require a bit more patience than the quick-growing annual vegetables and herbs. "My pawpaw had fruit this year for the first time — seven years as advertised!" she says with a laugh. Her pomegranates may never bear fruit in her rather cool climate, though she still holds out hope.

Vining interest. To take advantage of vertical space, Nan trains vines like kiwi and grape to climb pillars, trellises, and the two big posts near her stair garden, where she weaves the vines along the railings as they grow. Permanent gravel pathways lead the way around the yard, connecting each section of the garden and permitting easy access to the edible plants.

Nan's Favorite Plants

- **Mixed ornamentals and shrubs:** Spring bulbs such as daffodils, iris, daylilies, liriope, pansies, oriental lilies, peonies, crinum lilies, crape myrtle (dwarf cultivars), boxwood, holly (dwarf cultivars), self-seeding annuals, butterfly weed, butterfly bush, phlox, astilbe, lamb's ears, sedum, ferns, hostas, and bee balm

- **Mixed vegetables, planted in succession:** Onions, artichokes, lettuce, spinach, kale, Swiss chard, garlic, carrots, peas, beans, potatoes, soybeans (edamame), broccoli, cauliflower, cabbage, beets, pak choi, popcorn, kohlrabi, okra, peppers (hot or sweet), and tomatoes

- **Fruit:** 'Callaway' crab apple and 'Concord', muscadine, or other table grape

- **Herbs:** Parsley, sage, rosemary, thyme, oregano, fennel (bronze or Florence), tarragon, chives, anise hyssop, spearmint, horseradish, lemon verbena, chamomile, and lovage

- **Wildflowers:** Jerusalem artichokes, goldenrod, and ramps

Partially Shaded Vegetables

Marjorie Harris knows shade, and she understands the challenges that go along with trying to grow food in reduced light. Her design includes the best edibles for less-than-ideal light conditions, and Marjorie offers a handful of sneaky ideas to help ensure a decent harvest.

> Designed for partially shaded sites

> Features a charming checkerboard pattern with 2-foot-square stones and planting pockets

> Uses leafy shade-tolerant edibles like kale, Swiss chard, lettuce, and beets

"You can put these crops together and make something absolutely glorious — a tapestry of color and texture," says Marjorie Harris.

Marjorie Harris lives and gardens in downtown Toronto, where she has tended the same plot since 1967. Over the years, maturing trees have drastically reduced the amount of light her garden receives, and since she turned into an "obsessive gardener" in the 1980s, space has also become rather scarce. When she didn't have enough sunlight to grow the same vegetables she had been growing for years, she had to find new edibles. That's when she discovered that many vegetables and herbs will still grow and produce a harvest when shaded slightly.

Of course, there are varying degrees of shade, and those with full or deep shade will find it difficult to bring any type of edibles to a harvestable stage. Still, there are possibilities for these gardeners as well. "Even if you've got what seems to be a hopeless sun situation, you can grow some vegetables," Marjorie says, advising a light-challenged gardener to stick to leafy crops like kale, spinach, leaf lettuce, and Chinese cabbage, which can still produce a harvest with just 3 to 4 hours of sunlight. "You can put these crops together and make something absolutely glorious — a tapestry of color and texture."

Tips for working with shade. In dappled or partial shade, gardeners will have more luck, but they should still look for a bright spot to site their gardens. If possible, choose a location with a nearby shed or wall that can be painted white to reflect light into the garden. Rich, healthy soil will also help give edibles a head start, so loosen and amend your soil well before planting. If nearby trees are shading your garden, their roots may be stealing nutrients and water from your vegetables; in that case, raised beds might be a good idea.

Creating the checkerboard. Marjorie's plan is extremely flexible in that you can place the plants wherever you like, and it can be quickly installed in a large or small yard. To create the checkerboard, Marjorie has staggered 2-foot-square patio stones, set in sand, with 2-foot-square garden plots.

Picking stones. When selecting stones, keep in mind that light-colored ones will reflect sunlight back to the plants, giving your shady garden a boost. This formal pattern offers visual interest to the garden, but Marjorie is quick to point out that the stones also absorb heat, extending the growing season and creating a small microclimate.

Between the stones, the tidy planting squares allow you to focus your gardening efforts on a small area, making seeding or transplanting a snap. In addition, when growing in such compact squares, the decorative foliage of vegetables such as Swiss chard and dinosaur ('Lacinato') kale can be fully appreciated. In the middle of the garden, an obelisk for pole beans or peas is a practical choice, adding vertical interest and support for vining crops.

Producing fruit in the shade. To grow fruiting crops like baby eggplants and cherry tomatoes even in light shade, consider planting in large pots that are positioned in the sunniest parts of the garden. Marjorie notes cherry tomatoes will mature more quickly than large-fruited types and be more likely to produce a harvest, and "baby eggplant is delicious and colorful, but it needs at least 6 hours of sun per day to bear a decent crop." Try 'Little Fingers', 'Listada De Gandia', or 'Fairy Tale'.

MARJORIE'S TRICKS FOR OVERCOMING SHADE

- **Look up.** Trying to find a spot with enough light to grow edibles can be a challenge, especially when the available location is situated under tall trees. Before you give up, look up! Are there any branches that could be thinned (possibly professionally, if the trees are mature) to let in more light?

- **Reflect it.** Planting a vegetable garden near a brightly colored wall or fence, or applying a reflective mulch to the soil surface, will bounce light back to the plants.

- **Amend it.** Vegetables growing in shade will need all the help they can get to produce a decent crop, so make sure that your soil is well amended with compost or aged manure.

Leafy crops like lettuce, kale, and spinach work well in shady sites.

Use light-colored patio stone to create a checkerboard pattern and reflect light back to the plants.

Marjorie's Garden Plan

10' DEEP X 14' WIDE

1. Spinach
2. Lettuce
3. Beets
4. Pak choi
5. Kale
6. Swiss chard
7. Obelisk with pole beans

Find a sunny spot for Marjorie's mix of fine herbs:

8. Basil
9. Parsley
10. Mint
11. Sage
12. Thyme
13. Rosemary

10.	1.		11. + 12.		3.	13.
8.		5. + 9.		5. + 9.		2.
	6.		7.		6.	
4.		1. + 5.		5. + 9.		2.
	1.		2.		3.	

Windy City Harvest

THE COMMUNITY IMPACT OF THE CHICAGO BOTANIC GARDEN can't be overstated. The garden has ties with such programs as the Cook's County Sheriff's Vocational Rehabilitation Impact Center, and Windy City Harvest, a project that also includes a summer internship program for junior and high school students called Green Youth Farm. Windy City Harvest is an outreach program that offers hands-on training and experience in organic vegetable and plant growing for 15 to 20 adults each year who are interested in obtaining jobs in the "green industry." Graduates of the course at Windy City Harvest receive a certificate in sustainable horticulture delivered by the Chicago Botanic Garden in partnership with Richard J. Daley College.

Windy City Harvest also provides local, healthy, and affordable food for community residents. Between 2009 and 2012, it produced 55,920 pounds of produce that was sold to wholesale suppliers like Midwest Foods, and it also contributed 26,158 pounds of produce through government-subsidized outlets like Women, Infant, and Children's centers and at farmers' markets that accept SNAP benefits and senior coupons. "Growing food is the scaffold that supports real training, the possibility of self-sufficiency, and the way forward for a more sustainable and community-centered local economy," said Angela Mason, Director of Community Gardening for the Chicago Botanic Garden.

The largest production site of Windy City Harvest is located at the Rodeo Garden, an urban plot that covers nearly 2 acres. Over the course of a single season, the Rodeo Garden produces approximately 15,000 pounds of vegetables. It provides transitional jobs for graduates of Windy City Harvest as well as the young men who have completed their four-month residence at the Vocational Rehabilitation Impact Program. When baseball season is under way, food from this garden is shared with fans of the Chicago White Sox at Levy Restaurant, located in U.S. Cellular Field.

Along with organic urban farming methods, students learn essential business skills. After six months of hands-on instruction at Windy City Harvest, students spend three months in a paid internship before graduating. After they've completed their course, many graduates become employees of the Chicago Botanic Garden.

Small Space Beds

Often described as a "living museum," the Chicago Botanic Garden occupies 385 acres on and around nine islands and boasts 26 distinct gardens, including the popular Regenstein Fruit and Vegetable Garden, where the Small Space Beds are located. The garden focuses on innovative techniques and ideas for growing more food with less land.

❯ Relies on intensive cropping, interplanting, and succession planting techniques

❯ Vertical supports and structures, as well as containers and window boxes, boost production

❯ Diverse plantings attract beneficial and pollinating insects

Visitors to the Regenstein Fruit and Vegetable Garden at the Chicago Botanic Garden will enjoy breathtaking scenery and colorful plant combinations as they stroll around the island, but they may be surprised to learn that the focus of this amazing space is on edible, rather than ornamental, plants. A closer look will reveal that the real stars of the show are the hundreds of different types of organically grown vegetable, herb, fruit, berry, and nut plants — most of which are well suited to the Chicago climate.

One of the more popular exhibits is the Small Space Beds. Here, six garden beds make up the prime production area: three long, narrow plots and three smaller geometrically shaped beds. These six gardens are densely planted with plenty of high-producing crops to provide food from spring through late autumn. "The narrow beds allow easy access to all parts of the garden without the gardeners needing to walk on the soil," says Lisa Hilgenberg, a horticulturist at the Chicago Botanic Garden. "By not walking on the beds, the soil remains loose and well aerated for good root development."

Learn new gardening methods. Most urban gardeners won't have enough room to re-create the entire small-space garden, but its style and the methods used to maintain it — such as intensive planting, intercropping, and succession planting — can be transferred to a home garden on a smaller scale. "A big advantage of growing crops intensively is that with thoughtful planning, large amounts of produce can be harvested from a small garden space," says Lisa, who also points out other advantages to growing crops intensively: soil moisture retention and weed reduction. "With the plants spaced close together, as they fill in and shade the ground, there are fewer weed problems," she notes.

Experiment with diversity. The Chicago Botanic Garden also uses the Regenstein Fruit and Vegetable Garden to illustrate the diversity found in the vegetable world. For example, gardeners there plant three different varieties of each vegetable to allow visitors to see how each plant responds to the Chicago climate. Diversity is well recognized by organic gardeners as a key to maintaining a healthy plot, and a garden planted with a wide range of vegetables, flowers, and herbs also will draw in more beneficial and pollinating insects, helping to minimize pest populations and ensure good fruit set on crops like cucumbers and zucchini.

Grow up. To grow more food in less space, many crops are grown vertically. Vining crops such as pole beans, grapes, kiwi, and cucumbers are grown up supports. Compact edibles like garden cress, violas, and kohlrabi are planted in pots, window boxes, or hanging baskets. "This garden says, 'Wherever there is a sunny spot, there's room for a pot, planter, trough, or garden bed to grow edible plants' — you can do this at home!" says Lisa.

THREE BASICS OF SMALL-SPACE GARDENING

1. Intensive planting. Minimize wasted space by planting crops close together. Raised beds are a cornerstone of intensive planting and allow you to easily prepare soil and care for closely spaced crops without the need to walk on — and compact — the soil.

2. Interplanting. This technique involves growing two or more vegetables in the same space at the same time. Generally vegetables are matched by maturity times (long versus slow), plant size (tall and upright versus short and spreading) or nutritional needs (heavy versus light feeders).

3. Succession planting. Once a crop has finished, it is immediately pulled and tossed on the compost pile, and the empty space is replanted with fresh seeds or seedlings.

For Intensive Beds

1. **Beets:** 'Red Ace', 'Kestrel', and 'Touchstone'
2. **Scallions (spring onions):** 'Nebechan', 'Guardsman', and 'Deep Purple'
3. **Spinach:** 'Space', 'Corvair', and 'Red Cardinal'
4. **Radish:** 'Rudolf', 'Crunchy Red', and 'Shunkyo Semi-Long'
5. **Parsnips:** 'Panache'
6. **Lettuce:** 'Rouge Grenobloise' ('Red Grenoble'), 'Merlot', and 'Black Seeded Simpson'
7. **Cabbage:** 'Caraflex', 'Gonzales', and 'Savoy Express' (early varieties)
8. **Carrots:** 'Berlicum 2', 'Purple Haze', and 'Atomic Red'
9. **Turnips:** 'Purple Top White Globe', 'Tokyo Cross', and 'Tokyo Market'
10. **Collards:** 'Top Bunch'
13. **'Hon Tsai Tai' mustard, claytonia, 'Surrey' arugula, and 'Wildfire' lettuce mix**
14. **Pak choi:** 'Win-win Choi', 'Mei Qing Choi', and 'Joi Choi'
15. **Roses:** 'Nyveldt's White' hybrid rugosa (2012 Herb of the Year)
16. **Kale:** 'Toscano'
17. **Culinary herbs:** Chervil, chives, sage, salad burnet, parsley, coriander, thyme

For Vertical Beds

11. **Lettuce, garden cress, and violas in hanging baskets**
12. **Kohlrabi (purple and white), garden cress, violas, and snapdragons in window boxes**
18. **Espaliered apples underplanted with rhubarb:** 'Baldwin' apples, 'Canada Red' rhubarb
19. **Kiwi:** Hardy 'Arctic Beauty'
20. **Espaliered apple:** 'Wolf River'

The Small Space Beds Plan

105' DEEP X 100' WIDE

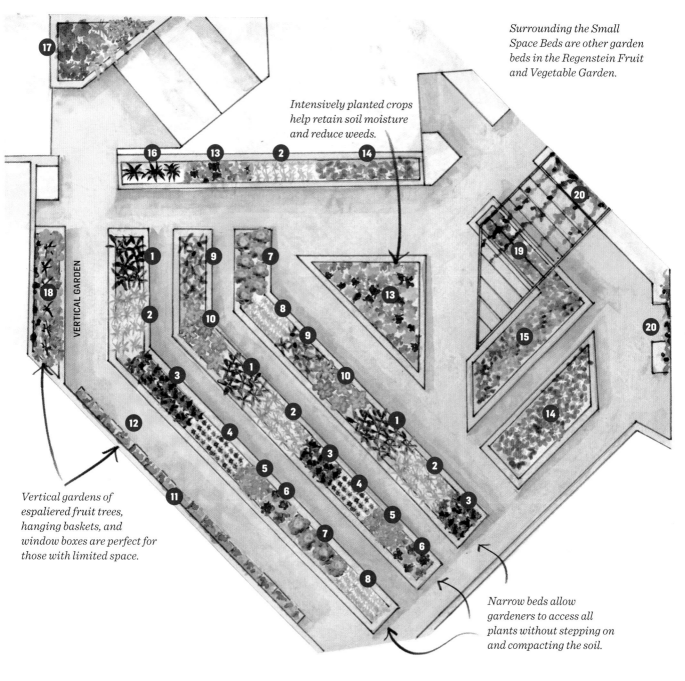

Surrounding the Small Space Beds are other garden beds in the Regenstein Fruit and Vegetable Garden.

Intensively planted crops help retain soil moisture and reduce weeds.

VERTICAL GARDEN

Vertical gardens of espaliered fruit trees, hanging baskets, and window boxes are perfect for those with limited space.

Narrow beds allow gardeners to access all plants without stepping on and compacting the soil.

The Circle of Life

E mma Cooper's plan creates an ecosystem with multiple functions. In addition to providing a space to grow food, it produces ample compost, comfrey tea (a natural nutrient source rich in potassium and nitrogen), and chicken manure for enriching the soil. The garden is designed as a series of concentric circles to emphasize the importance of recycling nutrients through compost and back into the garden soil, which itself is a closed-loop system.

> A closed-loop design that comprises a series of concentric circles for chicken and food production

> Includes six beds for fruits, berries, and vegetables, and a compost area to recycle chicken and garden waste

> A central flower bed provides food for beneficials and pollinators, as well as blooms for bouquets

> A comfrey tower creates high-nutrient tea to nourish food plants

The entrance to the garden is through an arbor that can do double duty in spring, summer, and autumn by supporting climbing vegetables such as pole beans and cucumbers, or ornamental gourds and flowering vines. The outer ring is a chicken run, which provides a secure space for a small flock of backyard hens that "recycle kitchen scraps, crop residues, and garden pests into a supply of high-nitrogen fertilizer and compost activator," says Emma. Plus, the chickens supply eggs and help clean up the garden beds when empty or in winter. The manure can be conveniently disposed of in the adjacent compost bins.

Hot composting. The second ring of the garden includes three compost bins. An avid composter, Emma explains that the three compost bins "allow the composter to practice hot composting — building up layers of green and brown materials (high-nitrogen and high-carbon matter) which then heat up and rot down quickly." Once the first pile starts to cool, it is turned into the second bin.

This transfer adds oxygen that reignites the hot composting process. When the heap in the second bin cools, it is turned into the third bin to mature.

If the hot-composting method is too labor-intensive, Emma suggests cold composting, in which both green and brown materials are added to the bin and left there. This method proceeds more slowly but is much easier. When the first bin is full, composters begin adding materials to the second bin, and when that is full, to the third. "By the time all the bins are full, it's time to empty the first one," says Emma.

Using a comfrey tower. Near the composting area Emma has planted a patch of comfrey, the rotting leaves of which are used to fertilize her vegetable and berry crops. "Comfrey is a leafy perennial plant with deep roots that bring up nutrients from the subsoil," notes Emma. The leaves rot quickly with very little residue and contain much of the nutrients brought up by the roots. To capture

Emma's Garden Plan

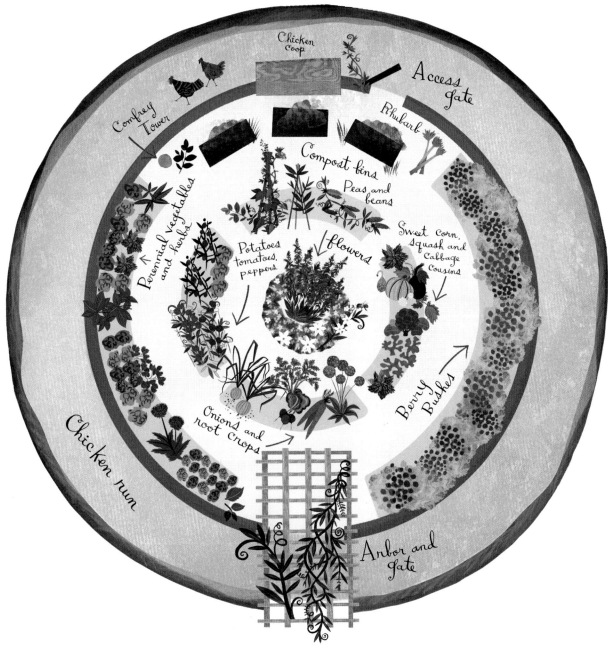

Chicken Coop

Access Gate

Comfrey Tower

Rhubarb

Compost bins

Peas and beans

Perennial vegetables and herbs

Sweet corn, squash and Cabbage Cousins

Potatoes tomatoes, peppers

flowers

Onions and root crops

Berry Bushes

Chicken run

Arbor and Gate

the goodness of comfrey, Emma uses a "comfrey tea tower," which is simply a section of 8-inch-diameter PVC pipe fixed to a fence post (see illustration on next page). A piece of mesh is placed over the bottom of the pipe, and just-harvested leaves are inserted into the top. A bottle or bucket can be placed beneath the mesh to collect the concentrated liquid released from the rotting leaves. This "tea" should be diluted with water (approximately 15:1 water to comfrey tea) before it is used to sidedress any crops. "Tomatoes and peppers love the high-potash

Just-harvested comfrey leaves go in top of an 8-inch-diameter PVC pipe.

Comfrey leaves rot within the pipe.

A bucket catches the concentrated liquid from the rotting leaves, to be used as fertilizer in the garden.

liquid," says Emma, who also uses it for all of her fruiting plants. She recommends growing a sterile cultivar of comfrey, such as Bocking 14, to prevent prolific self-sowing.

Near the third compost bin, a clump of rhubarb supplies both stems for cooking and leaves (toxic to humans) for the compost pile. Flanking the compost bins are the beds of perennial vegetables and herbs and berries, which Emma mulches with garden compost in the spring.

Beautiful focal point. The central rings of Emma's "Circle of Life" garden include four beds for vegetables and an inner circle for flowers. The round flower bed is decorative, but it also serves multiple purposes: attracting pollinators and providing cut flowers.

Emma has assigned a vegetable family to each bed: potatoes, tomatoes, and peppers in one; peas and beans in another; sweet corn, squash, and cabbage "cousins" (brassicas such as broccoli and kale) in a third; and onions and root crops in the last. The beds are rotated each year to keep the soil and the plants healthy, resulting in a four-year cycle. Emma says that crop rotation helps prevent the build-up of pests and disease. In addition, "as each crop has different nutrient requirements and a differing ability to shade out weeds, these things are balanced out as well," she says.

The size of the garden can be adjusted, but a diameter of 32 feet will offer plenty of room.

Emma's Favorite Varieties

For a dual crop, sow salad greens like lettuce and spinach between and underneath the slower-growing tomatoes, peppers, broccoli, kale, and pole beans.

- **Bush beans:** 'Royal Burgundy', 'Dragon Tongue', and 'Provider'
- **Pole beans:** 'Emerite', 'Purple Podded Pole', and 'Blue Lake'
- **Beets:** 'Touchstone Gold', 'Chioggia', 'Early Wonder', and 'Cylindra'

- **Broccoli:** 'Arcadia' and 'Premium Crop'
- **Carrots:** 'Purple Dragon', 'Yaya', 'Atomic Red', and 'Rainbow Mix'
- **Kale:** 'Red Russian', 'Winterbor', and 'Rainbow Lacinato'
- **Onions:** 'Red Beauty', 'Candy', 'Rossa di Milano', and 'Ailsa Craig'
- **Peas:** 'Super Sugar Snap', 'Sugar Ann', and 'Oregon Sugar Pod II'
- **Peppers:** 'Jimmy Nardello', 'Jalapeño', and 'Miniature Red Bell'

- **Potatoes:** 'Russian Banana', 'All Blue', and 'Yukon Gold'
- **Summer squash:** 'Costata Romanesco' and 'Yellow Scallop'
- **Sweet corn:** 'Earlivee' and 'Honey & Cream'
- **Tomatoes:** 'Persimmon', 'Pineapple', 'Kellogg's Breakfast', and 'Chocolate Cherry'
- **Winter squash:** 'Sweet Dumpling' and 'Bush Delicata'

Sunburst Veggie Garden

Who would have thought that growing food could be so controversial? Yet in many regions, front-yard vegetable gardeners have been met with opposition by their neighbors and municipalities over their right to tear up grass and replace it with edible plants. In her plan, Shawna Coronado sides with the food, demonstrating that a vegetable garden can be pleasing to the eye *and* the palate.

> The unique sunburst design draws attention to the color and texture of each crop or ornamental plant

> Includes a bench to enjoy the view

> Adds value to the neighborhood and provides diversity for pollinators and beneficial insects

"My gardens beautify the community, improve our home values, help feed the community, and make a difference for my neighbors," Shawna Coronado says.

Traditionally the front yard has been reserved for grass, but with the increased interest in green living, more homeowners are putting their front yards into food production. For Shawna, necessity was the major motivation. She wanted to grow vegetables, but "the only sunny spot was the front lawn, so my solution was to rip out all the grass and plant sun-loving vegetables," she says.

Because the garden would be so open to the neighborhood, Shawna wanted it to be both beautiful and edible. As she laid out the curved pathway and shaped the large garden bed, she realized it resembled a setting sun. "When I imagined the sun, it was only a quick jump to realize I might build the vegetable beds into a sunburst shape," she says.

Creating rays of beautiful color. Using ornamental vegetables such as 'Bright Lights' Swiss chard or 'Bull's Blood' beets, she created swaths of color and texture for each "ray." By using a different shade of green or burgundy in every other row, she made the rays more pronounced and attractive. In fact, Shawna says that

most people who walk by the garden don't even realize that most of the plants are vegetables.

A simple approach. Shawna insists that "this is a creative solution that anyone can create around a patio garden." To create the straight lines that define each ray, Shawna used thin rope fastened onto wooden stakes. Within each roped section, she planted edibles or perennials, depending on the amount of light that part of the garden received. In the shadiest section of the garden, she planted rays of low-light ornamentals such as hostas and heucheras. In the brighter sun, she began to lay out the vegetable ray rows.

In the first vegetable ray, she chose a decorative vegetable such as 'Bright Lights' Swiss chard; 'Premium Crop' broccoli; 'Bull's Blood' beets; or red, white, and yellow onion sets. The second vegetable ray features hybrid cabbage seedlings, the third 'Yummy Snacking' sweet peppers, the fourth pineapple sage plants (ornamental), and the final vegetable ray in the garden holds Brussels sprouts. Gardeners lucky enough to have full sun can use edible plants for the full sunburst design, including favorites such as tomatoes, peppers, bush beans, and basil.

Deterring rabbits. To help repel the local bunny population, which devastated her vegetables in the first season, Shawna surrounded the sunburst garden with marigolds. "The secret is to get the old-fashioned 'smelly' varieties," she advises, since the rabbits shy away from the scent. Try 'Dwarf French', 'Queen Sophia', or 'Brocade Mix'.

Beating the heat. As summers in Chicago have grown longer, hotter,

and drier, Shawna has turned to a few "secret weapons" to ensure her garden stays lush and healthy all summer long, such as 1 to 2 inches of mulch (leaves and chipped wood) and a dedicated watering program. She also takes care of the soil by adding compost and composted manure as well as soil additives like worm castings and organic fertilizers, all without tilling. "Strong soil means strong microbes for the plants to interact with and more water holding capacity," she says. "By strengthening the soil you strengthen the plant. Think of it as vitamins to help your organic vegetables grow to their very strongest."

Beautifying the neighborhood. Growing food in the front yard has gotten many gardeners in trouble, since many towns prohibit the planting of edibles in such a highly visible location. Luckily for Shawna, her community has been extremely supportive, and her front-yard garden has been a rewarding experience for both her and her neighbors. "Fortunately, my neighbors know I'm the 'crazy garden lady' and have supported me wholeheartedly from the very beginning," she says. "My gardens beautify the community, improve our home values, help feed the community, and make a difference for my neighbors," she adds.

Shawna's Garden Plan

25' DEEP X 26' WIDE

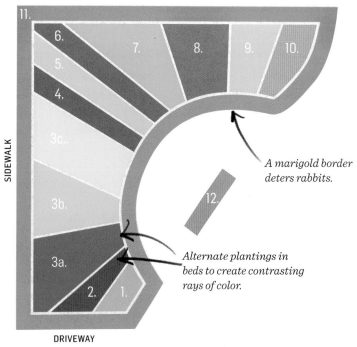

A marigold border deters rabbits.

Alternate plantings in beds to create contrasting rays of color.

SIDEWALK

DRIVEWAY

1. 'Rozanne' and 'Biokovo karmina' perennial geraniums
2. 'Dolce Blackcurrant' heuchera
3a–c. 'Patriot', 'Gold Standard', 'Halcyon', 'August Moon', or 'Guacamole' hostas
4. 'Bright Lights' Swiss chard
5. 'Premium Crop' broccoli
6. 'Bull's Blood' beets
7. Hybrid cabbage
8. 'Yummy Snacking' sweet peppers
9. Pineapple sage
10. Brussels sprouts
11. Marigolds
12. Bench

Living Walls

FOR ROBIN PLASKOFF HORTON, a creative director for over 30 years, design has always been a passion. When the idea for her award-winning website Urban Gardens came to her during a post-professional design workshop with iconic designer Milton Glaser, she felt she had found her niche.

Unlike suburban or rural gardeners who typically have sufficient space for a vegetable plot, urban gardeners face many challenges, with the need to find a suitable site often being the overriding issue. A trend spotter and design writer, Robin tackles these issues on her website in a way that both encourages and inspires. Her frequent updates feature innovative ideas, products, and techniques for cultivating a garden where there is little or no growing area.

Vertical gardens are one such way for urban gardeners to economize their small site and leave valuable floor space for furniture, grills, or décor. When picking edible plants for a vertical garden, Robin says to base your selections on the amount of sunlight your garden receives. Most vegetables and herbs require full sun for optimum growth, but leafy herbs and greens will grow well with 3 to 5 hours of light. "For pockets in vertical systems, choose compact crops like spinach, lettuce, parsley, Asian greens, or strawberries, mixing up plants with various colors and textures," says Robin.

Robin says that many urban gardeners have created their own vertical gardens using "upcycled pallets, bookshelves, and DIY pocket gardens from hanging shoe bags." For those looking for something more straightforward, there are also a number of commercially available vertical gardening units and kits available for purchase (see Resources for websites).

✦ HANG-A-POT. This clever product allows you to attach 4- to 10-inch pots to any surface — brick, wood, lattice, vinyl fencing, and more. Robin suggests hanging a collection of pots to cover an entire wall or fence, or just a portion of it.

✦ CLINGER CLIP. Similar to Hang-A-Pot, the Clinger Clip also allows you to mount a pot on just about any surface. Simply install the clip, plant your pot with your desired edible, and slip it into the device. Voila! You have an instant edible garden for an underused space.

✦ FLOWALL. A rectangular panel (15 by 16 inches) with 16 removable small pots, Flowall is perfect for compact herbs and salad greens. A water reservoir keeps the plants irrigated for up to six weeks, making this a low-maintenance and innovative choice.

✦ URBIO. A modular, magnetic, versatile vertical surface, Urbio can be used for plants, garden décor, and more. "Urbio's magnetic system can transform any wall or ferrous surface into a beautiful vertical garden," says Robin. Choose from a range of eco-plastic pots with strong magnets that will keep your plants secure on the wall.

✦ PLANTS ON WALLS. According to Robin, many vertical gardening products use a pocket design with a feltlike material made from recycled plastic water bottles. "Plants on Walls offers a root-wrapping system that enables you to move the various modular pieces without disrupting the plants," she says.

Formal Herb Garden

Herbs are both useful and decorative, adapting easily to formal and informal designs. Kate Copsey has arranged a selection of popular culinary herbs in a pleasing symmetrical design in her formal herb garden. A hedge of fragrant lavender surrounds the plot, and a crisscross of compact germander or upright thyme separates the tidy beds.

› Situate the compact plan off the back deck for convenient harvesting or in the front yard to inspire neighbors

› Low-growing herbal hedges divide the garden into triangular sections

› Freeze or dry herbs for the winter pantry

Using symmetry. A formal herb garden can take many forms, including knots (see page 127), geometric shapes, and beds arranged in grids. Whatever the design, symmetry is important. In Kate's rectangular plot, the garden is divided into four main planting beds — two of green basil and lemon balm or golden sage and two of purple basil and Italian or Greek oregano, with alike plots directly diagonal from one another. Formal gardens require more maintenance than cottage gardens, as they will need to be trimmed to stay neat and preserve the visual symmetry.

Kate's plan can easily be adapted to different spaces, though she recommends that the garden be at least 8 by 10 feet. In a larger garden, a path of stepping stones could be tucked between the plants to allow easy access. When it comes to site selection, Kate advises choosing a sunny spot with well-drained soil close to the house.

Historically, formal herb gardens included plants such as germander, upright types of thyme, rosemary, lavender, and santolina. Kate chose the majority of the plants in her design based on their culinary uses and appearance. "Most have good flavor," she says, "but they also have contrasting colors or leaf form to give some aesthetic appeal to the garden." The plan includes perennial, biennial, and annual herbs, as well as a pot of bay that can be brought indoors to overwinter in areas colder than Zone 8.

Defining edges. For the double border around the garden, Kate chose a combination of lavender on the outside and curly parsley along the inside edge. "Plants like tightly curled parsley or 'Boxwood' basil make excellent edging plants," notes Kate. Since many formal gardens are subdivided into smaller planting sections, she has added two low hedges that crisscross the middle of the plot. A hedge of germander or upright thyme runs diagonally from the four corners to the center of the plot, while stretches of sage create a cross.

Tucked into the small triangular garden beds are popular culinary herbs, including basil, oregano, and lemon balm. Greek and Italian oregano are both tender perennials

Kate's Garden Plan

8' DEEP X 10' WIDE

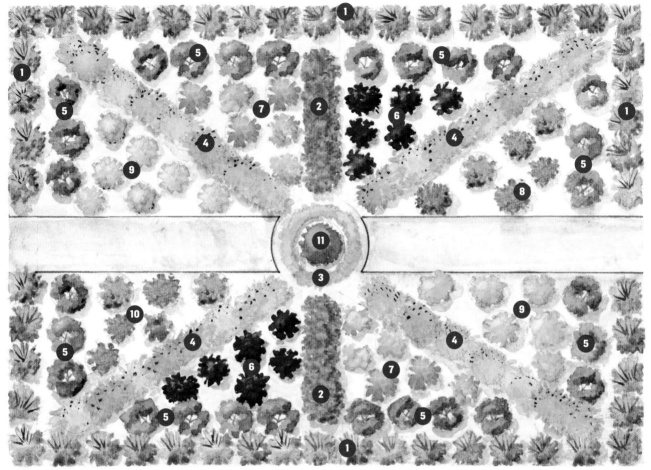

north of Zone 5, so they may need to be replanted each year, depending on where they are grown. Green and purple basil are also warm-season herbs. They can be purchased as plants in late spring or grown directly from seed. For the purple basil, Kate suggests the cultivars 'Purple Ruffles' and 'Round Midnight'.

Best time to pick. To preserve top flavor, Kate recommends harvesting herbs in the morning, once the dew has dried from the leaves. She makes herbal vinegars to use in the winter, but garden herbs can also be frozen or dried for later use. To dry, bundle a small group of stems together and hang them in a cool, well ventilated place that is out of direct sunlight, until the plants are completely dry.

Edging Plants

1. Lavender
2. 'Aurea' golden sage
3. Lemon thyme
4. Germander

Center Plants

5. Curly parsley
6. 'Purple Ruffles' or 'Round Midnight' purple basil
7. Green basil
8. Italian oregano
9. Lemon balm
10. Greek oregano
11. Bay tree (in a center pot)

Chile Lover's Garden

Those who prefer their food on the spicy side will enjoy Dave DeWitt's "Chile Lover's Garden". He offers plenty of tips on growing great peppers, and he highlights the diversity of chile peppers, including the superhots 'Scorpion', 'Bhut Jolokia', and 'Fatalii'. Just keep a glass of milk handy in case you can't take the heat!

❯ Features some of the hottest peppers in the world

❯ Includes 24 different varieties of peppers

❯ Grown in raised beds to offer early spring warm-up and improved drainage

Like many other gardeners — from the North to the South — Dave DeWitt, known as the Pope of Peppers, has become hooked on collecting and cultivating these ancient plants. Peppers originated more than 5,000 years ago in what is now known as Bolivia. According to Dave, there are about 25 species of *Capsicum*, but only five have been domesticated. Of those five species, there are thousands of cultivated varieties, but only around 20 varieties are significant to commercial growers. The good news for home gardeners is that they have free rein to experiment with the countless chile varieties that seed companies offer in varying degrees of flavor and heat.

Soil for chiles. To grow great peppers, Dave advises growing in raised beds that receive plenty of sunshine and decent, but not heavily amended, well-drained soil. He notes that too much nitrogen can reduce yield. His ideal soil medium is a combination of topsoil, aged compost, and unfertilized potting soil. Cold-climate gardeners can get a jump on the season by purchasing plants or starting seeds indoors or in a greenhouse. Once the pepper seedlings are set in the ground, he advises applying a mulch of shredded tree bark.

Packing on the heat. To spotlight the diversity of chile peppers, Dave has selected 24 different varieties, all of which are available through seed catalogs, as well as in transplant form through Dave's website. Pepper enthusiasts will appreciate Dave's superhot pepper bed, which includes some of the world's hottest peppers. 'Scorpion' and 'Bhut Jolokia' are considered extremely hot, rated over 1,000,000 on the Scoville Scale (a measure of a chile pepper's heat).

Cooking with chiles. Countless dishes around the world are enhanced by the scorching heat of chile peppers, including chili, salsa, and curries. Dave prefers serranos and habañeros in fresh salsas; New Mexican chiles in sauces with enchiladas, tamales, and *carne adovada*; and dried red chiles in curries. Just remember to wash your hands extremely well after handling chile peppers to avoid skin or eye irritation. Or wear rubber gloves.

Beauty with a Bite

With their assortment of colors, shapes, and sizes, it's easy to see the beauty in the following peppers. However, it would be a mistake to confuse beautiful with sweet, as many of these fruits are smoke-coming-out-of-your-ears hot and should be approached with caution.

MILD

'Bishop's Crown'. The flattened, three-sided shape of the mild (heat level 6), almost sweet fruits of this pepper give rise to its name. The plants themselves are quite large, growing 3 to 4 feet tall and yielding dozens of green fruits that mature to red.

'Ancho 101'. A mildly hot, heart-shaped pepper, it produces 3- to 4-inch-long fruits that are 2 to 3 inches wide. The green fruits age to red and are known as ancho when dry and poblano when fresh.

'Angkor Sunrise'. Pretty pale peppers (heat level 5) are initially soft yellow but mature to red. The plants can grow up to 4 feet tall, producing a good yield of the 1½-inch-long and ½-inch-wide fruits.

MEDIUM HOT

'Lemon Drop'. The vinelike plant of 'Lemon Drop' will grow about 3 feet tall, producing sunny yellow, cone-shaped fruits (heat level 8 to 9) that grow around 2 to 3 inches long and have a pleasing citrusy flavor.

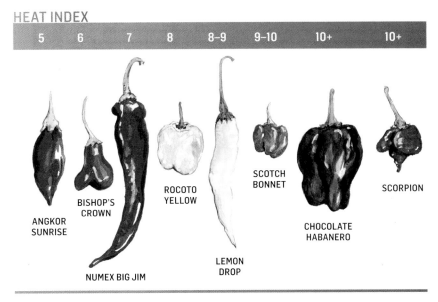

| 5 | 6 | 7 | 8 | 8–9 | 9–10 | 10+ | 10+ |

ANGKOR SUNRISE

BISHOP'S CROWN

NUMEX BIG JIM

ROCOTO YELLOW

LEMON DROP

SCOTCH BONNET

CHOCOLATE HABANERO

SCORPION

'Aji Rojo'. The peppers (heat level 7) grow about 1 inch wide and 5 to 6 inches long. They are initially green but turn chocolate brown and eventually mature to orange-red.

'NuMex Big Jim'. Considered to be the longest chile pepper in the world. The 2-foot plants yield peppers that typically grow to be around 9 inches long but have been known to exceed a foot in length! The cone-shaped fruits (heat level 7) mature green to red.

'Tabasco'. Upright pods are held in profusion on 3-foot plants. The fruits (heat level 7) begin as soft yellow-green but eventually turn red.

'Siling Labuyo'. Small, cone-shaped fruits (heat level 8) grow just 1 to 1½ inches long and ¼ to ¾ inches wide. The green fruits turn red as they mature.

'Rocoto Red'. Small, apple-shaped fruits (heat level 8) grow to be 1½ inches long by 1½ inches wide, starting green but aging to bright red.

'Rocoto Yellow'. Similar in shape and size to 'Rocoto Red', this variety has yellow fruits (heat level 8).

REALLY HOT

'Orange Habanero'. A really hot chile (heat level 10), its bright orange fruits grow 1 to 1½ inches long.

'Red Habanero'. The size and shape of these fruits (heat level 10) are similar to those of 'Orange Habanero', but the skin color is a bright cherry red.

'Scotch Bonnet'. Named for its resemblance to the traditional Scottish hat called a tam, the 'Scotch Bonnet' pepper has an aroma and flavor often described as fruity or sweet.

Yet don't underestimate its heat, as it ranks high among the hot peppers (heat level 9 to 10).

'Chiltepin'. A unique variety thought to be a wild form. Its tiny 1/4- to 3/4-inch fruits (heat level 10) are green, aging to red.

SUPERHOT

'Scorpion'. The Scorpion is one of the world's hottest peppers, measuring up to 1,400,000 on the Scoville rating (heat level 10+). The name comes from the shape of the fruits, which have a pointed end said to look like a scorpion's stinger.

'Bhut Jolokia'. An elongated-type habanero, this extremely hot pepper (heat level 10+) bears 2- to 3-inch-long fruits that mature to a bright red. Also called 'Ghost Chile', it boasts a Scoville rating over 1,000,000!

'Chocolate Habanero'. Chocolate lovers be warned! The 2-inch-long fruits of this fiery habanero (heat level 10+) are named for the chocolate brown color of their mature pods, not for any sweetness in the flavor.

'Fatalii'. This habanero-type pepper bears eye-catching, cone-shaped, bright yellow fruits that can grow to be over 3 inches long. 'Fatalii' fruits are considered among the hottest of the chiles (heat level 10+), so handle with care.

TASTY ORNAMENTALS

'NuMex Centennial'. Sometimes referred to as just 'Centennial', this pepper was developed by New Mexico State University for its 100th anniversary. It has purple foliage, flowers, and (initially) purple fruits. As they mature, the small pods ripen from purple to yellow to orange and finally to red.

'Black Prince'. This is an unusual ornamental with dark-colored foliage and purple-black pods that mature to red. It's great for container gardens!

'Chilly Chili'. This compact hybrid has dense growth and clusters of long-lasting, tapered fruits that emerge yellow but mature to red. It's considered childproof, as it is non-pungent.

'Orange Peter'. Considered a medium-hot pepper, this variety is often grown as an ornamental for its 3-inch-long, blunt-shaped peppers. The fruits ripen from green to orange.

Peppers by Species

Dave likes to group his peppers by species. If you like, follow the Pope of Peppers and arrange your pepper beds in these groups!

CAPSICUM ANNUUM

- 'Ancho 101'
- 'NuMex Big Jim'
- 'Chiltepin'

CAPSICUM ANNUUM ORNAMENTALS

- 'NuMex Centennial'
- 'Black Prince'
- 'Chilly Chili'
- 'Orange Peter'

CAPSICUM BACCATUM

- 'Bishop's Crown'
- 'Lemon Drop'
- 'Aji Rojo'

CAPSICUM CHINENSE

- 'Orange Habanero'
- 'Red Habanero'
- 'Scotch Bonnet'

CAPSICUM FRUTESCENS

- 'Tabasco'
- 'Siling Labuyo'
- 'Angkor Sunrise'

CAPSICUM PUBESCENS

- 'Rocoto Red'
- 'Rocoto Yellow'

Starter Kitchen Garden

R oger Doiron has made it his life's mission to encourage and support those who like to grow food, even if it means ruffling the feathers of city and town officials who think food gardens belong out of sight. Roger's plan is a great stepping-off point for those would-be gardeners who are unsure of how and where to start. Though just 10 by 10 feet, this small garden provides enough space to make a dent in the weekly grocery bill and introduce some basic gardening concepts.

> A small-scale design for novice gardeners or those with little space

> Organized into six beds for ease of planting, tending, and harvesting

> Uses interplanting and succession planting for continual cropping

> Features popular and easy-to-grow edibles

Roger's basic design is small enough for all but the tiniest properties. Roger says that it's best to start with a small garden, so that you can gain an understanding of growing vegetables without being overwhelmed. One of the biggest mistakes a novice gardener can make is going too big too fast. A kitchen garden should be a place of enjoyment. Tending your plants is good for both the body and the soul, and once you are comfortable with the yearly rhythm of growing a garden, you can always expand your current plot.

Roger's garden has six beds, each measuring just $2^1/_2$ by $4^1/_2$ feet. An easy way to build up beds is to shovel the soil from the pathways on top of the growing areas and add compost or aged manure to enrich the native soil. One-foot pathways separate the beds and allow ease of seeding, tending, and harvesting. To keep the paths clean and mud-free, mulch them with several inches of straw, shredded leaves, or bark mulch. Alternatively, you can pave the paths with stepping stones or bricks.

What to grow? When trying to decide what to grow, Roger encourages gardeners to think about what they and their families like to eat. You may also want to grow vegetables that are expensive to buy if grown organically — such as leeks, heirloom tomatoes, and eggplant — or those that are hard to find. Roger has included a selection of traditional favorites in his design, but feel free to substitute other crops that pique your interest.

Try interplanting. To get more out of your space — and more bang for your buck — use interplanting, a common technique that allows you to grow more than one crop in the same space. Simply sow seeds of fast-maturing crops like salad greens between slower-growing vegetables such as peppers, broccoli, and cabbage. You can plant successive crops of salad plants like lettuce, arugula, spinach, and Asian greens — sowing fresh seed in beds that have just been harvested.

To supply fresh herbs to the kitchen, Roger's plan also includes common but indispensible flavorings such as dill, thyme, parsley, spearmint, and basil. The mint, which has an extremely aggressive growth habit, should be grown in a pot beside the garden so it doesn't take over the entire plot. The herbs also increase the productivity of the vegetable crops because if allowed to flower they, along with the edible nasturtiums, attract beneficial and pollinating insects.

Make it enjoyable. No matter what you choose to grow in your kitchen garden, remember Roger's most important words of advice: "Have fun!" He recalls a conversation he had with a gardening friend who pointed out that, unlike our ancestors, gardening for us is a choice, not a necessity in order to ensure survival. "For us, there's a Plan B — the grocery store — if all of our best-laid garden plans go up in flames (or to the deer)," he says. "Knowing that should allow us to approach each season with lightness and a 'what will be, will be' attitude."

A SUBVERSIVE PLOT

"When we encourage people to grow some of their own food, we're encouraging them to take power into their hands: power over their diet, power over their health, and power over their pocketbooks."

— Roger Doiron, from his TED talk "A Subversive Plot: How to Grow a Revolution in Your Own Backyard"

Roger's Favorite Varieties

Growing some of your own vegetables and herbs can save money, but it will also introduce you to the incredible flavors of outstanding heirloom and hybrid varieties like the ones listed below.

- **Tomatoes:** 'Sungold' cherry and 'Costoluto Genovese'
- **Peppers:** 'Ace' and 'Early Jalapeño'
- **Basil:** 'Windowbox' bush and 'Genovese'
- **Cucumbers:** 'Chelsea Prize'
- **Zucchini:** 'Raven' and 'Magda'
- **Carrots:** 'Napoli' and 'Rainbow Mix'
- **Beets:** 'Early Wonder' and 'Detroit Dark Red'
- **Radishes:** 'French Breakfast' and 'Easter Egg II'
- **Lettuce:** 'Allstar Gourmet' mix

- **Spinach:** 'Winter Bloomsdale' and 'Tyee'
- **Leeks:** 'Bleu de Solaize'
- **Onions:** 'Candy' and assorted red, yellow, and white sets
- **Garlic:** 'Music'
- **Kale:** 'Winterbor' and 'Red Russian'
- **Swiss chard:** 'Bright Lights' and 'Ruby Red'
- **Pole beans:** 'Kentucky Wonder', 'Emerite', and 'Fortex'
- **Eggplants:** 'Fairy Tale' and 'Rosa Bianca'

Roger's Garden Plan

10' DEEP X 10' WIDE

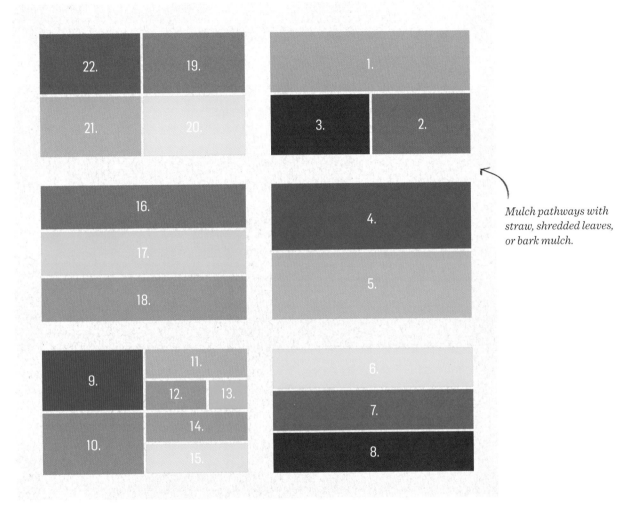

Mulch pathways with straw, shredded leaves, or bark mulch.

1. Tomatoes	9. Lettuce mix
2. Peppers	10. Spinach
3. Basil	11. Dill
4. Cucumbers	12. Thyme
5. Zucchini	13. Spearmint (potted)
6. Carrots	14. Parsley
7. Beets	15. Nasturtiums
8. Radishes	16. Leeks

17. Onions
18. Garlic
19. Kale
20. Swiss chard
21. Pole beans on teepees
22. Eggplants

Lasagna Gardening

THE IDEA OF LASAGNA GARDENING was pioneered by Patricia Lanza, whose inspiration came from nature. During a walk in the woods, she realized that by piling organic materials on top of one another, she could create rich soil, just as the layers of fallen leaves and twigs in the forest decompose and become earth. The soil would be ready for plants — shrubs, perennials, annuals, vegetables, or herbs — with no digging required.

In her 2004 book, *Lasagna Gardening with Herbs* (Rodale Books), Pat describes her method in less than 50 words: "Pick a site. Cover site with wet newspaper. Cover paper with peat moss and other organic materials. Layer materials using 1 part green stuff (nitrogen) to 4 parts brown stuff (carbon) until your garden is deep enough to plant in. Pull back the layers and tuck in plants. Water."

This simple but ingenious method sparked a gardening revolution where would-be gardeners no longer needed to tediously remove sod and weeds, as well as pick for rocks, prior to planting. By simply layering organic materials including chopped leaves, straw, compost, pine needles, kitchen scraps, topsoil, and aged manure on top of wet newspaper, they could create a lasagna-style garden that was ready to plant right away.

For novice gardeners, a lasagna-style plot is a very easy way to grow food. Pat recommends building the bed the autumn before you intend to plant, if possible, so that the materials have a head start on the decomposition process. If you don't have an ample supply of leaves from your own property, you may be able to source a few bags from your neighbors or gather them in autumn as they're piled at the street curb for pickup. Once you've collected your organic materials, choose a sunny, relatively flat site. Frame in the bed with boards to make the garden look tidy and to help keep the layers of organic materials in place as they compost. A 4- by 8-foot bed is an ideal size for beginners; as your plants grow and your skill level increases, you can always add another bed (or two!). When Pat built her original lasagna garden, she piled the layers of organic matter 24 inches high in November; by the time spring arrived, the materials had composted down to an 8-inch-deep garden bed with dark, rich soil and plenty of worms.

Keep the garden well watered in the first year to ensure the plants have plenty of moisture, and also to support the decomposition process. As the layers of organic materials decompose, you will need to top up the garden bed to maintain an appropriate soil depth and to ensure that the roots of your edibles are not exposed. The easiest way to continue building the bed is to keep a few bags of shredded leaves, a bale of straw, or a compost pile nearby, which can then be spread around your plants when necessary. The lasagna method may be an easy way to build a garden, but remember that the decomposition process takes time. "Practice patience," says Pat with a smile. "What started as a walk in the woods has resulted in a new way of life for me."

Formal Kitchen Garden

What better way to enjoy an alfresco meal of homegrown vegetables and herbs than with family and friends at a table in the heart of the garden? In her design, Ellen Ecker Ogden highlights the age-old connection between the garden and kitchen by planting the four formal beds with a carefully chosen selection of gourmet edibles and annual flowers.

> A central table invites outdoor meals and moments with friends and family

> Includes a gourmet selection of vegetables and herbs chosen for their outstanding flavor

> Edible plants are arranged in ornamental fashion and interplanted with flowers

"Enjoying the magic that happens around the table with good food and friends is key to building connection, and what better place to do this but in the garden?" says Ellen Ecker Ogden.

Table as centerpiece. A passionate cook and gardener, Ellen believes that the garden and the kitchen go hand in hand. At the center of her design, she has a placed a table where homegrown food can be celebrated with family and friends. "Enjoying the magic that happens around the table with good food and friends is key to building connection, and what better place to do this but in the garden?" says Ellen. Even when the table is not used for eating, it's a good place to sit and watch the birds and pollinators.

Ellen's garden measures 30 feet long by 35 feet wide and is compact enough to fit comfortably within the boundaries of all but the smallest properties. The design has only four beds, but Ellen's arrangement makes the garden a very productive space. The outside beds are a manageable 3-foot width, which allows easy planting, maintenance, and harvesting from the interior side of the garden. The two inner beds are a bit roomier, measuring from 3 to 6 feet wide, since they can be accessed from more than one side. For a clear separation from the lawn, Ellen suggests a border — such as a low stone wall, a split rail fence, or a boxwood hedge — around the perimeter of the garden.

Soil-level beds. Depending on the site and the whims of the gardener, the beds can be raised or left at ground level. Ellen admits that she prefers traditional soil-level beds. "Soil is key, and it's important to add compost, plant cover crops, and work the earth — which is harder to do with a raised bed," she says. She also finds that soil-level beds provide more flexibility when designing the shape and size of your garden plots. If building raised beds, use untreated, rot-resistant lumber such as cedar or hemlock; other options include stone, brick, or even low wattle fencing.

When choosing edibles for her garden, Ellen selects for flavor and ornamental value. She also picks her vegetables based on what she likes to cook and what is not available for purchase locally.

Select high-value plants. "The fruits and vegetables that I grow can't always be bought at the market, or they cost a lot to buy organic," she says. Another factor is the length of the harvest season — Ellen aims for a steady return from spring through late autumn. About 80 percent of her plants are her favorite, tried-and-true varieties, and the remaining 20 percent are new and different each year.

Arrange for color. Ellen also pays particular attention to how the plants she chooses are arranged. For the two beds that surround the table, Ellen has interplanted green butterhead lettuce with red radicchio, which (after being cut back) will produce purplish-red heads to take center stage once the lettuces mature and are harvested. In the center of one of these beds, 'Bright Lights' Swiss chard and dinosaur ('Lacinato') kale provide color and structure, as well as a steady supply of nutritious greens. She adds that most hearty greens can be grown practically year-round.

Clumps of small to medium-sized sunflowers such as 'Autumn Beauty' and 'Valentine' break the large outer beds into smaller planting plots. Between the cheerful sunflowers, tomatoes are supported on Texas-style cages and interplanted with 'Sweet Genovese' basil. Texas-style tomato cages are extremely sturdy wire supports that are 18 to 24 inches in diameter and up to 6 feet tall. Bush and pole beans, cucumbers, potatoes, cabbage, broccoli, and herbs fill the remainder of the beds. In front of the cucumbers, a low edge of 'Lemon Gem' signet marigolds adds a pop of color and provides edible blooms that add a hint of citrus to homegrown salads.

Ellen's Garden Plan

30' DEEP X 35' WIDE

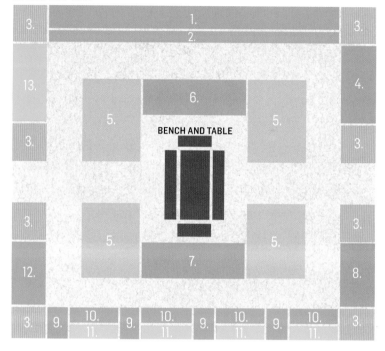

1. Tomatoes
2. Basil
3. Sunflowers of mixed heights
4. Artichoke
5. Mixed butterhead lettuce varieties and radicchio
6. Leeks, onions, and garlic
7. Swiss chard and kale
8. Potatoes
9. Rosemary, chives, tarragon, sage, marjoram, dill, cilantro, and basil
10. Beans
11. Cucumbers
12. Broccoli
13. Cabbage

Ellen's Favorite Varieties

- **Tomatoes:** 'Brandywine', 'Persimmon', 'Big Rainbow', 'San Marzano', 'Green Zebra', 'Sungold', and 'Sweet 100'
- **Basil:** 'Sweet Genovese'
- **Artichoke:** 'Green Globe'
- **Leeks:** 'King Richard' and 'Bleu de Solaize'
- **Onions:** 'Candy' and 'Walla Walla'
- **Garlic:** 'Early Red Italian'

- **Swiss chard:** 'Bright Lights'
- **Kale:** Dinosaur ('Lacinato')
- **Potatoes:** 'Red Bliss'
- **Cucumbers:** 'Boston Pickling', 'Northern Pickling', 'Lemon', 'Diva', and 'Suyo Long'
- **Beans:** 'Fin de Bagnols', 'Royal Burgundy', 'Roc d'Or', and 'Blue Lake 274' bush; 'Trionfo Violetto', 'Kwintus', and 'Blauhilde' pole

- **Sunflowers:** 'Autumn Beauty', 'Teddy Bear', 'Valentine', and 'Moulin Rouge'
- **Marigolds:** 'Lemon Gem' signet
- **Broccoli:** 'Green Sprouting Calabrese' and 'Waltham 29'
- **Cabbage:** 'Early Jersey Wakefield' and 'Late Flat Dutch'

Tall sunflowers provide privacy and delineate the ends of the outer rows.

Choose colorful varieties of vegetables for the beds surrounding the table.

A low stone wall creates a border between the garden and the yard.

Grocery Garden

J enks Farmer wants you to know that you can easily, quickly, and inexpensively grow food from what you buy at the grocery store. "Many vegetables and fruits have seeds, roots, and shoots that can be used to grow more plants just like them!" he says. In his own yard, Jenks has created an edible oasis in which the majority of the plants have come from regrowing or propagating food that comes from the supermarket.

> ❯ Grow seeds, roots, and shoots from the grocery store
>
> ❯ Create a backyard oasis with your leftovers
>
> ❯ Clumps of rooted rosemary and mint, replanted leeks, and direct-seeded beans and flax offer a homegrown harvest

Jenks's inspiration for a grocery garden came from his travels. "When traveling and living in other countries, I would see things in markets that fascinated me," Jenks recalls. "I remember once in Cambodia buying a tiny, tiny round eggplant at the market, and from it, I got about a dozen seeds and planted them at my friend's house." Since then, he's experimented with many vegetables and fruits from grocery stores and farmers' markets, trying to sprout seeds and root anything that comes with a stem.

A beautiful combination. A couple of Jenks's favorite grocery-store goodies are flax and elephant garlic (not a true garlic but a cousin that is closely related to leeks). In the fall, he simply divides the garlic head into bulbs and pushes them into the soil, leaving a tiny bit of the tip exposed. Then he sprinkles the top with flax seeds and covers them with another quarter-inch of soil.

To grow bulbous stem crops like leeks and lemongrass, Jenks advises looking at the base of the plant. "Leeks will almost always have a basal plate, which is the bottom of a bulb where the roots initiate," he says. The basal plate on lemongrass has often been removed before it is displayed in the supermarket, so you may need to dig to find one that has a little bit of base and, if possible, a few roots. For peanuts, you'll need to find a supplier with uncooked pods. They don't have to be organic, Jenks says, but he tries to find organic peanuts.

Where to shop. The best places to source vegetables and fruits to root or plant are a local organic grocery store, the organic section of a large supermarket, or an ethnic grocer. Jenks finds that small, organic stores tend to have the best stock of vegetables and fruits ready for planting, since they don't have the overly meticulous expectations of perfection that some giant chains do. Jenks lives and gardens in Zone 8b, but those in cooler regions can also employ many of his methods, and grow the more tender specimens in pots and move them indoors for winter.

It's not about quantity. Growing a grocery garden may not be the

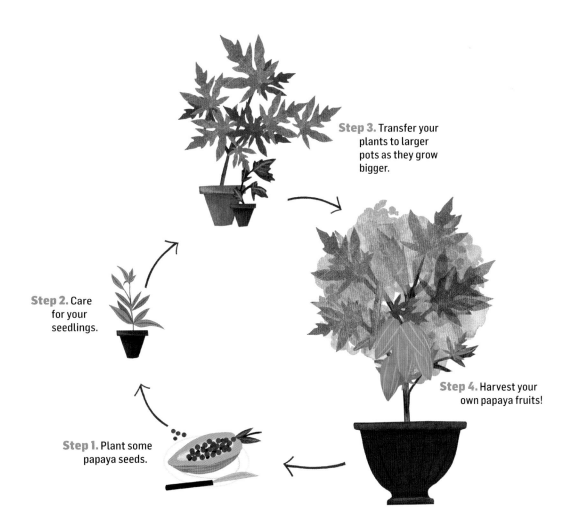

Step 3. Transfer your plants to larger pots as they grow bigger.

Step 2. Care for your seedlings.

Step 4. Harvest your own papaya fruits!

Step 1. Plant some papaya seeds.

best way to produce large quantities of food — planting the basal plate of a leek or a stalk of lemongrass will yield a single plant, for example, though peanuts or beans can yield a much larger harvest when planted in quantity — but that isn't Jenks's goal. "It's not about a meal; it's about making connections, and it's a story for the garden to tell," he says. "It's also a reminder that plants are food and food can become plants."

Grocery Goodies for the Garden

With a little creative thinking, it's amazing what you can do with the leftover bits of vegetables and herbs bought at the supermarket. That last sprig of mint? Root it! A handful of dried beans? Plant them! The stem end of a leek? Grow it!

Flax. Direct-seed in the garden or in pots alongside elephant garlic.

Elephant garlic. Best bought in the organic produce aisle.

Beans. A summer crop that is direct sown in late spring. "Lima beans from the grocery store usually make vines, but lots of beans grow on bushes," Jenks says.

Jicama. With this native Mexican vine, Jenks says to look for a tuber with a bit of green on the top (avoid polished ones), and grow it on the fence in summer.

Peanuts. Plant uncooked, natural peanuts in a sunny spot.

Potatoes. In later winter, plant organic potatoes bought at the grocery store.

Mints. Grocery-store spearmint or other mint roots easily and can be planted in a garden or a pot. Just remember, it can be extremely invasive, so give it an isolated spot.

Ginger. Look for plump roots with well-developed "eyes."

Leeks. Plant the rooted basal plate.

Rosemary. "If you get a young, fresh bunch from the grocery store, you can root them [the stems] in water," says Jenks.

Lemongrass. Plant the rooted basal plate.

Papaya. Save the seeds from a fruit and start them inside. "Harvest the fruits when green for green papaya salad!" Jenks suggests.

Chrysanthemums. Jenks advises buying potted mums or cut flowers from the florist section, rooting them, and using the dried flower petals for tea.

Citrus. Jenks suggests trying to grow citrus plants from seeds. "They're easy to grow, and I just let the seeds dry a few days, before planting them."

JENKS'S TIPS FOR SPROUTING AND ROOTING GROCERY STORE TREASURES

- **Start with raw.** Be sure that any beans, nuts, grains, flax, or other seeds you buy are raw. Cooking, baking, and even salting can inhibit germination.

- **Start with organic.** Many conventionally farmed products have growth inhibitors sprayed onto them. Potatoes and onions, for example, are treated so they won't sprout in the bag or in your pantry. They won't sprout if you try to grow them either.

- **Set the goal.** You don't have to raise an orchard or have 100 percent germination. Often, my goal is to teach the lesson that food is made up of seeds, so that we can recognize the cycle.

- **Moisturize.** Chrysanthemums, rosemary, lemongrass, and other plants sold as cut stems are often dried out by storage in coolers and transportation. Before you try to root anything, soak it in water for a few hours and allow it to recover.

- **Seek out the specialty stores.** Often the produce at smaller international stores is less processed than that in big stores. I find great stuff, and produce that sprouts more readily, at many Mexican and Korean groceries.

Backyard Orchard

Colby Eierman wants us to rethink our landscape choices and opt for more fruiting plants like apples, pears, plums, and cherries. Traditionally, fruit trees were reserved for large gardens, but Colby points out that even a small urban garden can yield a bumper crop of homegrown fruits. His plan includes a range of ornamental and edible plants, as well as a spot for outdoor meals and an oven for homemade pizza.

> Creates an edible orchard oasis in the city

> Includes a pizza oven and picnic bench for outdoor meals

> Vining crops take up little space, but offer big harvests and increase privacy

Why grow a maple when that same sunny spot can be used to produce ripe, juicy plums? or cherries? or apples? Contrary to popular belief, most fruit crops are actually low-maintenance garden plants. Plus, they can be grown in small spaces. "Many small urban or suburban lots offer plenty of space for planting and growing food," says Colby. "Quite often, planting a small vegetable garden is just the beginning, as we eventually realize that adding perennial fruit trees can provide a big return on a small investment."

Colby's pocket-sized fruit garden is based on the backyard of his former home and measures roughly 30 by 30 feet. He recommends enclosing it with a fence to provide a structure to support the espaliered plants and to increase privacy, giving the garden a courtyard ambiance.

Select trees carefully. Colby says the key to a successful backyard orchard is to choose the right trees for your region and to plant them in the right spot, so that they can add both bounty and beauty to your landscape.

Like most edibles, fruit trees will grow best and produce the largest harvest when grown in a location with full sun and decent soil. Colby gardens organically, so he notes that taking the time to find the best site for fruiting trees can go a long way in reducing the occurrence of pests and diseases and boosting overall tree health.

Let fruit trees ring the garden. The majority of the beds are laid out around the perimeter of the property. A 'Frost' peach, an 'Emerald Beaut' plum, and a 'Blenheim' apricot anchor the corners of the garden. Between the fruit trees, vining kiwis and espaliered apples and figs are trained to grow on or against the fence. (In a colder climate, substitute additional apples, pears, or grapes for the figs and kiwis.) At the foot of the plum and peach, Colby has tucked short grasses such as dwarf fountain grass (*Pennisetum alopecuroides*), Japanese forest grass (*Hakonechloa macra*), or blue or even red fescue (*Festuca glauca, F. rubra*). In front of the espaliered 'Honeycrisp' and

'Cox's Orange Pippin' apples he has placed a compact hedge of ornamental oregano.

Try espaliering. No matter how small your garden, Colby says, it can fit an espaliered tree. It is particularly important that you select the right cultivar, however. "If, for example, fireblight is an issue in your area, apples and pears can easily lose a limb each year to this bacterium, and if your tree only has six limbs (as with certain espalier patterns), it has a lot to lose. Disease resistance becomes a very important issue," Colby explains.

Colby also points out that a home orchard isn't necessarily "all about the fruit." "I see fruit trees as one component of a diverse edible landscape," he notes. "If your trees are part of a landscape that is a gathering space for friends and family, you will pay closer attention to the trees and harvest a rich experience, as well as tasty fruit," he says. He advises making room in your backyard orchard for other edibles like vegetables and herbs, as well as for an eating area, wood oven, fire pit, or even a hot tub! In his plan, Colby finds space for a picnic bench and a wood oven to emphasize the connection between garden and food.

Behind the wood oven, Colby has planted two kiwi vines, which are extremely vigorous and will appreciate the strong support provided by the fence. Just remember that you will need separate male and female plants to ensure fruit set.

Make room for vegetables. Stepping stones lead the way from the wood oven to the back deck, where a ground-level bed for assorted vegetables skirts the stairs and edge of the deck. Some outstanding edible picks are the wonderful Italian 'Bianca di Maggio' onion, 'Veronica' Romanesco cauliflower ("It has psychedelic color!" says Colby), dinosaur ('Lacinato') kale and the traditional Mediterranean vegetable, cardoon, whose spiky gray-green leaves offer interesting architecture to edible gardens. A deck-level assortment of herbs is easy to gather, and the flowering herbs draw beneficial pollinated insects to the fruit trees. A nearby potted Meyer lemon supplies aromatic fruits and can be moved indoors for winter in colder regions.

ESPALIER

Espaliering is a technique of training trees or shrubs against a flat surface such as a wall, fence, or trellis, or onto a system of wires and posts to create a living fence. An espalier adds a formal and decorative element to a garden. Because the plants are grown vertically, it's also a practical way to grow fruit trees in small gardens. Plus, the open pruning of an espalier allows ample air circulation, reducing the occurrence of disease.

In terms of edible plants, pears and apples are among the best choices for an espalier, as they take well to frequent pruning and are available in dwarf forms, but even grapes and red currants can be trained in this manner. There are numerous designs for espaliers; two of the more common ones are the horizontal cordon and the candelabra. A horizontal cordon has a vertical leader (main stem) and branches that grow horizontally on both sides of the center stem. A candelabra has several tiers of branches that are trained in a U-shape to resemble a branched candlestick.

HORIZONTAL CORDON

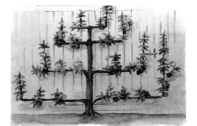

CANDELABRA

Colby's Garden Plan

Plum

Kiwi Vines

Apricot

Compact ornamental grasses

Wood oven

Espaliered apples

Ornamental oregano

Picnic bench

Deck

HOUSE

Herbs at deck height

Compact ornamental grasses

Mixed vegetables

Meyer Lemon

Herbs

Peach

Espaliered fig

Colby's Favorite Orchard Fruits

APPLES

- **'Cox's Orange Pippin'.** Beautiful yellow-blushed fruit in orange-red with crisp texture and complex flavor
- **'Honeycrisp'.** Aromatic, crisp, and exceptionally flavored fruit

FIGS

- **'Panache Tiger Stripe'.** Soft yellow fruit with deep green striping; late to mature, with sky-high sugar content

- **'Black Mission'.** Deep purple-black skin and soft pink flesh that is flavorful and jamlike
- **'Celeste'.** Small fruit with brownish-purple skin and excellent flavor; ripen in early summer
- **'Black Jack'.** Large, tear-drop-shaped fruit with purple-brown skin and deep pink flesh

OTHER TASTY FRUITS

- **'Blenheim' apricot.** Early ripening; outstanding flavor and medium-large yellow fruits
- **Meyer lemon.** Bright yellow fruits with sweet flavor
- **'Frost' peach.** Good choice for colder climates; ripens in early August
- **'Emerald Beaut' plum.** Fruits have greenish-yellow skin and a yellow-orange interior

Front-Yard Foraging

Sarah Elton's quest to offer her children "real" food prompted her to dream up a front yard full of forage-able berries and brambles including raspberries, strawberries, and black raspberries. Her plan, which is based on her raspberry garden, concentrates on native edibles that are hardy and drought-tolerant and require less fussing than introduced species.

> ❯ Features forage-able plants like brambles and strawberries
> ❯ Design works in full sun or partially shaded spaces
> ❯ Supports beneficial insects and pollinators

"I've benefited from the drought tolerance of having native plants in my front yard. Even in the deep heat of summer, and with my sandy soil, I still rarely have to water," Sarah Elton says.

Sarah's first foray into growing her own food plants began about eight years ago, when a "volunteer" raspberry popped up in her front yard. She moved the raspberry bush to the backyard three times, but it kept coming up in the front. Eventually, she says, she "realized how lovely it was to have food on the front lawn." She soon expanded to tomatoes and beans, growing them in pots in the backyard where there is more sun.

Blending in with the neighborhood. Like many urban properties, her home sits beside a busy street. "I have tried to take good care of the garden so that it still fits in with the neighborhood," Sarah says. "Most people don't seem to notice, but those who pay attention to local botany frequently stop to ask me about the different plants growing in the yard," she adds.

The range of edible plants provides a steady supply of food from spring to autumn, a large portion of which Sarah's family enjoys as they harvest — hence, a "foraging" garden. Children will particularly love the berry plants.

No-fuss plants. Careful plant selection with a concentration on natives has also reduced the need to fuss over the garden. "I've benefited from the drought tolerance of having native plants in my front yard," she says. "Even in the deep heat of summer, and with my sandy soil, I still rarely have to water."

Sarah has also included edible ornamental plants, such as milkweed, daylilies, and wild ginger. The young shoots (under 6 inches) of milkweed can be boiled and used like asparagus, while the roots of wild ginger offer a mild, but pleasing, peppery-ginger flavor to dishes. Sarah's family enjoys adding the daylily buds to omelets.

A narrow pathway traverses the space between the food plants, allowing one to easily harvest food and transport organic materials. Sarah admits that the raspberries occasionally overtake that path, but she doesn't mind — the plants provide her family with about $100 worth of organic berries every season.

Sarah's Favorite Forage-able Varieties

- **Black raspberries:** 'Jewel', 'Black Hawk', and native
- **Raspberries:** 'Boyne' (early season) and 'Heritage' (fall bearing)
- **Jerusalem artichokes:** 'Stampede' and 'Mammoth French White'

- **Pawpaw trees:** 'Shenandoah', 'Susquehanna', and 'Potomac'
- **Strawberries:** 'Kent', 'Veestar', and 'Chambly' June-bearing; 'Albion', 'Tribute', and 'Tristar' day-neutral (everbearing)

- **Gooseberries:** 'Poorman', 'Hinnomaki Yellow', and 'Achilles'
- **Currants:** 'Pink Champagne' red; 'Titania' and 'Consort' black

Sarah's Garden Plan

Front Porch — Herbs in pots

Cultivated black raspberries — Native black raspberries

Common milkweed

Jerusalem artichokes

Pawpaw

Canada wild ginger

Low-growing thyme

Rhubarb — Daylilies — Strawberries

Currants

Gooseberries

Sidewalk and street

Canner's Garden

Daniel Gasteiger is able to enjoy a year-round bounty from his own vegetable garden by preserving, canning, drying, and freezing his spring, summer, and autumn harvests. In his plan he combines fruit trees, vegetable crops, and herbs in quantities that will provide enough of a harvest that some may be enjoyed fresh from the garden and the excess preserved.

> ❯ Crops are succession planted to continue the bountiful harvest well into autumn

> ❯ Vegetables are mulched to reduce watering

> ❯ A series of bean tripods supports rampant bean vines

Daniel has created a garden that is very similar to a classic American kitchen garden. "Traditionally, [a classic American kitchen garden] was located close to the house — in many cases, the entire front yard and then some," says Daniel. "Homeowners harvested from it in small quantities to prepare meals, and in huge quantities to fill canning jars; fermentation jugs; cold stores; and drying trays, blankets, or hangers."

Estimating how much to grow. This sizable garden measures 108 feet by 137 feet and is best suited to a large property where fruit trees, berry crops, vegetables, and herbs have plenty of room to grow. To figure out how much of each crop he needs to grow, Daniel begins by asking, How much of this will my family eat in a year? "I serve certain vegetables once a week and others two or three times a week," he says. "To decide how many bean plants I need to grow, for example, I start with the notion of harvesting 52 meals' worth of beans." He notes that some of those beans will be eaten in summer as they are harvested, but most go into the freezer or are canned for future meals. With a list of expected yields for each vegetable, Daniel calculates how much he will need to plant. He suggests planting more than you estimate because preserved food will last longer than a year.

Some of Daniel's favorite varieties are shown in the box on the opposite page, but he encourages gardeners to look for varieties that grow best in their individual regions. If you're not sure which varieties are best for your area, ask the experts at your local garden center or garden club, or seek varieties available from regional seed companies.

Watering a large garden. Once you've picked and planted your crops, Daniel suggests mulching them heavily to save on water. "For a large garden — one that feeds you for a year — you'll need a watering system that is more efficient than hand-watering, in the event of a dry season," Daniel warns. He suggests a drip irrigation system, though they can be costly. He also recommends water barrels, which are inexpensive and will collect and store rainwater that can then be used to irrigate the garden.

To support the rampant growth of climbing beans, Daniel uses tripods made from 8-foot stakes (see page 85). You can use 8-foot lengths of 1½- by 1⅛-inch boards (often called "furring strips" by building supply stores) or bamboo posts. The tripods could also double as tomato stakes.

Keeping your garden productive. When the early, cool-season crops like peas, lettuce, and spinach run out of steam by July, replant the beds with squash, melons, cole vegetables (brassicas), and beans. "If you're starting winter squash in July, choose short-season varieties such as 'Early Butternut'," advises Daniel.

Adding fruit. Daniel's plan includes peach, pear, cherry, plum and apple trees — the bounty of which can be used for fresh eating, baking, and preserving, as well as making juice, cider, vinegar, wine, and much more. However, Daniel notes that full-size trees require a lot of space and their production varies from year to year. Pears, especially, can produce widely different numbers of fruits from one season to the next. He also notes that while dwarf fruit trees take up less space, they will also yield fewer fruits than full-size trees.

Daniel has also included two strawberry patches, which will provide years of sweet berries. "Strawberries hit their stride in their second year and usually fade in their third, but with good management, you can stretch a bed for four to six years," says Daniel. If disease becomes an issue, he advises eliminating the beds and starting fresh in a different location.

EXPECTED CROP YIELDS PER 100-FOOT ROW

This list comes from the Louisiana State University Ag Center and is an estimate for Southern gardens. Yields may vary depending on your region; check with your local extension agent.

LIMA BEANS (BUSH): 1 bushel shelled (32 lbs.)

SNAP BEANS (BUSH): 1.5 bushels (30 lbs.)

SNAP BEANS (POLE): 2 bushels (30 lbs.)

BEETS: 100 lbs.

BROCCOLI: 70 heads

CABBAGE: 85 heads

CANTALOUPE: 120 melons

CARROTS: 150 lbs.

CAULIFLOWER: 60 heads

CHINESE CABBAGE: 100 heads

COLLARDS: 175 lbs.

CORN: 120 ears

CUCUMBER: 170 lbs.

EGGPLANTS: 150 lbs.

GARLIC: 350 heads

KOHLRABI: 75 lbs.

LETTUCE: 100 heads

MUSTARD: 100 bunches

OKRA: 175 lbs. (6 bushels, about 30 lbs. each)

ONIONS: (dry) 220 lbs.

PEAS (SOUTHERN): 20 lbs. shelled

PEAS (ENGLISH): 40 lbs.

PEAS (SNOW): 65 lbs.

PEPPER (BELL): 125 lbs.

PEPPER (CUBANELLE): 200 lbs.

POTATO (IRISH): 200 lbs.

POTATO (SWEET): 200 lbs.

PUMPKIN: 150 lbs.

RADISH: 30 lbs.

RUTABAGA: 90 lbs.

SHALLOT (GREEN): 350 bunches

SPINACH: 40 lbs.

SQUASH (SUMMER): 80 lbs.

SQUASH (WINTER): 150 lbs.

STRAWBERRIES: 170 lbs.

TOMATOES: 250 lbs.

TOMATOES (CHERRY): 450 lbs.

TURNIPS: 100 bunches

WATERMELONS: 20 melons (20 lbs. each)

Daniel's Favorite Varieties for Preserving

For the best-quality canned produce, opt for fruits and vegetables that are young, tender, and harvested within the past 12 hours. The less time a crop spends traveling from the garden to a jar, the more flavor and nutrition you can expect in your finished product (a great reason to grow your own!). Many of Daniel's picks offer excellent flavor and are extremely high-yielding, making them good choices for a Canner's Garden.

VEGGIES

- **Beans:** 'Golden Wax' and 'Tendergreen' bush; 'Blue Lake Pole' and 'Kentucky Wonder' pole
- **Onions:** 'Stuttgarter' and 'Yellow Globe'
- **Carrots:** 'Red Cored Chantenay'
- **Potatoes:** 'Katahdin' and 'Kennebec'
- **Peppers:** 'Purple Jalapeño', poblano, 'Orange Bell', and 'Corno di Toro' (red)
- **Tomatoes:** 'Cornue des Andes' ("It's a paste type, but a sensational all-around variety!"), 'Moonglow', and 'Big Boy'
- **Sweet corn:** 'Bodacious' and 'Silver Queen' (interplant with cosmos to reduce ear worms)
- **Broccoli:** 'Waltham 29'
- **Cauliflower:** 'Snowball'
- **Peas:** 'Wando'
- **Squash:** 'Black Beauty' summer; butternut, 'Neck Pumpkin', and 'Blue Hubbard' winter
- **Cabbage:** 'Late Flat Dutch'

- **Lettuce:** 'Ithaca' and 'Parris Island Cos'
- **Cucumber:** 'Marketmore 76', 'Boston Pickling', and 'Bush Pickle'
- **Asparagus:** 'Mary Washington' and 'Jersey Night'
- **Rhubarb:** 'Victoria'

FRUITS

- **Raspberries:** 'Latham'
- **Blueberries:** 'Liberty', 'Jersey', and 'Blueray'
- **Grapes:** 'Reliance', pinot noir, cabernet, chardonnay, reisling, and 'Chenin Blanc' (6 trellised vines)
- **Strawberries:** 'Cavendish', 'Jewel', and 'Ozark Beauty'
- **Peaches:** 'Elberta' and 'Hale Haven'
- **Pears:** 'Bartlett' and 'Moonglow'
- **Sour cherries:** 'Montmorency'
- **Plums:** 'Mount Royal'
- **Apples:** 'Pink Lady' and 'Honeycrisp'

WINTER SQUASH 101

When I give a presentation about preserving, there is always someone who asks whether it's best to can or freeze winter squash to make it last. My answer: If you have a guest bedroom, roll your winter squash under the bed in that room. Winter squash stores amazingly well where it's cool and dry (about 50°F/10°C).

I keep winter squash on the floor of my dining room near the glass doors that lead out to our screen porch. The floor is naturally cool and we often have "fresh" squash as late as April or May — seven months after harvest. Check the squash periodically and use any that start to shrivel. If you have pets, beware that they may turn winter squash into chew toys!

— Daniel Gasteiger

Daniel's Garden Plan

137' DEEP X 108' WIDE

1. Bush beans
2. Onions
3. Carrots
4. Potatoes
5. Peppers
6. Tomatoes
7. Sweet corn
8. Broccoli
9. Cauliflower
10. Peas followed by winter squash
11. Summer squash
12. Cabbage
13. Lettuce and spinach
14. Cucumbers
15. Asparagus
16. Pole beans
17. Annual and perennial herbs
18. Raspberries
19. Blueberries
20. Grapes
21. Rhubarb
22. Strawberries
23. Peaches
24. Pears
25. Sour cherries
26. Plums
27. Apples

Growing pole beans on tripods saves valuable garden space. Daniel's tripods are quick and easy to make. Just insert three 8-foot-tall stakes about 4 feet apart in a circle, securing the top with garden twine or wire. Plant three to five seeds around each leg.

Slow-Food Garden

The members of the global organization Slow Food know that fresh, local food is the key to great meals, which should then be shared with family and friends. In the spirit of enjoying the freshest food possible and using heirloom seeds, Growing Places Indy has created a relatively small "Slow-Food Garden" that is succession planted and divided into eight main planting beds surrounded with herbs and flowers. The innovative design includes a crafty combined composting and water-gathering system, as well as a living mulch to support pollinators and beneficial insects.

> An extremely ornamental design intended to promote the enjoyment of fresh, homegrown food

> Features eight main planting beds for food production

> Garden waste is recycled in the compost and water-collection area

> Flowers and herbs surround the garden to attract beneficial insects

The organization Slow Food was founded in 1989 to challenge the rapid rise of both fast food and fast life. At its core, the organization's aim is to connect the pleasure of good food to community, which includes encouraging people to grow some of their own food. Inspired by the work of Slow Food, this compact and highly ornamental yet productive design from Growing Places Indy requires just 400 square feet of space, making it a practical garden for most sites.

Easy to lay out. The square plot has been divided into eight formal planting beds, surrounded by narrow garden strips on three sides. To create the pattern, begin by marking out the eight beds using a tape measure, stakes, and twine. Once you have laid out the design, remove the turf, adding it to the nearby composting area. The small circle at the center of the garden is ideal for a dwarf fruit tree or berry shrub. Even a space-saving trellis could be set in the middle circle to support vining pole beans

or cucumbers, or ornamentals like gourds.

Herbs and flowers are important. One-foot-wide strips of herbs and flowers enclose the central square of the garden on three sides. One of the long, narrow beds could be used for perennial herbs and ornamentals, including lavender, thyme, sage, purple coneflower, bee balm, daylilies, and milkweed — plants that also support populations of bees, butterflies, hummingbirds, and numerous beneficial insects. The other two strips could be planted with annual herbs for kitchen use — such as chamomile, parsley, rosemary, tarragon, and basil — as well as colorful flowers for fresh bouquets. Popular flower choices include zinnias, cosmos, calendulas, celosia, cleome, sunflowers, larkspur, strawflowers, and stock.

Creative recycling. Along the remaining open side of the garden, a clever composting and water-collecting station is located within convenient distance of the growing beds. The sloped roof above the compost bins keeps the decomposing materials from becoming too soggy and allows rainwater to drain directly into the three rain barrels for easy irrigation. To minimize environmental pollutants in your rain barrels — pollen, molds, bird droppings, industry pollutants — consider including a "first flush" diverter or only use the collected water for ornamental plants. As well, clean your rain barrels occasionally, rinsing well at the beginning and end of each growing season.

Tucked beside the rain barrels, the folks at Growing Places Indy have left a 2- by 4-foot area that can be used to grow several fruit bushes, brambles, or a small fruit tree. This extra space can be used for a pollinating partner if a fruiting shrub such as highbush blueberry or honeyberry (Haskap berry) is planted at the center of the garden, as these fruits need two different cultivars to ensure adequate pollination.

Using a living mulch. The 1-foot-wide walkway that runs between and around the garden beds has been cleverly planted with a low-growing clover such as white Dutch. This living mulch will foil weed growth, but it will also attract pollinating and beneficial insects. Plus, the carpet of clover will prevent muddied feet, fix atmospheric nitrogen, and is tough enough to withstand frequent foot traffic.

Succession planting. The team at Growing Places Indy has planned the garden based on continuous succession planting from spring through autumn, to ensure maximum production (see the chart on page 88 for recommendations). Once the last crops in each bed have been harvested in fall, they suggest sowing a cover crop to build up the soil and prevent winter erosion.

Growing Places Indy recommends selecting Slow Food USA Ark of Taste varieties. Some of their favorites include those on the following page. Many of the varieties listed may take a bit of effort to track down, but the reward of flavor will be worth it.

Inspired by the work of Slow Food, this compact and highly ornamental yet productive design from Growing Places Indy requires just 400 square feet of space, making it a practical garden for most sites.

CLEVER RECYCLING STATION

The composting and water-collecting station at the side of the garden recycles garden waste and provides plenty of irrigation water and organic matter to the crops.

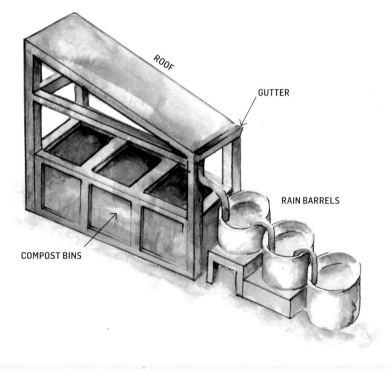

ROOF

GUTTER

RAIN BARRELS

COMPOST BINS

SUCCESSION PLANTING PLAN

Bed	Spring	Summer	Fall	Winter
1	lettuce/arugula/cover crop	tomatoes	lettuce/arugula/cover crop	cover crop
2	scallions	scallions	scallions	cover crop
3	lettuce/arugula/cover crop	tomatillos/husk cherries	lettuce/arugula/cover crop	cover crop
4	peas	pole beans	peas	cover crop
5	leeks	leeks	leeks	cover crop
6	radishes/cover crop	peppers	radishes/cover crop	cover crop
7	greens (kale, Swiss chard, collards, mustard)	greens (kale, Swiss chard, collards, mustard)	greens (kale, Swiss chard, collards, mustard)	cover crop
8	carrots	carrots	carrots	carrots
9	beets/turnips	beets/turnips	beets/turnips	cover crops
10	potatoes or sweet potatoes	potatoes or sweet potatoes	cover crop	cover crop
11	onions	onions	cover crop	cover crop
12	garlic	garlic	garlic	garlic
13	fruit (tree, bramble, or bush)	fruit (tree, bramble, or bush)	fruit (tree, bramble, or bush)	fruit (tree, bramble, or bush)
14	clover walkway	clover walkway	clover walkway	clover walkway
15	herbs	herbs	herbs	herbs
16	flowers	flowers	flowers	flowers
17	compost bin	squash/melons planted in compost	squash/melons planted in compost	compost bin
18	compost bin	compost bin	compost bin	compost bin
19	rain barrels	rain barrels	rain barrels	store or disconnect rain barrels
20	fruit (tree, bramble, or bush)	fruit (tree, bramble, or bush)	fruit (tree, bramble, or bush)	fruit (tree, bramble, or bush)

Laura's Garden Plan in Summer

20' DEEP X 20' WIDE

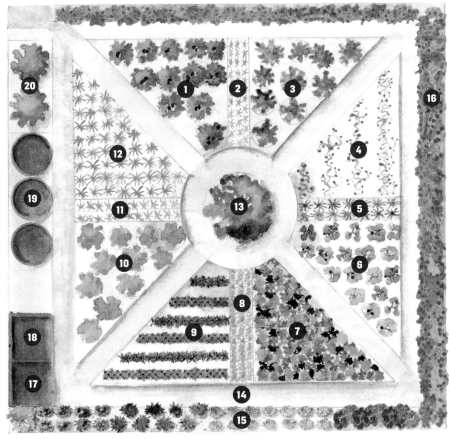

See Succession Planting Plan at left for key to plant beds.

Recommended Slow Food USA Ark of Taste Varieties

- **Beans:** 'Cherokee Trail of Tears' bush beans, 'Hidatsa Shield Figure' pole beans, 'Lina Cisco's Bird Egg' bush bean
- **Beets:** 'Early Blood Turnip-Rooted'
- **Garlic:** 'Lorz Italian', 'Inchelium Red'
- **Husk (ground) cherries:** 'Aunt Molly's'
- **Lettuce:** 'Grandpa Admire's', 'Speckled Lettuce', 'Tennis Ball'

- **Peppers:** 'Beaver Dam' sweet pepper, 'Jimmy Nardello's Sweet Italian Frying', 'Sheepnose Pimento'
- **Potatoes:** 'Green Mountain', 'Ozette'
- **Onions:** 'I'itoi'
- **Sweet potatoes:** 'Nancy Hall', 'Ivis White Cream'
- **Winter squash:** 'Amish Pie', 'Boston Marrow'

- **Tomatillos:** 'New Mexico Native'
- **Tomatoes:** 'Aunt Ruby's German Green', 'Cherokee Purple', 'German Pink', 'Orange Oxheart'
- **Turnips:** 'Gilfeather'
- **Watermelons:** 'Moon and Stars', 'Yellow-Meated'
- **Cover crops:** Annual ryegrass, winter rye, buckwheat, oats, red clover

Power Foods

When planning an edible plot, Dan Jason suggests that you consider including power foods like beans, quinoa, amaranth, and flax. "They pack a wallop, both in their amazing ability to multiply themselves (via their edible seeds) and in their ability to provide carefree means for the home gardener to obtain the highest-quality protein and oil," he says. Not only are his plant picks easy to grow, but many are also extremely decorative and can be grown across much of North America.

> Plant a power food crop like quinoa, flax, beans, or kale in each bed of your garden

> Plants were chosen based on their nutritional value and ease of cultivation

Essentially, power crops are just nutrient-dense foods. They include the aforementioned high-protein seed crops as well as beans, soybeans, kale, and even hull-less oats and barley.

Organize your space. For a well-organized and productive power food garden, Dan recommends planting the crops in 4- by 8-foot rectangular beds. For a comfortable working area and room for a wheelbarrow, allow at least 2 feet of space between the beds.

Top three power foods. Dan's top picks are the protein-packed quinoa, amaranth, and flax. "They are easily as gorgeous as any ornamental you might choose for your garden," Dan says. A cool-weather crop, quinoa is native to South America, where it has been cultivated for more than 5,000 years. Amaranth also hails from South America and, like quinoa, has edible foliage and seeds. It grows 4 to 8 feet tall, depending on the variety, with bronze- and burgundy-toned flower heads. Flax, a pretty plant with a light blue flower, is grown for its seeds that

are high in fiber and omega-3 fatty acids.

Cooking with power foods. Flax seed is often eaten raw in granola, yogurt, and smoothies, or baked into breads and muffins. Amaranth and quinoa can be ground into a gluten-free flour or cooked as healthy whole grains. Dan points out that amaranth and quinoa grains have an amino acid balance that is close to ideal for human nutrition, while flax seeds have a similar optimum fatty acid balance. And the leaves of amaranth and quinoa are among the most nutritious of vegetable greens. Combine this with their limited care demands, ornamental appearance, and healthful yield (one amaranth plant can produce a quarter of a million seeds in one season!), and it's not hard to see why more and more gardeners are starting to take notice.

Planting seeds. To plant these crops, simply sprinkle the small seeds evenly over the entire bed, tamping down lightly to ensure good seed-soil contact. Alternatively, seed them in two shallow furrows.

"The same broadcast planting technique [used for quinoa, amaranth, and flax] can also be used to sow wheats, hull-less oats, hull-less barleys, triticale, and other grains intended to be sprouted, juiced, or eaten as whole grains," Dan says. Soybeans and bush beans should be planted in two lengthwise rows per bed, sowing each seed about 1 inch deep and 3 inches apart.

If you are growing quinoa and amaranth for seed production, thin plants so that they are spaced 12 inches apart on center. If you are growing them for leafy greens, they can be allowed to grow more densely.

Great grains. Dan also believes that more gardeners should experiment with grains like wheat, hull-less oats, and barley. Hull-less oats are gaining popularity as a backyard grain because they require less processing after harvesting when compared with hulled oats. During the growing season, they are very carefree, requiring only an occasional watering in the event of a prolonged drought.

Hull-less barley is a good choice in regions with short seasons, as it matures earlier and tolerates cooler weather better than wheat. Hull-less barley varieties "are hardy, carefree crops that provide hearty and satisfying food," Dan says. He also notes that the plants have a graceful nodding effect that is attractive in the garden as well as in dried arrangements.

"Grains are a surprisingly easy and very rewarding crop for home gardens," he says, adding that grains are a good choice for less-than-ideal soils, as they tend to "lodge" or fall over when the earth is overly fertile. To plant, Dan suggests scattering the seeds over the beds or planting them in rows, with seeds spaced 1 inch apart. Cover the seed lightly with soil, and toss a row cover over the beds if birds are a problem. To harvest, pick or cut individual ripe wheat seeds when the plants have dried completely and thresh by hand. Hull-less barley and oats have very loose hulls that are removed quickly and easily by rubbing.

Super kale. A more common member of the power foods family is kale. He recommends growing it because it is packed with vitamins, minerals, and many phytonutrients (natural compounds found in plant-based foods that can enhance health).

Kale is very easy to grow and can be sown thickly in spring or early autumn for a bed of baby leaves (ideal for salads, stir-fries, or smoothies), or young plants can be transplanted into the garden in early spring and allowed to grow to maturity. In a 4- by 8-foot bed, eight kale seedlings will quickly fill the plot. In zones colder than 6, the bed can be covered with a mini hoop tunnel in late autumn to allow easy winter harvesting. Kale is sweeter when harvested after the first frost.

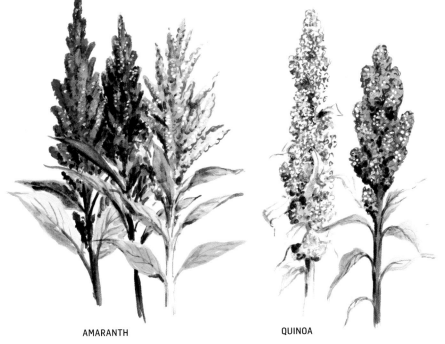

AMARANTH

QUINOA

FLAX

Dan's Favorite Power Foods

Quinoa. The foliage of this cool-weather native of South America can be enjoyed as a green in the same manner as spinach. The seeds (once rinsed to remove the bitter saponin) can be cooked and eaten like rice or used in a wide assortment of dishes. Dan suggests 'Multi-Hued' or 'Bright Beauties'.

Amaranth. Amaranth hails from South America and, like quinoa, has edible foliage and seeds. It is an extremely decorative plant, described by Dan as "majestic." It grows 4 to 8 feet tall, depending on the variety, with bronze- and burgundy-toned flower heads. Look for 'Burgundy Grain', 'Hopi Red Dye', 'Manna de Montana', or Dan's own 'Amaranth Mix'.

Flax. A pretty plant with a light blue flower, flax is grown for its seeds that are high in fiber and omega-3 fatty acids. There are two main types of flax: brown and golden, and Dan has found much success growing golden flax seed. A few seed companies offer flax seeds for gardens, but you can also plant the organic whole seeds found at bulk food stores.

NO-FUSS WHEAT

"Few people realize that wheat can be sprouted or cooked as the whole wheat 'berries' they are. In fact, these delicious ways of eating wheat provide much more nutritional benefit than consuming it as bread or pasta," says Dan.

Wheat. There are many varieties of wheat, so have fun experimenting with the diverse types and flavors. Dan suggests trying kamut (*Triticum turgidum* var. *durum*), an ancient wheat with a silvery-blue seedhead and large kernels. It contains 29 percent more protein and 27 percent more lipids than common wheat, as well as increased levels of vitamins and minerals. He also recommends 'Blue Tinge Ethiopian' for eating as a whole grain and 'Brazilian Lavras', or 'Thatcher' for making flour.

Hull-less oats (*Avena nuda*). These are gaining popularity as a backyard grain because they require less processing after harvesting when compared with hulled oats. During the growing season, they are very low-maintenance, requiring only an occasional watering in the event of a prolonged drought.

Hull-less barley. This is a good choice in regions with short seasons, as it matures earlier and tolerates cooler weather better than wheat. Hull-less barley varieties "are hardy, carefree crops that provide hearty and satisfying food," Dan says. He also notes that the plants have a graceful nodding effect that is attractive in the garden as well as in dried arrangements. 'Ethiopian Hull-less Barley' is the easiest to thresh, the highest yielding, and the most reliable.

Beans. There are many types of beans that can be grown in a home garden, from bush to pole, snap to dry, and soybean to fava, garbanzo, and more. "Try a variety of different types to see what you like and what grows best in your area," says Dan. He suggests growing pole beans on trellises and soybeans and bush beans in two rows in the 4-foot-wide beds. He likes 'Trionfo Violetto' or 'Blue Lake' pole beans and 'Hidatsa', 'Agate', and 'Grand Forks' soybeans.

Kale. If you want to enjoy a winter harvest, opt for hardy and cold-tolerant varieties like 'Red Russian' or 'White Russian'.

Heirloom Sampler

*W**hat's old is new again*** as gardeners discover the joy of growing heirloom vegetables such as 'Cherokee Purple' tomatoes and 'Lolla Rossa' lettuce. Marie Iannotti celebrates the diversity and flavor of heirloom edibles in her plan, which includes six main planting beds to showcase her top heirloom picks.

> Showcases flavor-packed heirloom vegetables

> Promotes seed saving and genetic diversity

> Uses quick hoops to extend the season in early spring or late autumn

Marie Iannotti is passionate about heirloom vegetables (open-pollinated plants that are 50 years or older, the seeds of which can be collected and saved and grow true to type). Initially she was drawn to them for their outstanding flavor. "I was in search of a better-tasting tomato and stumbled upon heirlooms just as they were gaining popularity," she recalls. "I tried growing a few surprisingly wonderful tomatoes, peppers, and beans, and just kept going."

The importance of heirloom crops. Unfortunately, thousands of heritage varieties have been lost over time, but thanks to the diligence of avid seed savers and heritage seed companies around the world, many have been preserved and are once again available to gardeners. "We need to keep the enormous variety and genetic diversity of vegetables available, because one size does not fit every garden," says Marie. When sourcing seed, you'll discover that certain heirloom varieties, like 'Brandywine' tomatoes, are widely available, while others, like those on Slow Food's Ark of Taste, may take you on a bit of a wild-goose chase. Marie also notes that when gardeners save the seeds from their best-producing, healthiest heirloom varieties from year to year, the future generations of those plants will be better adapted to the climatic conditions of their specific areas.

Marie's heirloom sampler garden is a tidy 20 by 25 feet with six

manageable beds ranging in size from 9 by 4 feet to 9 by 3 feet. Marie favors raised beds, yet with the hot dry summers that seem to be an increasing trend, she is also intrigued by the thought of sunken beds, which are plots that are dug so that they are below soil level. "You're still working with a designated bed, but water drains into the bed, which is a nice feature during dry summers," she says.

Top heirlooms. Her favorite heirlooms include 'Cherokee Purple' tomatoes (she is partial to their musky, smoky flavor), 'Romanesco' broccoli ("It's slightly sweet, nutty,

and tender — if you can stop looking at it long enough to take a bite!"), and 'Charentais' melons ("perfumed, tropical, and sweet, they are worth the hassle of growing them in my less-than-ideal climate").

Making the most of your space. Marie decides where to put each crop based on its space demands. "I place the larger, space-hogging plants first and then allocate space for the perpetually harvested vegetables like the chard and greens," she says, adding that she tucks in herbs wherever there is a vacant spot. "I usually keep one bed dedicated to succession

planting so I don't have to go searching for spare space."

Heirlooms taste great. Whatever heirloom vegetables you choose to grow, remember that "variety is the spice of life." Marie encourages you to experiment with all sorts of heirloom vegetables. In her book *The Beginner's Guide to Growing Heirloom Vegetables*, she notes that heirloom crops are not dusty antiques, but rather prized champions grown and hand-selected for quality, flavor, and production. "Their true splendor comes from being too scrumptious to forget," she says.

MARIE'S SEED-SAVING TIPS

- **Save seed from the best of your vegetables.** Choose the tastiest, healthiest, and juiciest, so you can pass these traits along. Some of the easiest seeds to save are beans, peas, peppers, and squash. Garlic cloves are also a great way to get started with seed saving.

- **Isolate different varieties of the same vegetable** to prevent cross-pollination. The easiest ways to do this are to plant varieties that bloom at different times, or to stagger planting so that the varieties are not in bloom at the same time.

- **Allow the vegetables to over-ripen before collecting seed.** Vegetables like tomatoes, squash, cucumbers, and eggplant will be well past their edible stage when the seeds are ready to be collected. For most vegetables, you can simply scoop out and dry the seeds. Tomatoes require a wet processing method where the seeds are allowed to ferment in the tomato pulp for a few days before being rinsed clean and dried for storage.

- **Make sure your seed is thoroughly dry** — to the point of being brittle — before you store it away in an airtight container.

Marie's Garden Plan

20' DEEP X 25' WIDE

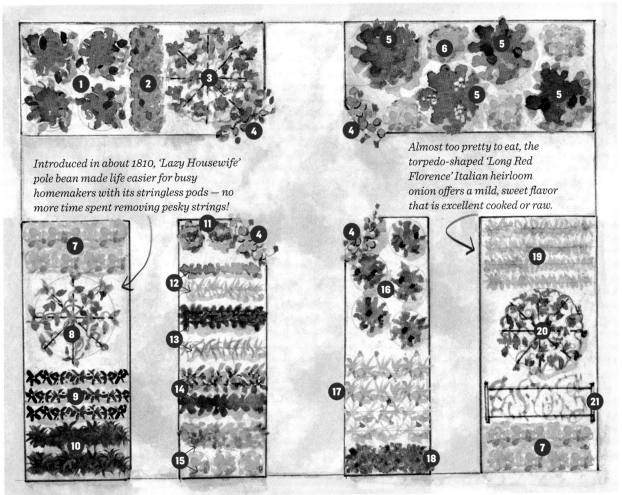

Introduced in about 1810, 'Lazy Housewife' pole bean made life easier for busy homemakers with its stringless pods — no more time spent removing pesky strings!

Almost too pretty to eat, the torpedo-shaped 'Long Red Florence' Italian heirloom onion offers a mild, sweet flavor that is excellent cooked or raw.

1. **Eggplants:** 'Louisiana Long Green' and 'Rosa Bianca' (2 plants each)

2. **Bush Beans:** 'Fin de Bagnol' French (filet)

3. **Zucchini:** 'Costata Romanesco' on a teepee

4. **Nasturtiums:** 'Double Dwarf Jewel Mix'

5. **Tomatoes:** 'Cherokee Purple', 'Italian Heirloom', 'German Pink', and 'Yellow Pear'

6. **Basil:** 'Lettuce Leaf' ('Italian Large Leaved') or 'Genovese'

7. **Lettuce:** 'Lolla Rossa', 'Four Seasons' ('Merveille des Quatre Saisons'), and 'Amish Deer Tongue'

8. **Pole beans:** 'Lazy Housewife' on a teepee

9. **Swiss chard:** 'Bright Lights'

10. **Kale:** 'Lacinato' (dinosaur or 'Nero di Toscana')

11. **Parsley:** Flat-leaved (Italian)

12. **Radishes and carrots:** 'French Breakfast' radishes and 'Paris Market' carrots

13. **Beet greens and scallions:** 'Bull's Blood' beet greens and 'Evergreen Hardy White' scallions

14. **Beets and spinach:** 'Detroit Dark Red' or 'Chioggia' beets and 'Bloomsdale Long Standing' spinach

15. **'Apollo' arugula and thyme**

16. **Sweet peppers:** 'Marconi'

17. **Garlic:** 'Music' (Zones 4–7) or 'Inchelium Red' (Zones 8–10)

18. **Greek oregano**

19. **Onions:** 'Long Red Florence'

20. **Cucumbers:** 'True Lemon' on a teepee

21. **Snow peas:** 'Golden Sweet' on a trellis

Wildlife-Friendly Garden

Tammi Hartung believes that gardeners should work with nature, and to celebrate that spirit, she has created an herb and food garden that is wildlife-friendly. Of course, not all critters are beneficial to a garden (Exhibit A: deer), but many are extremely valuable (Exhibit B: birds, bees, butterflies, and bats). The latter should be encouraged by including bird feeders, bat houses, mason bee boxes, and plenty of nectar- and pollen-rich plants.

> A wildlife-supporting design that includes fruit trees, vegetables, herbs, and berries

> Whimsical curving stepping stone paths wander between the garden beds

> The children's area includes a playhouse, a wagon-wheel garden, and a picnic table

> A wooden screen offers a secluded perch to enjoy the birds

Tammi Hartung's plan has many layers. First, there are the plants. Most are standard garden edibles; others such as goji berries and nettles are less familiar. Then there are the various wildlife-supporting features, including birdfeeders, bat houses, beehives, mason bee boxes, and hummingbird feeders. The garden also contains recreational elements: an outdoor eating area for summer feasts, a children's picnic table, a whimsical playhouse, several benches, and a bird viewing area. "I put this design together with the thought of a very earth-friendly family in mind," says Tammi of the 30- by 50-foot space.

Nettles and comfrey. Tammi's plan includes many vegetables, fruits, and herbs. Two plants, nettles and comfrey, are not often grown in conventional food gardens, but they offer many benefits to both the gardener and the health of the soil. "These are important plants in the world of herbal use," says Tammi, who uses nettles as a food plant in soups and casseroles. Nettles as well as comfrey are also good for building soil and activating compost. In permaculture, a design system that fosters ecological and sustainable agriculture, Tammi says that these plants are grown around and near fruit and nut trees, which need a lot of soil fertility to produce well.

Healthy plants need bees, bats, butterflies, and hummingbirds to pollinate them and manage pests. The bats are efficient at pollinating vines and night-blooming plants, while bees prefer plants with European origins — the fruit trees and many of the cabbage-family vegetables. Because these pollinators are so important to a garden, Tammi has included wildlife-friendly elements that they require in order to flourish. "There are food supplies, water sources, homes, and safe places to raise young and stay away from some of their predators," she says.

The benefit of roses. A rose hedge along the south side of the garden produces ample hips for birds, bears, squirrels, and deer, as well as for Tammi, who likes to use hips as a fruit and as an herb. The hedges "also provide shelter for homes and protection," says Tammi, adding that "all plants in the rose family are really good for bees, as well as anything with yellow or blue flowers, like lavender or helichrysum." Tammi's favorite roses are red leaf rose (*Rosa glauca*, also sold as *R. rubriifolia*) and Harrison's yellow (*Rosa × harisonii*). Her plan also includes seed-bearing plants for birds like goldfinches, which enjoy the ripe seeds of sunflowers, purple coneflowers (*Echinacea* species), and other types of coneflowers.

Within the herb bed, Tammi has added three birdfeeders to attract insect-eating birds that can help control any bad bug populations. A nearby bench is hidden behind a bird viewing screen — a wooden fence that is 6 to 7 feet tall and 6 to 8 feet wide, with portals or slots cut into the wood — to give garden visitors a close-up view without disturbing the birds.

A place to play. To encourage children to play in the garden, Tammi's plan includes an eating area for children's picnics or tea parties, a playhouse (or perhaps a treehouse?), and a wagon-wheel garden planted with kid-friendly edibles and herbs like cucumbers, carrots, cherry tomatoes, chives, and radishes. Clumps of violas and lamb's ears border the pathway that leads to the playhouse, inviting small hands to gather cheerful bouquets of the small violas or touch the soft, fuzzy leaves of the lamb's ears. This pocket of the garden plan is also in full view of several fruit trees, as well as the mason bee boxes and bird feeders, further introducing children to the diversity found in a garden.

Like many gardeners, Tammi must deal with marauding deer. Her fruit trees are caged until they are large enough to withstand the rutting bucks, and a fence around one small section of their food garden protects tender salad greens. See the box on page 98 for some of Tammi's favorite deer-repellant tools.

Tammi's Favorite Varieties

FRUIT

- **Apple trees:** 'Liberty', 'Macoun', and 'Albemarle Pippin'
- **Cherry trees:** 'North Star', 'Meteor', and 'Evans Bali' (tart varieties)
- **Raspberries:** 'Heritage' and 'Fall Gold'
- **Currants:** 'Red Lake' and 'Consort Black' currants
- **Strawberries:** 'Tristar' everbearing

VEGGIES AND HERBS

- **Children's herb and vegetable bed:** Dill, lemon balm, chives, cherry tomatoes, carrots, lettuce, 'Easter Egg' and 'French Breakfast' radishes, 'Marketmore', 'True Lemon', and 'Salt and Pepper' cucumbers
- **Salad greens:** 'Speckled Trout' romaine, 'Sylvestra' butterhead, and 'Wildfire' mixed lettuce; 'Bloomsdale Long Standing', 'America', and 'Whale' spinach
- **Onions:** 'Red Wethersfield' and 'Borettana Cipollini'
- **Sweet peppers:** 'Yankee Bell' and 'Round of Hungary'
- **Tomatoes:** 'Moskvich', 'Czech's Bush', 'Black Prince', 'Hungarian Heart', 'Red Robin', 'Sungold', and 'White Cherry'
- **Brassicas:** 'Red Express' and 'Bilko' cabbage; 'De Cicco' broccoli; 'Purple Top White Globe' turnips
- **Zucchini:** 'Ronde de Nice'
- **Carrots:** 'Scarlet Nantes'
- **Green beans:** 'Provider'
- **Swiss chard:** 'Five Color Silverbeet' and 'Orange Chiffon'
- **Beets:** 'Chioggia', 'Bull's Blood', and 'Early Blood Turnip-Rooted'
- **Potatoes:** 'German Butterball' and 'Dark Red Norland'
- **Winter squash:** 'Black Forest' Kabocha, 'Red Kuri', and 'Sweet Dumpling'
- **Herbs:** Lavender, purple coneflower (echinacea), fennel, garlic chives, marjoram, lovage, parsley, thyme, anise hyssop, sage, and sunset hyssop

TIPS FOR DETERRING DEER

When deer become an issue for Tammi, she finds that it's important to break up their daily routine for a few days, at which point they seem to give up and move on. Here are her favorite tools:

- **Yellow tape.** "If we need the deer to stop nibbling on a specific crop, we surround it with yellow caution tape tied to steel fence posts. It isn't pretty, but it works like a charm! After a few days, we take the tape down and don't have any more problems."

- **Soap.** "Put a highly scented bar soap like Dial or Irish Spring inside a sock or stocking. Knot the end and hang the soap sock in the area of the garden where deer are problematic."

- **Lavender or sage.** "Plant a border of lavender or sage around the food garden. The deer don't like the smell of these herbs."

- **Granular Plantskydd.** "If all else fails, I apply granular Plantskydd to the ground. It is a deodorized blood-meal product that is registered for use by organic growers and lasts for six months, even in wet weather!"

Tammi's Garden Plan

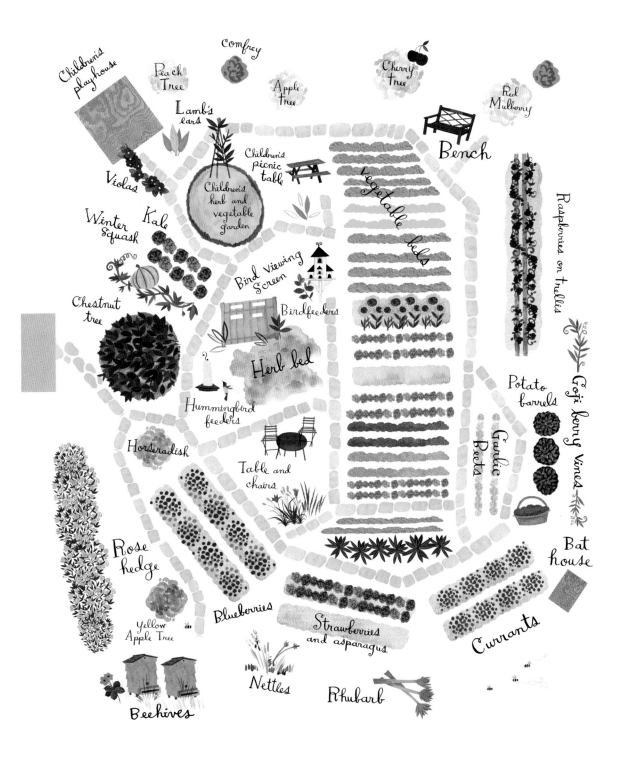

Children's playhouse

Peach Tree

Comfrey

Apple Tree

Cherry Tree

Red Mulberry

Lamb's ears

Children's picnic table

Bench

Violas

Children's herb and vegetable garden

Winter Squash

Kale

Bird Viewing Screen

Birdfeeders

Vegetable beds

Raspberries on trellis

Chestnut tree

Herb bed

Potato barrels

Goji berry vines

Hummingbird feeders

Horseradish

Table and chairs

Garlic

Beets

Rose hedge

Yellow Apple Tree

Blueberries

Strawberries and asparagus

Currants

Bat house

Beehives

Nettles

Rhubarb

Hanging Gutters

N *o garden? No problem!* With her design for a gutter garden, Jayme Jenkins proves that as long as you have a bit of sun, virtually any empty space can be used to grow food. "Gutter gardens are a great way to take advantage of the vertical spaces around your home to grow flowers and edibles, and create a stylish space divider or privacy screen without spending too much money," says Jayme.

> An easy way to turn an empty vertical space into an attractive edible screen

> Uses inexpensive or recycled gutters

> Can be customized to fit any sized space

> Ideal for compact crops such as leaf lettuce, parsley, or strawberries

Need more convincing? Just Google "gutter garden" and you'll find dozens of photos of gutters planted with compact vegetables such as leaf lettuce and baby spinach, herbs, and edible flowers. Gutter gardens are typically mounted on the side of a house, garage, or fence, but Jayme was reluctant to drill holes in the siding of her house; instead, she came up with the idea of a gutter garden that hangs from the roof of her front porch.

Jayme notes that gutter gardens are an attractive alternative to potted gardens, which can take up a lot of space and look cluttered. "This project is perfect for small-space gardens like balconies, or just to add visual interest to an otherwise boring patio," she says.

Protect your veggies. Gardeners weary of battling slugs, deer, voles, or rabbits will also appreciate that a hanging gutter garden keeps your tender lettuce and herbs safe from hungry critters. No more chewed leaves!

Water often. As with any container garden, you will need to water your hanging gutters much more often than in-ground crops. Water every couple of days, or as needed; a drip irrigation system will make watering much easier. Jayme recommends using a watering can with a narrow spout so that water hits the soil, not the plants. In such a small space, plants will quickly use up the nutrients in the soil, so give your gutter garden an occasional dose of a liquid organic food to keep food production high and your ornamental plants healthy.

Jayme's Hanging Gutters

Jayme suggests sticking to shallow-rooted edibles and annual flowers. As plants are harvested or production declines, replace them with fresh seedlings.

1. **Salad crops:** Arugula, spinach, pak choi, Swiss chard, kale (harvest and remove before plants reach full size), and all kinds of lettuce

2. **Annual herbs:** Cilantro, curly parsley, chives, thyme, rosemary, oregano

3. **Strawberries:** Jayme recommends buying bare-root plants to save money and make planting easier

4. **Root vegetables:** Baby beets, 'Easter Egg' radishes, and short carrot varieties like 'Tonda di Parigi'

5. **Annual flowers:** Marigolds, sweet alyssum, nasturtiums, pansies, and violas

6. **Sun-loving ornamentals:** Sedums, portulaca (purslane), and mecardonia

THREADED RODS

Stainless steel threaded rods support the top two layers of gutters, while the chain is just looped under the bottom gutter. Have your hardware store cut the threaded rods slightly wider than the gutter. The rods should be just wide enough so that, when the bolts are threaded, the gutter fits snugly between the chains.

"Let the hardware employee know that you need to be able to thread the bolts on and off the threaded rod," advises Jayme. If you will cut the threaded rod yourself, screw on the bolts before you make the cuts; otherwise you won't be able to screw them on.

HOW TO BUILD A THREE-TIER HANGING GUTTER GARDEN

These instructions are for a three-tier, 32-inch-long hanging gutter garden. For longer gutters or hangers, modify the materials accordingly. Jayme used zinc-plated chains, which will eventually rust, adding another design element to the gutter garden, but if you prefer shiny steel, go for galvanized chains.

MATERIALS

- 1 8-foot length of white gutter (PVC or other material) cut into three 32-inch sections (or longer lengths)
- 6 white gutter end caps
- 2 chains, cut to desired length. These are sold by the foot in hardware and building supply stores.
- 4 ⅛-inch stainless steel threaded rods (to support the gutters)
- 8 bolts (to be threaded onto the rods)
- 2 galvanized J-hooks
- Potting soil and plants

TOOLS

- Cordless drill with drill bit set
- Handsaw or hacksaw
- T-square or straightedge
- Tape measure
- Pencil or grease pencil
- Eye protection (always a good idea when working with tools)

1. Determine the center of each of the gutters; draw a reference line down the inside using your T-square to make the line straight. "This is to make sure your drainage holes are in a straight line, since the top levels will be visible from the bottom," says Jayme, explaining that it just looks better when the holes are even.

2. Using a ³⁄₁₆-inch drill bit, drill holes every few inches in the bottom of the gutters to make sure you provide good drainage. (Plant roots hate sitting in water for long periods of time.)

3. Locate a spot that gets at least 4 hours of sun. "I placed mine on the crossbeams of a pergola, but you could also hang it off a deck, balcony, or even the facia board on the eaves of your house," notes Jayme.

4. Measure in about 4 inches from the ends of your gutters and mark the corresponding positions on your support of choice. Drill pilot holes: "This is a hole slightly smaller in diameter than the screw's threads, which makes screwing in the J-hook a lot easier," she says.

5. Determine how far you want your gutter garden to hang down. Multiply that length by two to determine the length of chain you will need to hang one end of your garden. Using the handsaw, cut two pieces of chain to this length. Make sure each chain has the same number of links. (This is where elementary school math comes in handy!)

6. Loop the ends of one chain through the first J-hook, then loop the ends of the second chain through the second J-hook.

7. Cap the ends of your gutters, then fill with potting soil and plant them with succulents, shallow-rooted edibles, or — my favorite — strawberries!

8. Have a helper pull apart one hanging chain as you insert one end of the first gutter through the bottom of the chain loop, leaving about 4 inches of gutter extending beyond the chain support. Insert the other end through the other chain loop so it extends an equal distance beyond the chain.

9. Determine the mature height of your first gutter's plants, then insert a threaded rod through two chain links that are just higher than the eventual tops of the plants. Repeat for the other chain, making sure you insert the second rod at the same height as your first. (You can count the number of chain links from the bottom.)

10. Thread a nut on each end of the two metal rods. Tighten just enough to keep the gutter in place.

11. Repeat steps 8, 9, and 10 for your third gutter.

Modern Truck Garden

A *truck garden is traditionally a large garden* that grows food to be sold at market. Here, Leslie Land updated the concept. She created a plot that will produce plenty of vegetables, and she included varieties that aren't often found at supermarkets — 'White Currant' cherry tomatoes, 'Boothby's Blonde' cucumbers, and 'Red Noodle' yard-long pole beans.

> A fun design inspired by a traditional truck garden

> Features varieties that are often difficult to find at markets but easy to grow

> Organized by crop family to make rotation easy

> Includes a series of compost bins to recycle garden waste

It used to be that if you wanted to eat any of the more exotic varieties of vegetables, you had to grow them yourself. Happily, you can now find many more varieties of produce at markets, though Leslie lamented you're still unlikely to encounter edibles like "ferny, anise-flavored sweet cicely; earthy torpedo-shaped 'Crapaudine' beets (the oldest variety still being sold); or 'Monstruoso' basil, named for leaves large enough to wrap a jumbo shrimp." The solution? Enter Leslie's truck garden.

Unlike cottage gardens, which have informal beds of food and flowers not designed for production, truck gardens are laid out for easy care, with straight-edged beds and rows. Leslie's truck garden is a basic square

measuring 40 by 40 feet and divided by a series of paths. Although you may not wish to sell your harvest, you will certainly have enough to share with friends and family, or you may choose to preserve and can your excess.

No-fuss rotation. To keep crop rotation simple, the perennial crops such as asparagus, raspberries, strawberries, herbs, and flowers have been placed around the perimeter of the garden. At the back, near the asparagus bed, sit three compost bins: one for gathering fresh organics (kitchen and garden scraps), one for decomposing materials, and one for finished compost.

"The main production area for annual vegetables and herbs is in the center, where there are four beds, two large and two somewhat smaller to allow for different plants' space needs," said Leslie. "Tomatoes and squash take a lot more room than greens or trellised beans and peas, but as long as you organize your plants by family it will be easy to rotate the beds each year." To keep the production beds on a four-year rotation cycle, move the 3-foot horizontal path every two years, Leslie advised.

Leslie's Modern Truck Garden Plants

Leslie noted that this is a general plan; specific plants will vary depending on your taste and climate, but to get you started, she included a few of her favorite varieties.

NIGHTSHADES

'Aunt Ruby's German Green' tomatoes. "This super-juicy heirloom has a great balance of sweet and sour taste and is a brilliant emerald color," said Leslie. "It has a very short shelf life, but the fruits keep coming all summer after they get started, gradually dwindling in size as the season progresses."

'White Currant' cherry tomatoes. "The fruits are more of a cream color than white when fully ripe," she noted. "The tiny fruits are difficult to separate from the stem, but they are incredibly flavorful and beyond abundant." Plants become enormous and are very disease-resistant.

'Beaver Dam' hot peppers and 'Ashe County Pimento' sweet peppers. Listed in the Slow Food's Ark of Taste, 'Beaver Dam' is a Hungarian heirloom pepper with pointed fruits that ripen from green to bright red. They are medium hot and excellent in fresh salsa. 'Ashe County Pimento' is an heirloom pimento-type pepper with squat red ripe fruits that grow 3 to 4 inches in diameter and just $1\frac{1}{2}$ inches tall.

'Rosita' eggplants. Productive plants produce a generous supply of teardrop-shaped purple-pink eggplants that grow 8 inches long and 4 inches wide at maturity.

'La Ratte' potatoes. 'La Ratte' is a yellow-skinned and yellow-fleshed heirloom fingerling variety with a delectable buttery texture and flavor.

CUCURBITS AND ANNUAL HERBS

'Boothby's Blonde' cucumbers. A popular heirloom cucumber with oval-shaped fruits and soft yellow skin.

'Yellow Crookneck' squash. "Not a commercial animal, the plants are slower to bear than hybrids," said Leslie. "The squash, best picked around 4 inches long, get too big if you so much as look away." She also added that the tiny necks are vulnerable to breakage, but the flavor of this heirloom is fuller than that of other yellow squash, and when cooked it has a creamy texture.

Basil. "Basil is easy to grow from seed and expensive to buy," noted Leslie, adding that there are all sorts of flavors and shapes that are hard to come by unless you grow them from seed. "Replant several times over the summer so that young plants, which have the best flavor and texture, are always coming along."

LEGUMES

'Sugar Snap' peas. "There are about a dozen varieties of snap pea seeds available to gardeners, but none of the others is as sweet, crunchy, or prolific as the original 'Sugar Snap'," revealed Leslie. "Strictly a home garden plant, the vines are long and must be trellised and they're slow to start bearing, but once they get going they produce for a long time."

'Gold of Bacau' and 'Rattlesnake' pole beans; 'Red Noodle' yard-long pole beans. 'Gold of Bacau' is a Romano-type bean with flat butter-yellow pods that can reach 10 inches in length. The green, streaked-with-purple pods of 'Rattlesnake' pole beans are both beautiful and delicious. 'Red Noodle' beans are also rather unusual with lengthy 18-inch-long pods in an arresting shade of burgundy-purple.

Romano (flat-pod) bush beans. Compact, bushy plants yield a bumper crop of 6-inch-long, flat green beans. Exceptional flavor!

BRASSICAS AND ROOT CROPS

'Romanesco' broccoli. The apple-green heads of 'Romanesco' are almost too pretty to eat. Almost. Each domed head is composed of hypnotizing whorls of florets that have a mild nutty flavor and creamy texture.

(list continues on page 106)

To make it easy to rotate your beds, plant perennials around the perimeter of the garden.

Production-friendly straight beds and organized rows are hallmarks of truck gardens.

Move this path every two years to keep the beds on a four-year rotation cycle.

Leslie's Garden Plan

40' DEEP X 40' WIDE

1. Nightshades: Cherry and full-sized tomatoes, hot and sweet peppers, eggplants, and potatoes

2. Cucurbits and annual herbs: Cucumbers, squash, and basil

3. Legumes: Peas and pole and bush beans

4. Brassicas and root crops: Kale, broccoli, arugula, lettuce, and beets

5. Perennial flowers and herbs: sweet cicely, lovage, and bunching onions

6. Alpine and regular strawberries

7. Raspberries

8. Asparagus

9. Flowers

10. Annual herbs

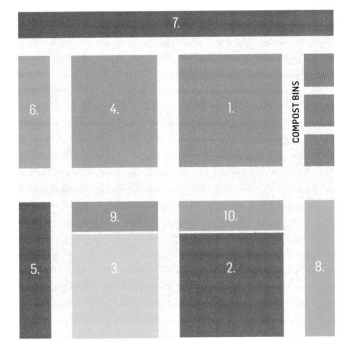

'Red Russian' and 'Lacinato' kale. 'Red Russian' kale is an extremely cold-tolerant variety with wide gray-green leaves highlighted by purple-red stems. 'Lacinato', on the other hand, is an heirloom kale with straplike dark blue-green leaves that are a bit softer in texture than curly kales.

Wild (rustic) arugula. "Garden arugula's spicier cousin, this stays tasty far longer than the common kind and is still a great salad addition when it has bolted and is peppery hot," said Leslie. "The plants are big and bushy, and the pretty, edible yellow flowers taste milder than the leaves."

'Merveille des Quatre Saisons' lettuce. This heirloom lettuce forms beautiful, dense heads that thrive in spring, summer, autumn, and even into winter if offered protection in the form of a cold frame. The tender, ruffled leaves have a pleasing, sweet flavor.

'Piracicaba' broccoli. "This Brazilian green is a twofer: it produces small, tender heads of broccoli as well as dark green leaves that are more tender than kale and more toothsome than cabbage," Leslie said, adding that the plant keeps producing from late spring to late fall.

'Crapaudine' and 'Lutz Winter Keeper' ('Lutz Green Leaf') beets. 'Crapaudine' beets are a heritage variety that "even look pre-modern, from their fat carrot shape to their rough, barklike skin," noted Leslie in her blog. "Of all the many beets I've grown, 'Crapaudine' is the tastiest, dense fleshed and sweet, with just enough — i.e. only a little — of beet's classic earthy taste." 'Lutz Green Leaf' is also considered a sweet-tasting beet, as well as an excellent keeper.

'Bleu de Solaize' leeks and 'Nebechan' scallions (if space allows). 'Bleu de Solaize' is an heirloom leek that produces fat shanks with attractive blue-green leaves, and with a thick mulch of straw, they can be enjoyed well into winter. 'Nebechan' is a Japanese scallion with upright foliage and no bulbing.

PERENNIAL CROPS

'Mignonette' alpine strawberries. "Aromatic and packed with flavor, the fruits from this plant are the tastiest of the little so-called wild strawberries that bear all season long," noted Leslie. "The fruits take forever to pick but are worth it."

'Tristar' strawberries. "This is an everbearing variety that produces a small crop in spring, a larger crop in fall, and sporadic berries over the summer," Leslie said. "The berries are larger and juicier than 'Mignonette', with a sharper flavor."

Sweet cicely. "This perennial herb is pretty enough for the flower garden," Leslie said. "All parts — the downy fernlike leaves, stems, flowers, and green seeds — are edible and taste like a cross between anise and tarragon."

Lovage. "This sturdy perennial herb has deeply cut leaves that taste strongly of celery," described Leslie. "It gives the biggest crops in spring and fall but will produce all summer if flower stalks are promptly removed and the tired growth cut back."

'Evergreen' bunching onions. "This is a hardy scallion that multiplies to form bunches," Leslie said, noting that it also makes a nice addition to the perennial bed.

Asparagus. "An all-male variety of green asparagus such as 'Jersey Knight' produces more spears over a longer time than a mixed-sex planting," said Leslie, noting that this is because female plants use energy to make fruits. The fruits will also self-sow, becoming weedy. " 'Purple Passion' is a mixed-sex variety, and even the male plants are less productive than green asparagus." However, she added that because it is so beautiful and delicious, it's worth giving garden space to a few plants.

Raspberries. These berries "are the grow-it-at-home fruit supreme, since they don't travel well and are very expensive," Leslie said. "Because they are quite climate-sensitive, the best varieties will be the ones recommended by the raspberry vendors at your local farmers' market."

LESLIE'S PICKS FOR HIGH-RETURN VEGETABLES

"If you are a gardener with limited space and time whose primary goal is the largest amount of tasty, organic food for the smallest amount of effort, the following crops are winners. They are easy to plant, easy to care for, easy to pick, easy to prepare, and — in some cases — all four," says Leslie.

- **Indeterminate tomatoes.** "These are named for their vines, which keep getting bigger and producing new fruit until felled by frost. There used to be a small selection of varieties sold as plants, but these days there is quite an assortment available at farmers' markets and garden centers. Unlike bush tomatoes, these varieties will need to be well staked to support the sprawling vines. An 8-foot wooden stake inserted into the earth before planting is ideal; as the plant grows, it can be continually tied to the support."

- **Nonhybrid pole beans.** "Like indeterminate tomatoes, old-fashioned pole beans keep growing and producing until frost — assuming you keep them picked. They may seem like more work than bush beans because you have to provide supports, but bush beans peter out much sooner and picking them is arduous. (There's a reason 'stoop labor' is a synonym for work nobody wants to do.)"

- **Zucchini.** "Everything they say about avalanches of zucchini is true, especially of hybrid varieties — none of which, unfortunately, is as delicious as 'Costata Romanesco'. This heirloom takes longer to start bearing than modern zucchinis; it has the prickly leaves characteristic of 'unimproved' varieties; and it makes big, sprawly plants instead of tidy bushes. It is not good for containers or for planting beside the front walk. The high return is the flavor. If space is tight, pass it by and go for a hybrid — most of them are fine if you pick them young."

- **Swiss chard.** "Plants hold without bolting from spring through fall in all but the hottest summer areas. There's no need to harvest whole plants; you can keep breaking off outer leaves for months. Every picking will be tender as long as plants get enough water."

Vintage Victory Garden

When LaManda Joy looks at all of the underused, weedy spaces in our cities, she sees countless possibilities for growing food. During World War II, sites like these were turned into "victory gardens" by civilians, supplying thousands of pounds of fruits and vegetables and relieving the pressure on the national food system. In her "Vintage Victory Garden" plan, LaManda has stepped back in time to a garden plan originally issued by the Illinois State Council of Defense to supplement the fresh food required by a family of five.

> Based on an original design for a World War II victory garden

> The large plot will supply a generous harvest of fresh food from late spring through autumn

> Vegetable varieties are also vintage, but still available through seed catalogs

In 1943, America was fully engaged in World War II, and across the country certain foods were becoming scarce. Not only was a significant portion of the workforce redirected to the war effort, so too were many of the vehicles and trucks that transported fresh vegetables and fruits.

The push to grow food. The materials used to can food were also used in the war effort, so even preserved food was difficult to find. The government encouraged the population to plant war gardens, commonly called "victory gardens," which relieved pressure on food resources and indirectly supported the war effort. In 1943 alone, more than 275,000 Chicago households started gardens.

Transforming urban spaces now. Fast forward to modern-day Chicago: Victory gardens, and the message behind them, are being revived by folks like LaManda Joy, who are transforming empty, weedy urban spaces into lush edible gardens. LaManda founded the Peterson Garden Project, a volunteer organization (3,000-strong) committed to teaching people how to grow their own food. "Our idea is simple: With so many empty lots within the city of Chicago, why not grow both food and community on them?" LaManda asks.

Vintage plan and plants. To celebrate the important role that victory gardens played during the Second World War, LaManda has shared this vintage plan originally issued by the Illinois State Council of Defense. The varieties listed in the plan have stood the test of time and are still available today through seed catalogs. Because it was intended to supply a long season of fresh food for a family of five, as well as vegetables to store for winter, it is a generously sized 25- by 50-foot plot.

The entire garden can be surrounded by a fence to exclude animals and provide a structure on which the pole beans can climb. If no fence is needed, 8-foot-tall wooden posts can be used to support the vigorous pole bean vines. Insert a post every 3 to 4 feet on the north side of the garden and hang pea and bean netting between the vertical supports.

Maximum yield. The 25-foot-long rows run north-south for maximum solar exposure and depending on the crop, the rows are spaced 12 to 30 inches apart. Suggestions for successive vegetables are given so that new crops can quickly replace the spent ones, to ensure the longest possible harvest.

LaManda's Garden Plan

50' DEEP X 25' WIDE

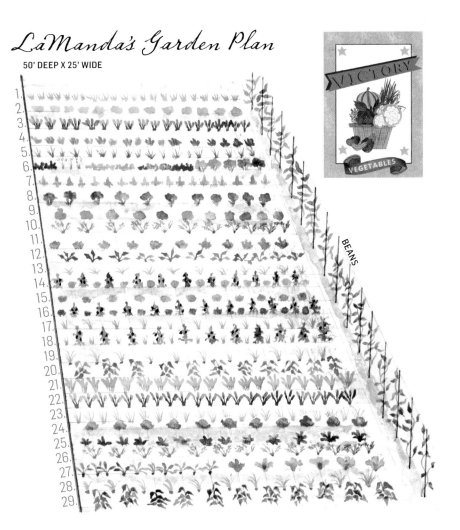

BEANS

VICTORY VEGETABLES

1. **Onions/lettuce:** 'Borettana Yellow Cipollini' onions, followed by 'Black Seeded Simpson' leaf lettuce

2. **Lettuce/spinach:** 'White Boston' butterhead lettuce, followed by 'Bloomsdale Long Standing' spinach

3. **Beets/collards:** 'Detroit Dark Red' beets, followed by 'Georgia Southern' collards

4. **Collards/beets:** 'Georgia Southern' collards, followed by 'Detroit Dark Red' beets

5. **Ebenezer' onions** for storing

6. **Parsley and mixed herbs**

7. **Endive/lettuce:** 'Broadleaf Batavian' endive, followed by 'Prizehead' leaf lettuce

8. **Broccoli/cabbage:** 'Green Sprouting Calabrese' broccoli interplanted with 'Golden Acre' early cabbage

9. **Cabbage/endive:** 'Late Flat Dutch' cabbage interplanted with 'Green Curled Ruffec' early endive

10. **Harris Model' parsnips**

11. **Lettuce/rutabagas:** 'Grand Rapids' leaf lettuce, followed by 'American Purple Top' rutabagas

12. **New Zealand spinach**

13. **Onion sets** (early maturing varieties)

14. **Tomatoes/lettuce:** 'Rutgers' tomatoes interplanted with 'Tom Thumb' butterhead lettuce

15. **'Iceberg' lettuce**

16. **Tomatoes/cabbage:** 'Abe Lincoln' tomatoes interplanted with 'Charleston Wakefield' early cabbage

17. **Onion sets**

18. **Tomatoes/onions:** Tomatoes interplanted with early onion sets

19. **Carrots/spinach:** 'Red Cored Chantenay' carrots, followed by 'Giant Noble' late spinach

20. **Beans/turnips:** 'Tendergreen' bush beans, followed by 'Purple Top White Globe' turnips

21. **Swiss chard:** 'Fordhook Giant'

22. **Beets/lettuce/radishes:** 'Early Wonder' beets, followed by ½ row 'Little Gem' head lettuce and ½ row 'Early Scarlet Globe' radishes

23. **Onions/lettuce/radishes:** Onion sets, followed by ½ row 'Deer Tongue' leaf lettuce and ½ row 'Crimson Giant' radishes

24. **Cabbage/limas:** 'Early Jersey Wakefield' cabbage, followed by 'Fordhook 242' bush limas

25. **Spinach/carrots:** 'Monstreux de Viroflay' spinach, followed by 'Scarlet Nantes' carrots

26. **'Hollow Crown' parsnips**

27. **Lettuce/radishes/beans:** ½ row 'Black Seeded Simpson' leaf lettuce and ½ row 'China Rose' radishes, followed by 'Golden Wax' bush beans

28. **'Red Cored Chantenay' late carrots for storing**

29. **'Fordhook 242' bush limas**

Asian Vegetables

Vegetable gardeners who enjoy experimenting with new foods and flavors will have fun with the selection of Asian vegetables and herbs featured in Wendy Kiang-Spray's plan. Wendy introduces us to time-honored Chinese gardening techniques and design ideas that she learned from her father, who still tends a large garden.

> ❯ Plants are traditional and popular Chinese crops

> ❯ Celebrates Chinese gardening techniques

> ❯ Uses raised beds that can be dismantled, shrunk, or enlarged from year to year

Wendy has modeled the design of her garden after her father's current plot, which measures approximately 19 by 35 feet, though the plan can easily be sized down to fit a range of sites. Chinese gardeners typically grow their crops intensively in raised beds that are laid out in long geometrical rows. "This system allows the area to be plowed or tilled, created and dismantled, season by season or year by year if desired," she explains. Because rural Chinese gardeners relied on rainwater to irrigate their gardens, the planting mounds for rambling crops like squash and pumpkins are large, above grade, and have a raised lip around the perimeter to help hold in as much water as possible.

Versatile vertical support. In her plan, Wendy has included both permanent and temporary structures for vining crops. The temporary trellises work well for supporting Malabar spinach vines as well as providing support for eggplants. The permanent arbor is both larger and sturdier than the trellises to support the heavier luffa gourds and bitter melons, also the tall yard-long beans. "The temporary structures are often made of bamboo — a cheap renewable resource that is strong, can be split, and comes in different widths and lengths," she says. Historically, scrubby trees such as mulberry were used to secure plants to their structures. The branches were cut and stripped of their bark, leaving behind a super-strong, thin material that could be used as a lashing.

To boost yield, Wendy suggests planting early, quick-growing vegetables like salad greens under the permanent arbor in spring. "However, keep in mind that Chinese summer vines like gourds, bitter melon, long bean, and luffa are all large and prolific and will quickly shade out any vegetables grown underneath," she cautions. Also, one needs to stand beneath the framework and reach up to harvest the vining crops, so if planting underneath, stick with fast-maturing crops that will be finished by the time harvesting begins.

Hilling up. Wendy shares some strategies Chinese gardeners use to encourage a delicious crop: To tenderize the stalks of the leeks, the plants are grown in a ditch and the soil is hilled up around the stems as they grow. Garlic (Chinese) chives are sometimes grown under pottery or a dark cloth to deprive them of light and create the coveted "yellow leeks," a more tender version of garlic chives. "Chinese chives are not used as an herb, but as a veggie, so having tender chives is desired," Wendy explains. Sweet potatoes, another favorite crop, are grown in raised hills rather than garden beds to improve drainage and keep the soil fluffy.

Cooking with other edible parts. Many of the vegetables in Wendy's plan will be familiar to North American gardeners, but she explains that Chinese gardeners often use different edible parts of these common crops. For example, sweet potatoes, beloved for their tasty tubers, are

Grow garlic chives under pottery to yield tender "yellow leeks."

grown by Chinese gardeners for their edible greens. "Snow peas are grown as much for their delicate shoots as their edible pods," notes Wendy. The unopened buds of daylilies are tossed in stir-fries and soups to add a delicious, sweet flavor. Her garden plan also includes luffa and bottle gourds, which yield bath sponges and dried bottles, respectively, but when harvested immature are superb for eating. "The dried mature bottle gourds can last through generations," she says, noting that they are used for many types of containers, including ladles, cups, and bottles.

Tasty Asian greens. Leafy greens are essential in Chinese cooking, and Wendy has included a range of popular greens. In summer, she concentrates on heat-tolerant vegetable amaranth, sweet potato leaves, Malabar spinach, garland chrysanthemum leaves, and mizuna. "Most leafy greens are best in the spring and fall," she says. "In the spring, gardeners find bolting and pests a problem, which is why I like to plant cool-weather greens in the fall." She also recommends tatsoi, pak choi, mustards, gai lan (her personal favorite), and napa-type Chinese cabbages.

Chinese gardeners grow popular plants for edible parts that are not customarily eaten — like the greens of sweet potatoes.

Wendy's Plants

There are many species and varieties of Asian vegetables. Wendy has chosen the vegetables that she finds reliable, as well as ones that are easily sourced from seed companies or Asian or international supermarkets (see Resources on page 245 for seed company suggestions).

MELONS AND GOURDS

1. **Luffa gourds.** Wendy notes that luffa gourds should be harvested when they are about 4 to 6 inches long. "At this stage, they are young, mild, and tender," she adds. "The fruits grow rapidly and can reach 2 feet in length, but they are generally too tough and bitter to eat at that point."

2. **Bitter melon.** Truly bitter in flavor, it's a squash everyone should try once!

3. **Bottle gourds.** The immature fruits are picked for stir-fries and other dishes. 'Long Opo' bears tender gourds that grow up to 15 inches long.

4. **Kabocha squash** (Japanese pumpkin). Vigorous vines will produce 4- to 8-pound dark green, slightly flattened pumpkins with a dry texture that is ideal in any recipe that calls for pumpkin or winter squash.

5. **Winter melon** (wax gourd). The heavy and extremely large fruits become covered with a waxy coating upon maturity. They are mild with a very high water content and are almost always cooked in soup.

GREENS

6. **Sweet potatoes.** Wendy grows a white-fleshed variety whose tubers she describes as "not fabulous," but whose greens are great. 'Nancy Hall' is a heritage variety with outstanding flavor.

7. **Malabar spinach.** This is an easy-to-grow, trouble-free vining vegetable with a flavor like spinach and a mucilaginous texture that makes it a great addition to soups or stir-fries.

8. **Tatsoi.** Also known as rosette pak choi or flat cabbage, this Chinese green grows nearly flat on the ground in a perfect rosette and is delicious when frost-sweetened in late fall.

9. **Vegetable amaranth.** This mild-tasting, quick-cooking leafy green is related to the ornamental amaranth 'Love Lies Bleeding'. There are many varieties of vegetable amaranth, and many are streaked with red.

10. **Chinese mustards.** There are leafy types and heading types of Chinese mustard, and both are coveted for their slightly spicy bite.

11. **Garland chrysanthemum** (*tong ho* in Chinese, *shungiku* in Japanese). The leaves of the garland chrysanthemum have a lovely aromatic flavor that is similar to the fragrance of ornamental chrysanthemum.

12. **Pak choi.** A type of Chinese cabbage with prominent, thick stems that are paler than the dark leaves.

13. **Mizuna.** A mild and tender leafy mustard, mizuna is excellent in spring and autumn salad mixes. Try purple mizuna to add color to salads.

OTHER ASIAN VEGGIES

14. **Yard-long beans.** Its pods are not quite a yard long, but this green bean is easy to grow. It's sturdier than most beans, making it ideal for cutting into workable lengths for a stir-fry.

15. **Leeks.** Wendy likes 'King Richard'.

16. **Bunching onions.** Try 'Tokyo Long White'.

17. **Garlic chives** (6 plants). Four of the plants are placed under pottery to blanch for tender yellow grassy leaves. In late summer, as the plants begin to send up flower stalks, these stalks are harvested before the buds open.

18. **Shallots.**

19. **Daikon radishes.** This enormous white elongated radish is extremely versatile in the kitchen.

20. **Assorted herbs.** Lemongrass, Thai basil, and cilantro are essential for flavoring Asian dishes.

21. **Soybeans.** Try 'Butterbeans', 'Tankuro', or 'Envy'.

22. **Gai lan** (Chinese broccoli). Looks similar to broccoli raab and is eaten stem, leaves, flowers, and all.

23. **Daylilies.** Blooms are edible; pick buds before they open for use in soups or stir-fries.

24. **Japanese eggplants.** Japanese varieties have a similar flavor to traditional eggplants but a slender elongated shape and a thinner skin. Try 'Choryoku', 'Black Shine', or 'Millionaire'.

25. **Thai eggplants.** Thai varieties produce beautiful, green-and-white-streaked eggplants the size of a golf ball. Try 'Thai Round Green' or 'Thai Round Purple'.

26. **Napa-type Chinese cabbage.** This upright Chinese cabbage forms thick, dense heads. Try 'Blues' or 'Green Rocket'.

27. **Hot peppers.** Try 'Thai Bird' or 'Thai Dragon'.

28. **Snow peas.** If a fence isn't available, provide support for the tall vines. Try 'Dwarf Grey Sugar', 'Mammoth Melting Sugar' or 'Oregon Giant'.

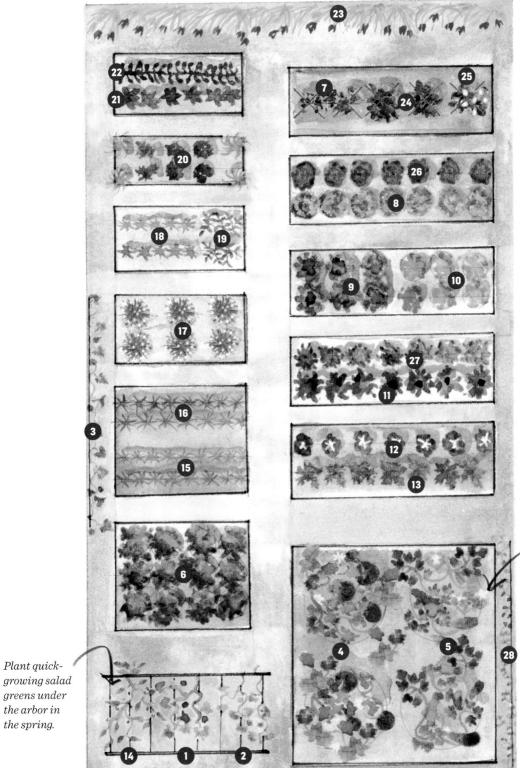

Wendy's Garden Plan

35' DEEP X 19' WIDE

Plant quick-growing salad greens under the arbor in the spring.

A raised lip around the squash mounds helps hold in as much water as possible.

Garden Squares for Kids

Gardens and children are a natural fit, and a great way to teach kids about food is by creating Karen Liebreich and Jutta Wagner's garden squares. This compact plan features four small square beds, each with a different theme to appeal to children of all ages: Jack's Beanstalk Teepee, Salad Hopscotch, The Magic Strawberry Carpet, and The Secret Fruit Arbor.

> A playful way to introduce children to food gardening

> Includes four distinct garden beds, each with a different theme

> Offers space to play, plant, and eat

> Features child-friendly fruits, berries, vegetables, and herbs

By mixing food with fun, Karen and Jutta's plan is a great way to introduce children to the wonders of growing their own food. "Our idea is based on four squares, mixing playfulness with tastiness to create an inspirational, easily maintained space that, without children even realizing it, will teach them about nature and food growing, while enabling them to graze on delicious and nutritious self-grown fruits and vegetables," says Karen.

Have fun with the shape. The compact size of each bed (just 4 by 4 feet) makes this design feasible for even a small site. The entire garden (including 2-foot-wide paths) measures only 10 by 10 feet, but it packs a lot of play into a small space. Because every location is different, Karen and Jutta suggest letting the characteristics of the site dictate the shape of the garden. "Depending on the space available, you could vary the size of each square or even the shape of the whole garden," notes Jutta. "The beds could be lined up, rather than arranged as a square grid, for example."

JACK'S BEANSTALK TEEPEE

For this magical garden, start by gathering 8- to 10-foot-tall bamboo canes or sturdy, straight saplings to make the framework of the teepee. To speed up the growing process, Karen and Jutta advise starting pole beans inside in pots in mid-April and keeping them protected until the risk of frost has passed. When ready to put the plants in the garden, leave a small space unplanted to act as an entrance to the living fort.

For additional color and edible flowers, sow seeds of mounding nasturtiums along the base of the teepee. "To make the teepee more interesting, pick several species of bean varieties, like those with purple or yellow pods, speckled borlotti beans, or beans with flowers in different colors," says Karen. With such a fun fort, even those who are well-established bean-haters will find it hard to resist a meal of their own homegrown beans!

Karen and Jutta's Garden Plan

JACK'S BEANSTALK TEEPEE

Pole beans on teepee

Mounding nasturtiums

SALAD HOPSCOTCH

Chives

4 Radishes

2 Lettuce 3

Spinach

1 Paving Stone

Basil

The Magic Strawberry Carpet

Lavender

'TRIBUTE' or 'OZARK BEAUTY' STRAWBERRIES

The Secret Fruit Arbor

raspberries

Garden Squares for Kids

SALAD HOPSCOTCH

A clever play on the classic children's game, this nine-squared garden features salad greens, herbs, and other compact crops. Simple paving slabs (painted with numbers, if you fancy) make it easier for small children to harvest the crops. Karen and Jutta recommend a first sowing or transplanting in early spring and replacing spent crops with fresh seeds or seedlings for a nonstop harvest until late autumn. Favorites include chives, arugula (rocket), radishes, and leaf lettuce, but you could also plant Asian salad greens, basil, 'Chioggia' beets, parsley, or spinach. "Just don't plant anything rampant like mint or lemon balm," they advise.

You can fit 12 to 16 plants into one square, although Jutta notes that regular picking allows closer planting. Karen and Jutta advise teaching children to leave about 3 to 5 leaves at the center when harvesting salad crops like lettuce, so that they can regrow.

THE MAGIC STRAWBERRY CARPET

Straight from the classic tales in *One Thousand and One Arabian Nights*, Karen and Jutta's design of a magic strawberry carpet will spark both your children's imagination and their appetite! They recommend growing day-neutral or everbearing varieties like 'Tribute' and 'Ozark Beauty', which produce fruit over a longer period of time than June-bearing types. In a larger garden, they suggest alternating the strawberry plants with fragrant lavender or — to allow for easy harvesting — stepping stones. In this compact 4- by 4-foot plan, however, strawberry fans will have no trouble reaching in from the sides of the square to pick the juicy berries. To keep production high, feed the plants every autumn with a berry food and replace them every three years, which is when production typically declines. "After flowering, mulch the plants with straw to keep the developing berries clean, and snip off any runners," advises Jutta. "And keep picking sweet berries throughout the summer!"

THE SECRET FRUIT ARBOR

What children wouldn't delight over their own secret garden where they can play, read, and daydream? This small square garden is surrounded by fruiting plants spaced 16 inches apart that create a lush, edible screen. Possibilities include raspberries (summer or autumn varieties), red currants, or vines such as grapes or kiwi. To support the plants, Karen and Jutta recommend surrounding the bed with a sturdy frame of wooden stakes joined by horizontal wires. The fence should be at least 5 feet tall. More experienced (or ambitious) parental gardeners could plant espaliered apples or pears (see box on page 78) along the arbor's outer border. "Let you and your child's fantasy run wild when planning the shape of the framework," says Jutta, "but leave a gap for an entrance archway."

Urban Homestead

Theresa Loe takes pride in her homestead, where she produces a bounty of homegrown food for her family of four and gathers fresh eggs from her chickens — all in the middle of busy Los Angeles on a property just one-tenth of an acre in size. How does she do it? She combines good design, vertical gardening, and sustainable practices to create a productive urban homestead.

> Grows a copious amount of veggies and fruits on just one-tenth of an acre!

> Includes chickens, worm composting, and traditional composting

> Edibles are planted in drifts for ornamental appeal

"This garden demonstrates how you can be more sustainable and garden organically even in a tiny urban lot," says Theresa Loe.

Theresa Loe fits the typical definition of an urban homesteader: a city or town dweller who wants to regain some control over her personal food security, as well as reduce her environmental footprint by growing a portion of her own food and keeping some type of livestock such as chickens. Although her property may be small, Theresa is able to grow a wide selection of edibles. Her family also has a flock of backyard chickens and a worm bin to produce vermicompost, as well as a traditional composting area for recycling kitchen and garden waste. "This garden demonstrates how you can be more sustainable and garden organically even in a tiny urban lot," she says.

Her plan for an urban homestead is loosely based on Theresa's own property and measures 45 by 36 feet. "I laid it out as a full-sun garden with raised beds," she says, "but it could easily be done in all pots and containers if someone had cement in the backyard."

Accommodates four hens. The chicken coop and run are an essential part of Theresa's homestead.

"The chickens are really wonderful family pets," she says, but adds that one should look into local city ordinances before bringing hens home. "Most cities only allow five or less hens, so I designed a coop and run area that would accommodate up to four hens, which will give you four eggs a day — a comfortable amount for a family of four," she explains. She advises allowing 3 to 4 square feet per chicken for the coop and about 8 square feet per chicken for the run. She also encourages people to let the chickens out of their pens as much as possible, so that they can "get exercise, look for bugs, do some weeding, scratch up the soil, and add a little fertilizer." If you're worried about them eating your plants, Theresa suggests that you let them out only when you are in the garden.

Drifting plants. For an ornamental look, Theresa generally prefers to grow her edibles in drifts, rather than typical long rows. The three 4- by 20-foot raised beds located in the center of the garden are intensively planted with popular edibles like tomatoes, carrots, spinach, peppers, and Swiss chard. Theresa's carrot bed is a great example of intensive planting and growing more in less space: The 10-foot bed is planted in three rows, so she has 30 feet of carrots in that one section.

Espaliered trees. To garner the most from her space, Theresa also grows vertically. In her plan, two espaliered apple trees have been planted along the west wall of the homestead for both their decorative and production values. (See page 78 for more on espaliered trees.) Unless you choose self-pollinating apples, she advises planting two different cultivars that bloom at the same time to ensure pollination. On the north side, vining beans and squash climb the wall, taking up little space in the garden but still offering high yields. She avoids varieties with long runners, such as spaghetti squash and watermelons, unless they are grown vertically. Bush types are grown on the ground to save space.

To take advantage of open garden space near the chicken run, Theresa has clustered together several containers of potatoes, lemon balm, and various mint plants. She opts to grow her potatoes in pots because she finds that they thrive in large containers and she is able to avoid bug problems.

Vining crops with long runners, such as spaghetti squash and watermelon, are best grown vertically in small urban spaces.

A cute chicken coop can become the focal point of the garden.

Theresa's Garden Plan

45' DEEP X 36' WIDE

Theresa has chosen plants for a summer garden. After these have been harvested, she recommends following them with fall and winter vegetables. Certain plants, like the kale and Swiss chard, can be left in place for the cold season.

Center Beds

1. **Tomatoes:** 'Brandywine', 'Green Zebra', and 'Amish Paste'
2. **Kale**
3. **Swiss chard**
4. **Carrots:** 'Cosmic Purple', 'Purple Dragon', and 'Romeo'
5. **Hot peppers:** 'Sweet Heat' and 'Hungarian Hot Wax'
6. **Spinach**
7. **Eggplants:** 'Rosa Bianca' and 'Black Beauty'
8. **Sweet peppers:** 'Purple Beauty' and 'Sweet Chocolate'
9. **Potatoes:** 'Butterfinger' and '(Swedish) Peanut Fingerling' (in containers)
10. **Mints, salad burnet, and lemon balm** (in containers)

Perimeter Beds

11. **Strawberry patch**
12. **Kohlrabi**
13. **Celery**
14. **Chives, thyme, and cilantro:** Ordinary chives and garlic chives; 'French', common (English), lemon, and silver ('Argenteus') thyme
15. **Stevia**
16. **Basil:** Thai basil or African blue perennial basil, 'Cinnamon' basil, and lemon basil (*Ocimum* x *citriodorum*)
17. **Sage and marjoram**
18. **Artichokes**
19. **Greek oregano and tarragon**
20. **Parsley and basil:** Flat-leaved and curly parsley; 'Spicy Globe' bush basil
21. **Zucchini**
22. **Various onions, leeks, and garlic**
23. **Squash:** 'Golden Scallop' and 'Early White Bush Scallop'
24. **Squash:** 'Yellow Crookneck'
25. **Zucchini:** 'Golden'
26. **Various lettuces**
27. **Various salad greens**
28. **Bush beans**
29. **Rosemary and dill**
30. **Sweet corn patch with trailing nasturtiums** (edible flowers) under corn

Plants Along Fence

31. **Grapes:** 'Concord'
32. **Grapes:** 'Flame Seedless'
33. **Apple:** 'Anna' (espaliered)
34. **Squash:** 'Trombetta' (climbing)
35. **Various bean plants** (against back wall)
36. **Miniature pumpkin**
37. **Salad cucumbers** (trained up the wall)

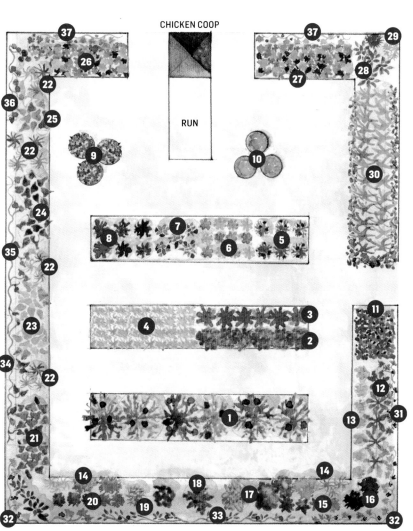

Teaming with Microbes

Jeff Lowenfels has a secret to creating a healthy, productive garden — team up with soil microbes! In his garden plan, Jeff makes a strong case for spending more time thinking about the fungi and bacteria that live in your soil and less money on pesticides and chemical fertilizers.

> The design emphasizes the importance of soil health

> Includes a greenhouse to stretch the season in cool and cold climates

> Four compost bins produce two types of compost — one that is fungi-dominated and another that is bacteria-dominated

> The surrounding fence omits deer or moose and supports vining peas and beans

Jeff says that microbes (microorganisms including bacteria, fungi, and protozoa) make the best soil. "Not only do they reduce organic matter down to usable forms for plants, but in the instance of some, such as mycorrhizal fungi, they go out and get the nutrients and bring them to the plant," he explains. By working to promote healthy microbe populations, you can encourage healthy soil and healthy plants. Jeff's plant choices, protective greenhouse, and moose fence were all determined by his northern location in Alaska, but his concept of creating a garden that sustains and encourages the soil food web applies to every region.

Because compost is key to a healthy garden, he has included four compost bins, as well as a compost tea brewer. "Organic gardens start with compost because this is the best way to supply the necessary microbial herd to both the soil and the plants the soil holds," explains Jeff. "These are the critters

at the bottom of the soil food web, and if you want soil structure, you need them. And if you want plants to be fed in the natural way, you need them."

Two types of compost. Jeff's plan has two active compost piles and two bins for storing the two types of finished compost. Of the two active piles, one is dominated by fungi and the other by bacteria. In their book, *Teaming with Microbes*, Jeff and Wayne point out that "some plants prefer soil dominated by fungi; others prefer soil dominated by bacteria." Bacteria-dominated compost should be used to feed your vegetables and annual flowers, while fungi-dominated compost goes on the trees, shrubs, and perennials. "Bacterial compost tends to have a higher pH than fungal composts," notes Jeff.

Making compost. To make a bacteria-dominated compost, he advises a blend of 1 part high-nitrogen green materials (grass clippings, green garden waste, hay) to 1 part regular green materials (food waste, cow manure mixed with bedding, alfalfa) to 2 parts woody materials (wood chips, leaves, twigs, shredded newspaper). A fungal compost is made by mixing 1 part high-nitrogen green materials to 2 parts regular green materials to 1 part woody materials. To ensure a steady supply of compost ingredients, Jeff keeps a holding area in his garden for ready-to-compost mulch, grass clippings, leaves, twigs, and sticks.

Moose fence. A 12-foot-tall moose fence surrounds the entire garden, including the composting area. In regions where moose aren't an issue, the fence can be omitted or tailored to exclude other pesky critters like deer. A 3½-foot-wide bed for a raspberry

hedge runs the inside perimeter of the fence, except on the north side, where Jeff recommends using the fence to support vining crops like snap peas, pole beans, and scarlet runner beans.

Season-extending greenhouse. The garden itself contains five square raised beds, each measuring 8 by 8 feet, with the center bed covered by a vented plastic hothouse to shelter warm-season crops. "You need a greenhouse to grow tomatoes in Alaska and also cucumbers and peppers," says Jeff. Each grows in a 5-gallon bucket inside the greenhouse. Black containers filled with water are warmed from the sun and stored by

the greenhouse entrance for quick and easy garden irrigation. Nearby, Jeff has included a line of logs for growing shiitake mushrooms.

To prevent recurring disease issues and nutrient depletion, the annual vegetable and herb crops should be rotated from bed to bed each year, but Jeff advises leaving the soil undisturbed when you do this. "*Don't* rototill an established garden," warns Jeff. "This destroys soil structure and greatly disrupts the soil food web." He uses a simple analogy to explain this logic: "When you cut a worm in half, you don't get two worms."

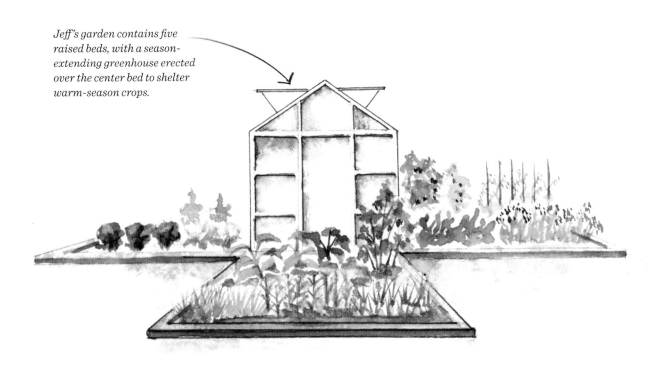

Jeff's garden contains five raised beds, with a season-extending greenhouse erected over the center bed to shelter warm-season crops.

Jeff's Garden Plan

23' DEEP X 23' WIDE

MUSHROOM LOGS

Jeff needs a moose fence. He gardens in Alaska!

Use bacteria-dominated compost on vegetables and annual flowers and fungi-dominated compost on trees, shrubs, and perennials.

COMPOST BINS

COMPOST TEA BREWER

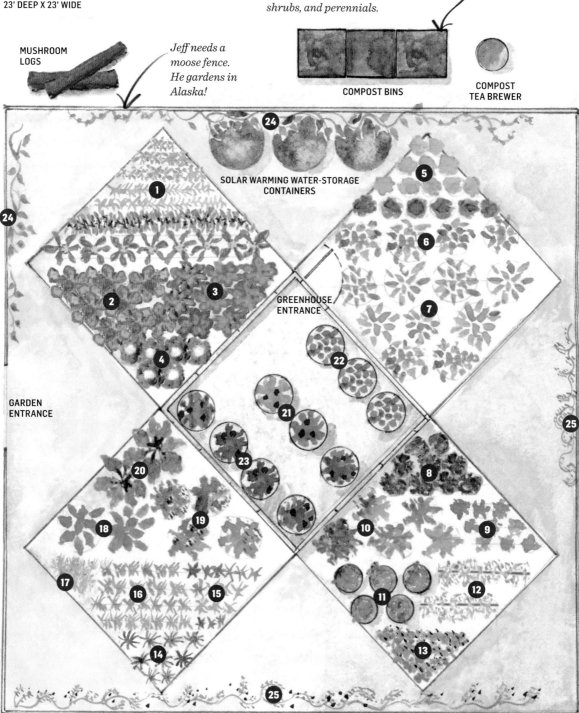

SOLAR WARMING WATER-STORAGE CONTAINERS

GREENHOUSE ENTRANCE

GARDEN ENTRANCE

1. **Radishes, carrots, beets, and kohlrabi:** 'Cherry Belle', 'Champion', and 'French Breakfast' radishes; 'Red Cored Chantenay' and 'Little Finger' carrots; 'Boltardy' and 'Ruby Queen' beets; 'Early White Vienna' and 'Early Purple Vienna' kohlrabi

2. **Broccoli:** 'Waltham 29'

3. **Brussels sprouts:** 'Jade Cross'

4. **Cauliflower:** 'Snowball Y' and 'Igloo'

5. **Cilantro and Lettuce:** 'Red Salad Bowl', 'Parris Island Cos', and 'Buttercrunch' lettuce

6. **Summer squash and zucchini:** 'Early Prolific Straightneck' summer squash and 'Black Beauty' zucchini

7. **Potatoes**

8. **Parsley**

9. **Oregano and thyme**

10. **Gooseberries:** 'Hinnomaki Yellow', 'Hinnomaki Red', 'Oregon Champ', and 'Jahns Prairie'

11. **Mints (contained in pots)**

12. **Peas:** 'Sugar Snap', 'Early Frosty', and 'Progress' (supported on poles)

13. **Borage**

14. **Leeks:** 'King Richard'

15. **Scallions:** 'Evergreen'

16. **Garlic**

17. **Chives**

18. **Yacons** (this South American plant produces edible dahlia-sized tubers)

19. **Currants:** 'Consort' black currants and 'Red Jade' red currants

20. **Rhubarb**

21. **Tomatoes:** 'Polar Beauty' and 'Sub-Arctic Plenty'

22. **Cucumbers:** 'Muncher' and 'Morden Early'

23. **Peppers:** 'California Wonder' and 'Hungarian Yellow Wax'

24. **Snap peas and beans:** 'Kentucky Wonder' pole and scarlet runner beans

25. **Raspberries:** 'Heritage', 'Boyne', and 'Latham'

JEFF'S #1 PLANTING TIP

"*Always* use mycorrhizal fungal spores or propagules when starting seed or transplanting," Jeff advises, noting that they can be applied as a powder or mixed with water and used for soil drenching. "These will help feed many of your plants, but they aren't used by cole crops like broccoli or cabbage." Any well-stocked garden center should have mycorrhizal products on their shelves, but they can also be ordered online (see Resources on page 245).

Urban Shade Garden

Kathy Martin is well aware of the challenges many urban gardeners face. Her own kitchen garden is small, at just 250 square feet. As well, she battles encroaching shade cast by two large trees that take away a little more sun each year. She has learned to work around these issues by growing the right plants for her dappled light conditions and relying on space at a local community garden to supplement the edibles she grows in her home garden.

> ❯ Ideal for a site that receives just 5 to 6 hours of sunlight

> ❯ The vegetable growing area measures just over 250 square feet — great for tight urban spaces

> ❯ Raised beds allow intensive planting and a cold frame stretches the harvest season

> ❯ Features low-light vegetables like pak choi, spinach, and kale

Kathy Martin's small vegetable garden is immediately recognizable by much of the online gardening community thanks to her popular blog *Skippy's Vegetable Garden*, launched in May of 2006 and named after her Portuguese water dog, a faithful garden companion. "My garden was actually just a muddy patch of soil then, but that was the beauty of it, knowing that it had such potential," she recalls. Through hard work and practical design, she has built it into a beautiful and productive space.

Maximizing space. Kathy's home garden includes both the 250-square-foot area for her edible plants as well as a spot for a 10- by 10-foot cold frame bed. To organize the plot, she divided it into five manageable raised beds, separated by narrow 2-foot-wide pathways, mulched with hay. The five beds each measure $3\frac{1}{2}$ by 9 feet. Opposite these tidy beds, Kathy has included an area for ornamental and fruiting plants, which add both color to the garden and habitat for birds and beneficial insects.

Extending the season. The 10-by 10-foot cold frame was built by Kathy's husband, Steve, a few years ago. "I like to fill it with greens that are ready to harvest by November," says Kathy. "They hold well in the frame, and we eat them as we want them during the winter." Once that winter harvest is finished, she fills the frame with fresh seedlings in March for more greens in April and May. A 4-foot-wide cobblestone walkway runs down the center of the garden, linking the beds together and providing comfortable access for a wheelbarrow.

Adaptibility to shade. At the beginning, Kathy's kitchen garden received enough sun to grow a wide variety of edibles, but as the years passed and the surrounding trees grew to shade more of her garden, Kathy has had to alter her plant choices to select for edibles that can still produce with less sun. "I've watched the shadows move across my garden and mapped out which parts get more and less light," she shares.

Kathy's Garden Plan

24' DEEP X 32' WIDE

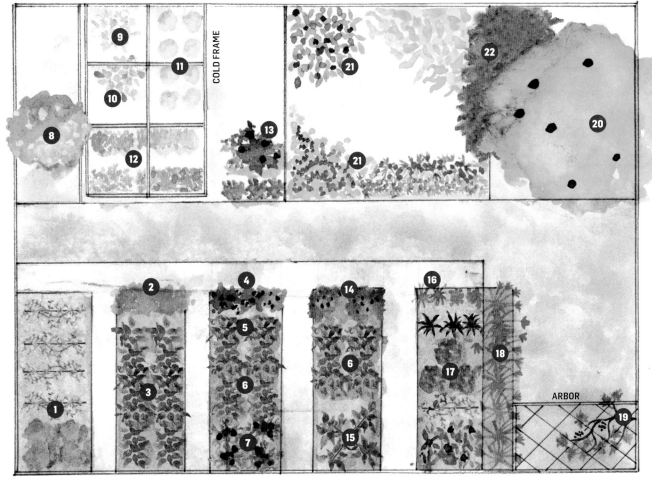

For 2 Hours Full Sun

1. **Peas and lettuce:** 'Sugar Ann' snap peas (first planting), then 'Oaky Red Splash', 'Red Sails', and 'Winter Density' lettuce (second planting)

For 3 Hours Full Sun

2. **Thyme**
3. **Beans:** 'Provider' and 'Royal Burgundy' bush

For 4 Hours Full Sun

4. **Alpine strawberries**
5. **Parsley**
6. **Soybeans:** 'Envy'
7. **Tomato:** 'Brandywine' and 'Sungold'
8. **Lemon:** 'Meyer' (potted)
9. **Cucumbers:** 'Diva', 'Sooyow Nishiki', and 'Sweet Success'
10. **Eggplants:** 'Tiger' and 'Black King'
11. **Kale, spinach, and pak choi:** 'Lacinato' (Tuscan) and 'Blue Curled Scotch' kale; 'Bloomsdale Longstanding' spinach
12. **Oregano, rosemary, and basil**
13. **Tomato:** 'Cherokee Purple'

For 5 Hours Full Sun

14. **Blueberries:** 'Bluecrop'
15. **Beans:** 'Orient Wonder' yard-long and 'Scarlet Emperor' runner
16. **Chives and sage**
17. **Peas, kale, and zinnias:** 'Oregon Giant' snow peas (first planting), then 'Lacinato' (Tuscan) and 'Blue Curled Scotch' kale and zinnias (second planting)
18. **Daylilies**
19. **Grapes**
20. **Apple:** 'Fuji'
21. **Mixed annual and perennial flowers**
22. **Rhododendron**

"Most parts of my garden now have 4 hours of midday light, but I do have a small 'prime' section that gets 5 to 6 hours of light." As well, like many small urban spaces, Kathy's garden is sheltered by nearby homes, creating a microclimate. This gives her an earlier start to the planting season, but also means that she needs to concentrate on heat-loving, shade-tolerant crops. "I've found that the best ones are beans, basil and other herbs, cucumbers, and kale," she says, adding that she also plants tomatoes and eggplants in the 'prime' beds with the most sun.

Testing crops. To discover the best crops for her garden, Kathy relies on trial and error, testing a wide range of varieties. For example, because she finds beans grow very well in her small plot, she is always on the lookout for new varieties to test. "I plant pole beans like red runner beans, Chinese pole beans including yard-long and a pale lemony variety that was given to me by a colleague, bush beans, dried beans, and soybeans," she says. "I have begun saving most of my own bean seeds and sharing them with other gardeners — a process that I am really enjoying." For gardeners with less room, growing pole beans is an easy way to boost food production as the vertical vines use less ground space than bush-type plants. "I grow them on 8-foot-tall teepees, five plants per pole," says Kathy.

Cucumbers are another standout crop in Kathy's small-space garden. "I've had great luck with cucumbers in my part-sun beds," she says, noting that they don't do well with less than four hours of light. "'Diva' is my favorite variety, but I also love the blocky white fruits and chartreuse interior of North Carolina pickling cucumbers." She uses 4-foot-tall lattice trellises to support the scrambling vines, and she plants them at the edge of the garden so they can scale the fence and roam into the yard.

Keeping up with compost. To keep production high in her challenging low-light conditions, Kathy adds generous amounts of compost. "I compost all of my kitchen and yard waste and end up with a very rich compost," she says. "In spring, I put 2 inches of compost on each bed and then I use liquid fish fertilizer or organic fertilizer during the growing season."

EXPANDING INTO A COMMUNITY PLOT

Because shade and lack of space limited her plant choices, and because she wanted the experience of growing with others, Kathy turned to a local community garden located just a mile away to supplement her home garden. Her 40- by 40-foot plot gives her plenty of sunny garden space for her edible crops and ornamental plants, which include perennials such as asparagus, rhubarb, raspberries, and several espaliered pear trees. Having a sunny alternative to her shady home garden has made a world of difference for Kathy. "Growing in full sun and very fertile soil is incredible," she says. The community garden has also given her the chance to learn many new gardening methods, watch a wide assortment of gardens grow, and connect with the other members. "Sharing the experience of growing food with others — in the community garden, in my home garden, and on the blog — is amazing," she says.

Edible Knot Garden

Though they are typically found in large, formal gardens, Karen Atkins believes that knot gardens make eye-catching elements in any landscape, even a suburban backyard. In her plan, she combines the aromatic foliage of 'Boxwood' basil with hardy dwarf lavender in a simple but visually appealing pattern that comes together with the help of a kiddie swimming pool.

> Compact 8- by 8-foot design is perfect for small spaces

> Adds a formal element to the landscape — but is easy to construct!

> Super-fragrant combination of basil and lavender

> When viewed from above — on a deck or from a window — gives your yard a "wow" factor

For centuries, knot gardens were a focal point in the landscapes of European kings and queens, and a major landscape feature in Tudor England. By the eighteenth century, these complex gardens fell out of favor when more naturalistic landscapes became popular. A century later, Victorian gardeners resurrected the style of knot gardening when they began to create elaborate and flamboyant formal flower beds and parterres.

Patterned on weaving. As the name implies, the history of knot gardens is intertwined with weaving. "A knot garden is a patterned garden where plants of contrasting habits and foliage are interlaced to mimic the 'over and under' effect created by two or more different colors of yarn," says Karen. Karen created this herbal knot garden pattern by simplifying a design first published in Gervase Markham's *The Countrie Farm,* in 1616. "A 10- by 10-foot space will give you enough room to plant the garden, with a 2-foot perimeter all around it," she says.

Easy to install. Today, knot gardens are often reserved for botanical gardens. They have not been widely adopted by modern gardeners, who fear the intricate and complex patterns, as well as the accompanying assumption of high maintenance. Yet Karen Atkins's design is easily installed, extremely manageable, and can be used as the centerpiece of a larger garden or just as a small jewel on its own.

Site to be seen. Choose a location that offers plenty of sunshine, decent well-drained soil, and a chance to be viewed at its best. "A patterned garden is best enjoyed from above," she says. "Therefore, you may choose to center your knot on an upstairs window or even a slightly raised porch for greatest effect." To keep the knot design distinct, Karen recommends that the lavender plants be trimmed annually. 'Boxwood' basil is an annual herb (with extremely aromatic foliage), and young seedlings can be transplanted into the pattern each spring once the risk of frost has passed.

Karen's Garden Plan
8' DEEP X 8' WIDE

The "over and under" effect of knot gardens is patterned on weaving.

1. **Dwarf lavender.** The fragrant blossoms of lavender can be used in scones, shortbreads, and other baked goods, as well as mixed with the tiny leaves of 'Boxwood' basil and sprinkled over yogurt and berries. Try 'Munstead Dwarf', 'Thumbelina Leigh', or 'Dwarf Blue'.

2. **'Boxwood' basil.** The 'Boxwood' basil is an aromatic cultivar of this annual herb with an attractive, rounded growth habit. Its extremely flavorful leaves can be used in place of regular basil in favorite recipes. If you'd prefer a perennial edible, common oregano could be substituted and clipped to shape, or the ornamental plant germander, which is hardy to Zone 5 and has attractive silvery foliage. If 'Boxwood' basil is difficult to source, 'Spicy Globe' or 'Pistou' could be substituted.

A STEP-BY-STEP GUIDE TO BUILDING A KNOT GARDEN

KNOT GARDEN MATERIALS

- 64 (6-inch) dwarf lavender plants
- 60 (6-inch) 'Boxwood' basil plants
-     Pea gravel
- 1 36-inch-diameter baby pool or hula hoop

1. Mark the center of your garden, preferably aligning it with an upstairs window or even a slightly raised patio or deck. At each of the outer corners of the 8- by 8-foot garden install a lavender plant (see drawing).

2. Plant each corner 'Boxwood' basil 4 feet from the center of the garden, centered inside the four lavender plants. Fill in the lines by planting one 'Boxwood' basil every foot between the corners of the inner diamond (see drawing).

3. Center a standard (36-inch-diameter) baby pool or hula hoop on one corner of the diamond. Arrange lavender plants every foot around the outside edge of the pool or hoop. Remove basil plants every other time they intersect, so that you establish an alternating "over/under" pattern (see drawing). Repeat this step for each corner of the diamond.

4. Plant the remaining lavender plants between the half-circles and the lavender plants at the outer corners of the garden (see drawing).

5. Using pea gravel, mulch the inside of the figures formed by the basil and lavender plants to emphasize the contrast between the two types of herbs.

Steps 1 & 2

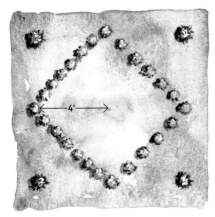

Step 3

Step 4

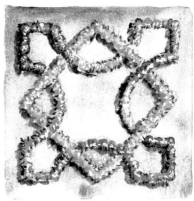

Vertical Vegetables

Gardeners are getting sneakier, and perhaps Rhonda Massingham Hart is to blame. Her design spotlights techniques and ideas that can be used for an in-ground garden or a container garden on a balcony. By putting unused vertical spaces like walls, railings, or other structures to work, Rhonda shows how you can grow a dramatically larger amount of food and turn a semi-private balcony into a mini urban farm.

> Includes trellises, a potato tower, veggie bags, planter boxes, and a mixed greens tower

> A garden arch adds a decorative element and offers more space for vertical crops

> Vegetables are arranged intensively in the planters for maximum harvest

Vertical vegetables are simply crops that are grown off the ground. There are many advantages to growing vegetables vertically, but perhaps the best reason is that it allows you to harvest more food from less space. Plus, upright and vining vegetables provide vertical interest on walls, fences, and structures — often screening an unsightly view. They also require less weeding and are less susceptible to pests and diseases when their foliage isn't lying directly on the soil.

Sun-loving design. Rhonda's design for a vertical balcony garden was inspired by her friend Jim, whose 6- by 12-foot balcony desperately needed some greening up. In addition to creating a privacy screen, the vertical plants also shaded his west-facing windows from the summer heat. This design needs full sun in order to thrive.

A dramatic entrance. Perhaps the most eye-catching element of Rhonda's small garden is the 7-foot-tall overhead trellis archway that leads from the sliding doors onto the balcony. Handy gardeners may wish

Upside-down tomato buckets are easy to make.

A columnar apple tree is perfect for tight spaces.

Compact crops like broccoli work well in the 1-foot-deep planters.

to make the arch from wood, or purchase a plastic or vinyl structure. This provides a grand entrance to the garden as well as a support for vining crops like pole beans or cucumbers.

Stacking greens. Underneath the trellis, in front of the sliding door that doesn't move, is the perfect spot for a mixed greens tower. This productive vertical structure can be a simple strawberry jar or a stacked set of containers, or you can make one by looping chicken wire in a cylinder shape, filling it with potting soil, and planting with seedlings. Rhonda suggests planting a single large edible, such as summer squash or cabbage, at the top of the cylinder and then filling the vertical pockets or holes with seedlings of lettuce, spinach, Swiss chard, or Asian greens.

Planter Picks. To the left and right of the trellis, Rhonda placed two 1-foot-deep planters filled with a good-quality potting mix. Sturdy wall-mounted trellises behind them provide support for vining vegetables.

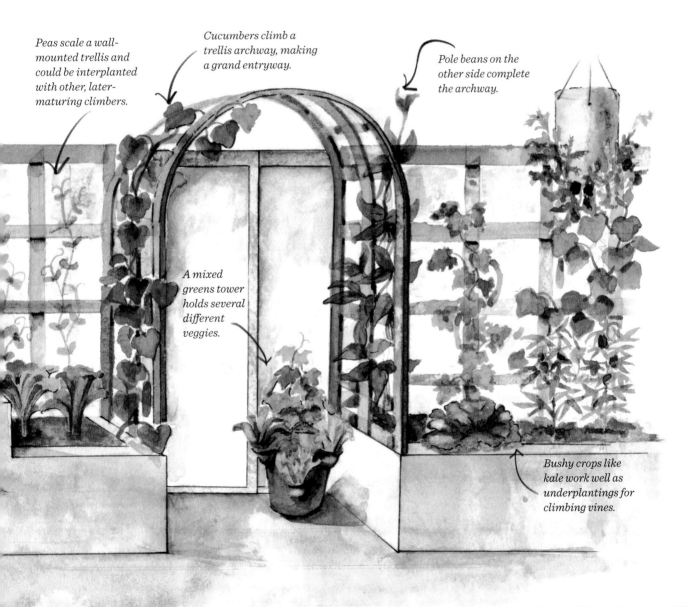

Peas scale a wall-mounted trellis and could be interplanted with other, later-maturing climbers.

Cucumbers climb a trellis archway, making a grand entryway.

Pole beans on the other side complete the archway.

A mixed greens tower holds several different veggies.

Bushy crops like kale work well as underplantings for climbing vines.

Inexpensive heavy-gauge wire panels make good trellises, and Rhonda recommends using those that are at least 4 to 6 feet tall to supply as much vertical space as possible. "Fill in the areas between the young plants with quick-growing smaller plants such as greens, scallions, and radishes while waiting for the larger ones to grow," she advises. Further, Rhonda notes that a wall or corner is a good spot for an espaliered apple or pear tree (see box on page 78). "Training a tree is simple, but takes several years," says Rhonda.

Planting wall-mounted trellises. Some good plant choices for the shorter planter trellises include melons (mini watermelons, muskmelons, and cantaloupes), cucumbers, peas, and vining types of squash. Rhonda recommends planting peas at every other upright so that you can enjoy an early harvest of peas before the slower melons, squash, or cucumbers are ready. When they are done producing, cut off the pea vines at ground level to give the other plants more room to grow.

Upside-down tomatoes. For a fun twist, Rhonda has planted upside-down hanging buckets and bags. Hang them from a top balcony railing (make sure your railing can handle the load!) or a sturdy ceiling beam. Fill the containers with tomato, pepper, or eggplant seedlings (see the box below for how to do this) and enjoy the adventure of watching your upside-down plants provide you with a bumper crop of tender fruits.

Vertical spuds. Balcony gardeners can also enjoy potatoes grown in a potato tower. The tower can be purchased, built out of scrap lumber, or created by bending wire mesh into a cylinder 18 to 24 inches in diameter. Rhonda advises aiming for a height of 2 to 3 feet and lining the cylinder with landscape fabric. Fill the bottom 6 inches of the cylinder with some soil and compost, and arrange 4 to 6 seed potatoes at the bottom. Cover the tubers with another 6 inches of soil and water well. As the green shoots pop up through the soil, continue to bury the stems. "Late-season potatoes tend to take better to this method than others," Rhonda says. "Look for 'German Butterball', 'Red Pontiac', 'All Blue', or 'Russian Banana'."

Fun baskets. Rhonda suggests including hanging baskets of strawberries, short-vined peas, patio tomatoes, and salad greens. "The baskets should be at least 1 foot in diameter and be decorative as well as functional," notes Rhonda, adding, "Staggering the hanging height of the baskets allows ample room for the growth and also creates a visual screen."

HOW TO MAKE AN UPSIDE-DOWN PLANTER

MATERIALS

- 1 sharp knife
- 15-gallon bucket, preferably white to reflect, rather than absorb, heat
  Potting soil
- 1 tomato, eggplant, or pepper seedling to grow upside down
- 3 basil seedlings to be planted at the top of the bucket as a living mulch to shade the soil and provide a secondary bounty. Alternatively, salad greens such as lettuce or Swiss chard could also be planted here.

1. Use the knife to cut a 1-inch hole in the bottom of your bucket.

2. Guide your tomato, pepper, or eggplant seedling root-first through the hole.

3. Turn the bucket over and fill it with potting soil and compost to within 1 or 2 inches of the top.

4. Plant the top of the bucket with basil, onions, salad greens, pansies, or other small plants.

5. Watch your plants grow! As the larger plant grows out the bottom hole, it will contort all over the place, but the fruit will hang free and clean.

Rhonda's Vertical Varieties

When choosing vegetables for a vertical garden, look for those with the words "vining," "climbing," or "indeterminate" in the descriptions listed in seed catalogs. Rhonda also encourages gardeners to use every every square inch of space by underplanting vertical crops with bushy edibles like peppers, kale, and broccoli.

FOR TRELLIS ARCHWAYS

- 'Lemon' or 'Garden Oasis' cucumbers
- 'Emerite' or 'Lazy Housewife' pole beans

FOR WALL-MOUNTED TRELLISES

- 'Lambkin' or 'Tigger' melons
- Cantaloupes, muskmelons, or mini-watermelons
- 'Zucchetta Rampicante' climbing summer squash
- 'Table Dainty' or 'Black Forest' F1 vining zucchini
- 'Acorn', 'Red Kuri', 'Delicata', 'Fairy', or 'Buttercup' vining winter squash

FOR HANGING POTS

- 'Quinalt' strawberries
- 'Red Robin', 'Micro Tom', or 'Patio' tomatoes underplanted with trailing nasturtiums
- 'Sugar Star' or 'Sugar Sprint' snap peas
- Assorted salad greens

FOR 1-FOOT-DEEP PLANTERS

- 'Ace' sweet peppers
- 'Early Jalapeño' hot peppers
- 'Red Russian' kale
- 'Caraflex' cabbage
- 'Luscious' sweet corn
- 'Arcadia' broccoli
- 'Cheddar' cauliflower
- 'Fairy Tale' or 'Hansel' eggplants
- Columnar 'Northpole' or 'Golden Sentinel' apple tree

FOR MIXED GREENS TOWERS

- Summer squash or cabbage (top)
- Lettuce, mesclun mix, spinach, Swiss chard, Asian greens (holes)

FOR POTATO TOWERS

- 'German Butterball'
- 'Red Pontiac'
- 'All Blue'
- 'Russian Banana'

Culinary Courtyard

Pioneered by Rosalind Creasy, edible landscaping is a technique that brings food and form together in a garden. With her plan for a culinary courtyard, Rachel Mathews has embraced the concept of edible landscaping and created a delightful spiral garden that combines fruits, vegetables, herbs, and ornamental plants in a way that is both sophisticated and calming.

> Sophisticated design features a low curved wall to contain edible crops

> Eye-catching arches along the pathway add height and support climbing vegetables and fruits

> Two cobblestone circle gardens offer secluded retreats for sitting and enjoying the garden

> Both ornamentals and edibles are included

Rachel Mathews's plan for a culinary courtyard garden is a modern take on growing food. "The idea was to create a place that people would want to spend time sitting and socializing in, and that would provide lots of fresh, organic fruit and vegetables," she says. The circular deck, curved cobbled pathway, and spiral design are both graceful and unique, adding character to any space but especially to a small, urban backyard. "Circular shapes are excellent in small gardens because your eyes follow the curves, which helps make the space look and feel larger," she notes. The garden measures just 35 by 26 feet, but it could be stretched to fit a larger property by extending the surrounding beds and adding more fruit-bearing trees and shrubs.

Getting the curves right. The centerpiece of the garden is the low curved wall. "It acts as both a retaining wall [for the] planter on the left-hand side of the garden and a divider in the middle, which helps create a secluded seating area," explains Rachel. She recommends calling in professionals to construct the complicated curves in this design. She also stresses the importance of having the curves built well, as even a slight straight edge to the curved sections will undermine the intended effect.

Arching style and support. Running along the cobblestone pathway, Rachel has included 8-foot-tall metal arches that serve a couple of purposes. "The fruit tree arches hug the inside of the rendered wall and also go over the path," she says. They offer vertical support to the fruiting trees — large plants that are often difficult to include in a small space. The arches also "provide height to the design and make it much more interesting because they prevent the entire garden from being seen in one go, which creates interest, especially in smaller gardens."

Rachel chose one apple, one plum, and five cherry trees to plant near her arches. Two of the cherry trees are early, one is midseason, and two are late, for a harvest that stretches over months, not weeks. Look for semi-dwarf or dwarf varieties of fruit trees to keep growth under control.

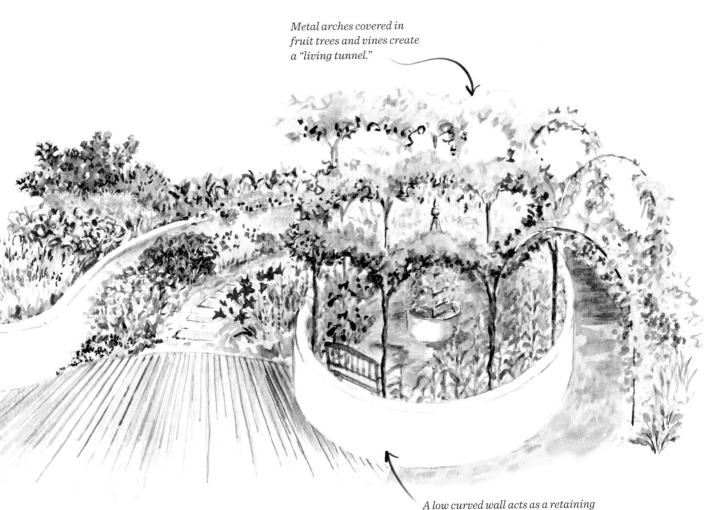

Metal arches covered in fruit trees and vines create a "living tunnel."

A low curved wall acts as a retaining wall and a space divider, creating a secluded seating area.

Rachel suggests trimming the trees tightly if an open feel is desired; for a more unruly, living tunnel (like Rachel's), the trees can be allowed to grow completely over the supports. As the fruit trees only cover half of the metal arches, Rachel has added a vining vegetable — 'Ashley' cucumbers, 'Wando' peas, and 'Polish Purple' pole beans — on the opposite side of each

arch to complete the tunnel effect. At the foot of each arch she has placed colorful — and edible — nasturtiums, 'Chrystal' lettuce, calendulas, and Swiss chard to soften the hardscape, attract pollinators, and provide a tasty snack while strolling down the garden path.

Secluded circles. The cobbled circles — one at the center of the

spiral wall and another tucked off the cobbled pathway that leads to the gate — create two secret sanctuaries in the middle of the city. The larger one has a bench for quiet contemplation and is surrounded by cherry trees, eggplants, and corn. Rachel likes to leave the corn in place through the winter to provide some structure, and she suggests mixing it with clumps of a tall grass such as *Miscanthus*. The smaller, more hidden circle is surrounded by edibles including blueberries and zucchini. At the center of each cobbled circle is an obelisk to support the vigorous vines of runner beans, which can be planted in the ground or in pots.

In addition to the strictly edible plants, Rachel has included ornamentals and plants that fall into both categories, such as artichokes and daylilies. "I definitely believe edible gardens can and should be attractive to look at," says Rachel. "For this garden I've chosen some of my favorite fruits and vegetables for flavor but also for looks." Some of the plants are annual, lasting just one season, while others are perennial in warmer climates. The perennial harvest will come from the fruiting trees and shrubs, as well as the strawberries, artichokes, and herbs such as rosemary, bay, chives, oregano, and thyme.

"Circular shapes are excellent in small gardens because your eyes follow the curves, which helps make the space look and feel larger," says Rachel Mathews.

Rachel's Culinary Plants

Plants Along Center Spiral

1. Common (English) thyme
2. Calendulas
3. 'Bronze' fennel
4. Chives
5. Oregano
6. Trees along "living tunnel": American (*Prunus americana*) and 'Weeping Santa Rosa' plum; 'McIntosh' and 'Winesap' apple; 'Sandra Rose', 'Rainier', 'Sweetheart', 'Sentennial', and 'Staccato' cherry
7. 'Amish Paste' tomatoes
8. 'Golden Bantam' sweet corn
9. 'Painted Lady' or scarlet runner beans
10. 'Long Purple' eggplants
11. Basil and 'Purple Italian' artichokes
12. 'Folgate' lavender
13. 'Crimson Pirate' daylilies

Plants Along Garden Perimeter

9. 'Painted Lady' or scarlet runner beans
12. 'Folgate' lavender
14. 'Cascabella' hot peppers
15. 'Red Express' cabbage
16. 'Cosmic Purple' carrots
17. 'Fatal Attraction' purple coneflower, ginkgo (kept as a large shrub), and 'Frimley Blue' rosemary
18. 'Sparkle' strawberries
19. 'Rainbow' Swiss chard
20. Vines along "living tunnel": 'Ashley' cucumbers, 'Polish Purple Stringless' climbing French (filet) beans, and 'Wando' peas
21. Nasturtiums
22. 'Caserta' zucchini and 'Killarney' raspberries
23. Bay tree
24. 'Chioggia' beets
25. Blueberries
26. 'Chrystal' lettuce
27. 'Crimson 'n Gold' flowering quince
28. 'American Flag' leeks
29. Swiss chard

Rachel's Garden Plan

26' DEEP X 35' WIDE

GATE

BENCH

DECK

METAL ARCHES

HOUSE

Concrete & Steel Garden

Making a vegetable garden from scratch can be rather expensive, especially if you build raised beds from rot-resistant wood and truck in large amounts of garden soil. Yet, as Laura Mathews illustrates, a vegetable plot doesn't have to break the bank. Laura builds her raised beds from recycled concrete blocks and creates soil by sheet mulching.

> Cost-effective design made with recycled building materials such as concrete blocks and old steel buckets

> Relies on sheet mulching, not trucked-in soil, to grow plants

> Two concrete block potato towers offer ample room for tasty tubers

In her plan, which measures 20 by 35 feet, Laura has constructed six raised beds from repurposed concrete blocks. The idea came from an industrial-inspired ornamental garden that she had seen at the Philadelphia Flower Show. "Given that there's a lot of energy around the idea of reusing or finding components for gardens, concrete blocks make sense for raised beds," she says. She recommends using standard 15⅝ by 7⅝ inch cinderblocks. Check with a local construction or demolition company to see if they have blocks you could salvage.

Maximizing the concrete blocks. To create the beds, Laura piled the blocks in two layers and staggered them to form 5- by 10-foot rectangles for the main beds and 5- by 5-foot squares for the potato towers. For a "bit of fun," she laid out the main beds in a zigzag pattern. This pattern also conserves blocks, as partial walls can be shared between beds. Laura suggests planting annual flowers, herbs, or small vegetables in the holes of the blocks to take advantage of all available space. Good choices

include curly parsley, nasturtiums, calendulas, and thyme. If you have the opportunity to break ground on the garden the autumn before you intend to plant, Laura recommends building the beds using a no-dig technique such as lasagna gardening (see box on page 70).

In the corner of the plan sit two pawpaw trees. "They're attractive, slow-growing, and ultimately small trees that will anchor the northwest corner of the garden without casting shade over the edible beds," says Laura.

Strong steel supports. The steel element of the garden comes from the stainless steel water trough in the center (which Laura says can be purchased from a farm store) and the series of paired steel buckets positioned throughout the garden. "Drainage holes should be made in all of the stainless containers," she advises. In the large trough, she has planted a 'Cardinal' cordyline in the middle and surrounded it with herbs and showy annuals: black petunias and red lantana. For the rest of the pails, she recommends repeating the annual flower and herb theme.

Towering tubers. Along the west edge of the plan, the two cinderblock potato towers encourage high production of tender tubers. "Potatoes grow best in loose, organic soil, rather than compact soil," says Laura. When you're ready to plant, place seed potatoes on the straw layer at the bottom of each tower, spacing them several inches apart. Cover the potatoes with 6 inches of garden soil. When the sprouts have pushed through the soil and grown about 6 to 8 inches in length, apply another 6-inch layer of soil to cover them. Continue this process until the tower is filled to the top. At the end of the growing season, the tower will be full of homegrown spuds, and you can dig for your buried treasure!

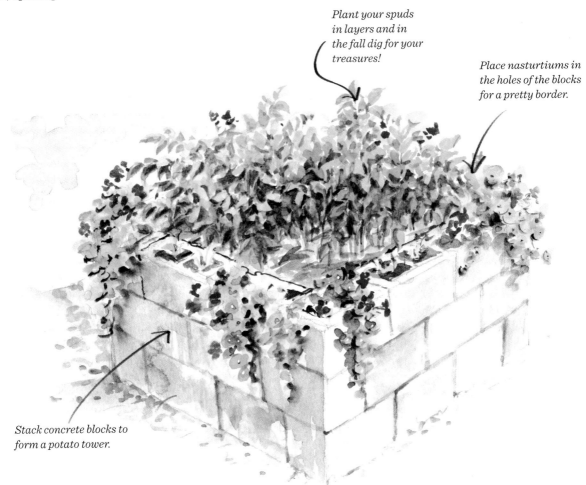

Plant your spuds in layers and in the fall dig for your treasures!

Place nasturtiums in the holes of the blocks for a pretty border.

Stack concrete blocks to form a potato tower.

A stainless steel water trough filled with flowers and herbs makes a stunning focal point.

Place steel buckets around the garden planted with your favorite herbs.

Concrete Beds and Steel Containers

1. **Tomatoes:** 'Zapotec Pleated', 'Virginia Sweet', 'Sungold', 'Indigo Rose', 'Jubilee', 'Black Prince', 'Cosmonaut Volkov', 'Aunt Ruby's German Green', 'Black Cherry', 'Tiffen Mennonite', and 'Green Zebra'

2. **Basil**

3. **Beans:** 'Windsor' fava and 'Fortex' pole

4. **Cabbage:** 'Minuet' napa-type Chinese

5. **Pattypan squash**

6. **Eggplants:** 'Rosa Bianca', 'Ping Tung Long', 'Rosita', and 'Applegreen'

7. **Peppers:** 'Feherozon' or 'Revolution' sweet; 'Hinkelhatz' hot

8. **Carrots:** 'Danvers Half Long', 'Jaune du Doubs', 'Purple Haze', and 'Nelson'

9. **Broccoli:** 'Arcadia'

10. **Radishes:** 'München Bier'

11. **Summer squash:** 'Lebanese White Bush'

12. **Lettuce:** 'Salad Bowl', 'Deer Tongue', 'Italienisher', 'Canary Tongue', and 'Kinemontpas' butterhead

13. **Spinach:** 'Bloomsdale' and 'Giant Winter'

14. **Potatoes:** 'Purple Viking' and 'Yukon Gold'

In-Ground Plants

15. **Annuals and herbs:** 'Cardinal' cordyline, black petunia, and red lantana annuals; oregano, dill, and Italian parlsey herbs

16. **Annuals and herbs:** petunia and lantana annuals; calendula, oregano, and thyme herbs

17. **Pawpaw trees**

18. **Winter squash**

19. **Lettuce:** 'Really Red Deer Tongue' and 'Merlot'

20. **Peas:** 'Sugar Ann' snap

21. **Kale, turnips, and onions:** 'Red Russian' and 'Winterbor' kale; 'Gilfeather' turnips; 'Copra' onions

22. **Garlic, spinach, and okra:** 'Bloomsdale' and 'Giant Winter' spinach; 'Red Burgundy' okra

23. **Melons and beets:** 'Hannah's Choice' muskmelons and 'Petite Yellow' watermelons; '3 Root Grex', 'Bull's blood', 'Detroit Dark Red', and 'Burpee's Golden' beets

Laura's Garden Plan

35' DEEP X 20' WIDE

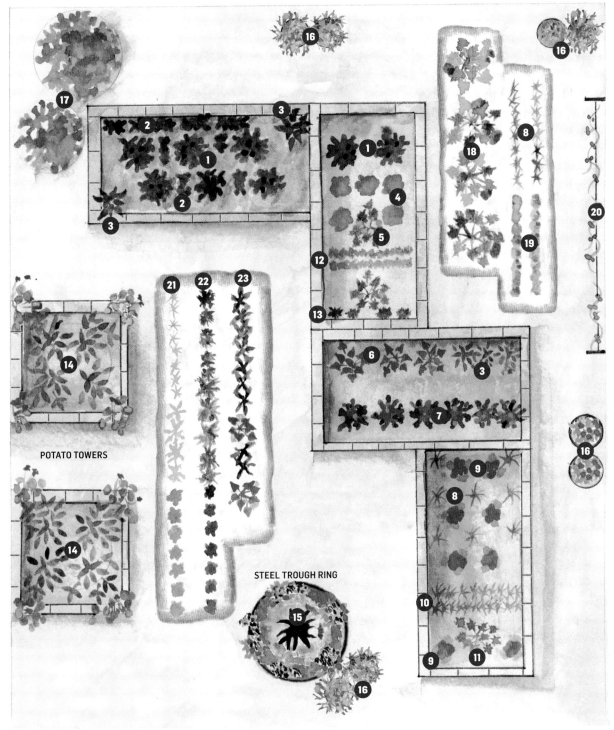

POTATO TOWERS

STEEL TROUGH RING

Front-Yard Suburban Farm

L ike many modern food gardeners, Chris McLaughlin is on a mission to get homeowners to rethink their front lawns. With her formal design for a front-yard suburban farm, she makes a strong case. Numerous decorative elements — checkerboard pavers, crushed granite pathways, and archway trellises — are pleasing to the eye, while vegetables from the well-filled garden beds tempt the palate.

> Formal design reflects a classic micro-farm approach

> Crushed granite pathways and arched arbors invite strolling (and grazing on the tempting veggies)

> Espaliered fruit trees provide homegrown fruit without taking up a lot of space

> Many of the crops are trellised on easy-to-build structures

Chris McLaughlin wants you to push the envelope in your urban and suburban front yards. "This design takes a classic micro-farm approach to the front yard and isn't for the faint of heart," she warns with a laugh. "It isn't about tucking food plants discreetly here and there into the foundation landscaping. Instead, it's rather boastful and proudly states, 'I am all about food production and I am *beautiful!*'" Do be sure to check into your local ordinances first so that you don't break the law when you break ground.

Making the space inviting. Besides producing homegrown food, a front-yard garden can also bring people together. In an effort to keep the garden neighbor-friendly and inviting, the garden paths are made of grass, and two grass-and-paver checkerboard walkways lead from the street to the yard and the yard to the house. Chris chose to include grass in the plan because, as the traditional front-yard ground cover, it may make food-skeptical neighbors a bit more comfortable.

The entire plot measures 26 by 26 feet and contains four 4- by 4-foot square beds, a central circle of chives around a wrought-iron obelisk, and a 3-foot-wide perimeter bed filled with fruits and sunflowers. The fruits include highbush blueberries, strawberries, espaliered pear trees, and columnar apple trees — beanpole trees with a single central trunk that produce full-size fruits all along their 8-foot length. (See page 78 for more on espaliered fruit trees.) A crushed granite pathway forms a cross in the middle of the garden, adding formality and permitting easy access for a wheelbarrow.

A showy entrance. An archway trellis marks the entrance of the garden from the street and bisects a highbush blueberry hedge that runs the length of the south perimeter bed. These hardy shrubs will supply a long season of sweet, juicy berries as long as at least two varieties are planted to ensure cross-pollination. "If you haven't planted blueberries before, they're quite the show!" raves Chris. "The new leaves are a stand-out,

Chris's Garden Plan

26' DEEP X 26' WIDE

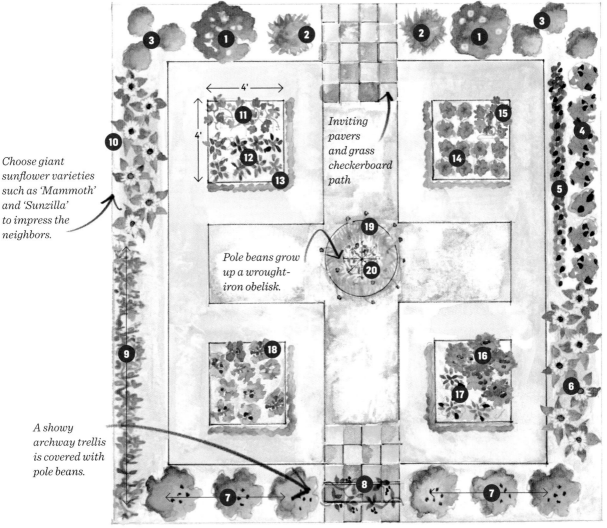

Choose giant sunflower varieties such as 'Mammoth' and 'Sunzilla' to impress the neighbors.

Inviting pavers and grass checkerboard path

Pole beans grow up a wrought-iron obelisk.

A showy archway trellis is covered with pole beans.

Perimeter Beds

1. **Lemon trees:** 'Meyer'
2. **Rosemary**
3. **Sage**
4. **Columnar apple trees:** 'Northpole', 'Golden Sentinel', and 'Scarlet Sentinel'
5. **Strawberries:** 'Quinault' everbearing
6. **Short sunflowers:** 'Teddy Bear', 'Baby Bear', or 'Orange Hobbit'
7. **Blueberries:** 'Sunshine Blue'
8. **Purple pole beans**
9. **Pear trees:** 'Moonglow' and 'Maxine' (also called 'Starking Delicious'), espaliered
10. **Medium to tall sunflowers:** 'Moonshadow', 'Velvet Queen', 'Mammoth', 'Kong', or 'Sunzilla'

Center Beds

11. **Melons:** 'Tigger' heirloom melons, 'Minnesota Midget' heirloom muskmelons, 'Golden Midget' heirloom watermelons, and 'Yellow Doll' hybrid watermelons
12. **Beans:** 'Nickel' and 'Dragon Tongue' bush
13. **Sweet alyssum**
14. **Kale:** 'Red Russian'
15. **Nasturtiums and pumpkins:** 'New England Sugar Pie' pumpkins (heirloom); 'Jack-Be-Little' (heirloom) and 'Baby Boo' (hybrid, white) mini pumpkins
16. **Tomatoes:** 'Cherokee Purple', 'Brandywine', 'Pineapple', and 'Vorlon' heirloom; 'Sungold' cherry; 'San Marzano' or 'Roma' heirloom paste
17. **Eggplants:** 'Rosa Bianca' (heirloom) and 'Fairy Tale' (hybrid)
18. **Peppers:** 'Banana' and 'Purple Beauty' sweet; 'Thai Dragon' hot
19. **Chives**
20. **Purple pole beans**

warm red color, followed by darling pink flowers and finally, the delicious blueberries." In autumn, the scarlet blaze of foliage color is dynamite.

Continuing east along the outside bed, short and sunny sunflowers add cheerful late summer color to the garden. "The shorter varieties are fun for small children and are great as food for wildlife or for fall crafts," notes Chris. Next to the sunflowers is a row of columnar apple trees, which are perfect for fruit lovers with limited space. She also points out that you will need a few different varieties for cross-pollination. 'Quinault' strawberries form an edible ground cover at the feet of the apple trees.

At the back of the garden, facing the house, two Meyer lemon trees, which could be planted in containers and brought indoors in the winter, yield an annual crop of aromatic fruits. The nearby rosemary plants, a magnet for beneficial insects, could also be grown in pots and moved indoors each autumn. The sage is hardy to Zone 5 and can be left in the ground in all but the coldest regions.

In the west perimeter bed, espaliered pear trees — again, two varieties for cross-pollination — provide a staggered harvest that runs from late summer to mid-autumn. " 'Moonglow' is a good pear for espalier," says Chris. "The fruit has good flavor with very little 'grit' to it, it ripens in mid-August, and it's highly resistant to fire blight." Medium to tall sunflowers finish the plot. If you're looking to impress (or astound!) your neighbors, consider monster-sized varieties like 'Mammoth', 'Kong', or 'Sunzilla'.

Maximizing the trellises. The four square beds in the middle of the plot contain a variety of both heirloom and hybrid vegetables, many supported on homemade trellis systems. The northeast bed contains trellised mini-pumpkins and climbing nasturtiums as well as kale. In the northwest square, melons and purple pole beans climb a wire panel tent, and heirloom bush beans fill in the rest of the space. Chris recommends succession planting for the bush beans, sowing fresh seed every few weeks for an extended harvest. In each of the southern squares, two mini rows of staked and pruned tomatoes occupy half of the plot, with peppers or eggplants filling the remainder of the beds. Along the inner edges of each of the four beds, Chris has planted a low hedge of sweet alyssum, whose fragrance is enticing to pollinating insects.

Southern Spring Garden

Cold-climate gardeners complain about their short seasons, but hot-climate gardeners don't necessarily have it any easier. They need to contend with drought and soaring temperatures as they try to get their lettuce to produce enough greens for a single salad. Here, Dee Nash shares her tips for coaxing a bumper crop of cool-weather vegetables like peas, onions, cabbage, and kale before the onset of summer.

> A compact design that allows Southern gardeners to enjoy an early harvest

> Includes heat-resistant salad crops

> A narrow trellised bed supports super-sweet peas, followed by summer cucumbers

> Cheerful edible flowers add color to salads and provide forage for bees

In order to produce a successful spring harvest of cool-weather crops such as turnips, salad greens, and radishes, Dee starts gearing up in late winter. "I plant most of my seeds for lettuce, spinach, Swiss chard, radishes, onion sets, and leeks outdoors in mid- to late February." Planting cabbages and related crops is a bit trickier, however; she needs to start the seeds indoors, setting the young plants out in the garden in early February under tunnels. "They need row covers because our last freeze date is about April 20," says Dee, "and if these plants don't have protection, the cold can be devastating to them." As an avid gardener and foodie, Dee knows the value of homegrown food, so the extra trouble is worth it to her.

Sow greens in autumn. She sows seed for salad greens like spinach and lettuce in the fall garden, knowing that they'll pop up and provide a late winter and early spring bounty. Because her spring weather is extremely variable, and since spinach will bolt at the first hint of heat, planting seed in late autumn ensures a good spring harvest even if the warm weather arrives early.

Best varieties for heat. Salad crops are among Dee's favorite vegetables to grow and to eat. To make sure that her greens last as long as possible in the garden, she selects heat-resistant varieties. "I look for types that are grown in places like Israel and Australia," she reveals. "I also buy most of my seed from Southern seed companies because they often have varieties that beat the heat."

Dee begins to harvest the salad crops when they are still small, cutting the outer leaves and allowing the center of the plants to continue growing. A piece of shade cloth can also come in handy for sheltering the cool-weather vegetables from the hot summer sun. With the arrival of May, her salad crops start to bolt and become bitter, signaling the switch from cool- to warm-season vegetables.

Good for small spaces. Dee's plan is perfect for a small garden, community plot, or starter vegetable garden. The 10- by 12-foot size is extremely manageable, but the garden will still

DEE'S FAVORITE LETTUCES

"I like all of the leaf types of lettuce, and a favorite which doesn't bolt early is 'Nevada.' It will turn bitter before it bolts. I also always grow 'Black Seeded Simpson' so that I can make my grandmother's wilted lettuce salad. It brings her back to me every time I take a bite," says Dee.

produce a respectable harvest from early spring to late autumn when succession planted. With a 2-foot-wide pathway, the two main planting beds would each be 5 feet wide. Dee recommends looking for a site that offers at least 6 to 8 hours of sunlight.

Mixing cool- and warm-weather crops. In a small garden space is precious, so to help make the shift from cool- to warm-weather crops easy, she plants her heat-loving vegetables (tomatoes, peppers, eggplants, and basil) in between the early edibles. "As the spring crops start to bolt, I pull them and leave the warm-season crops in place," she says.

An easy way to increase yields in a small garden is to include vertical crops. Dee recommends positioning a sturdy trellis at the back of her garden to support two varieties of super-sweet spring peas. Award-winning 'Sugar Snap' snap peas are planted on

one side of the trellis, while the crisp, flat pods of snow peas are seeded at the front. "Once the peas are finished, pull them out and replace with cucumbers and small melons for summer," advises Dee.

Flowers for the eye and the palate. The main section of the garden holds two beds, each planted with colorful mini-rows of salad greens, edible flowers, onions, and red or green cabbages. Clumps of early-blooming chives at the edges add their mild onion flavor to scrambled eggs, but the pretty pom-pom purple flowers can also be tossed into salads or steeped in homemade herbal vinegars. Within the salad beds, Dee's choices of 'Creamsicle' nasturtiums, johnny jump ups, and calendulas add cheerful color, attract pollinating and beneficial insects, and also bear pretty edible flowers.

FEBRUARY
Plant seeds outdoors: lettuce, spinach, radishes, leeks; plant onion sets

MARCH
Thin sprouts of seedlings of spinach and lettuce planted in fall

APRIL
Add shade cloth over lettuce to protect from full sun

Dee's Garden Plan

10' DEEP X 12' WIDE

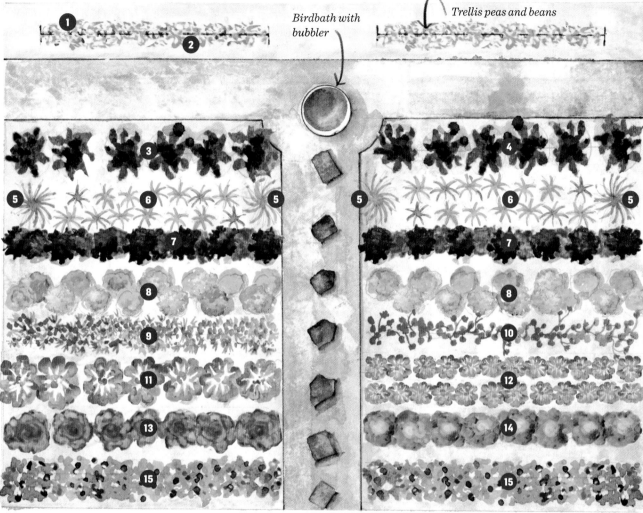

Birdbath with bubbler

Trellis peas and beans

1. **Snap peas:** 'Sugar Snap'
2. **Snow peas:** 'Oregon Sugar Pod II'
3. **Kale:** Dinosaur ('Lacinato')
4. **Swiss chard:** 'Ruby Red'
5. **Chives**
6. **Onions:** 'Red Wethersfield' red and 'Super Star' white
7. **Red lettuce:** 'Red Sails', 'Devil's Tongue', and 'Cimarron'
8. **Green lettuce:** 'Black Seeded Simpson', 'Slobolt', 'Forellenschluss', and 'Jericho'
9. **Calendulas:** 'Resina', 'Pacific Beauty Mix', and 'Flashback Mix'
10. **Nasturtiums:** 'Cherries Jubilee', 'Alaska', and 'Empress of India'
11. **Pak choi:** 'Ching Chiang'
12. **Tatsoi**
13. **Red cabbage:** 'Red Acre'
14. **Green cabbage:** 'Savoy Perfection'
15. **Johnny jump ups**

Founding Fathers Garden

Teresa O'Connor's "Founding Fathers Garden" design fuses elements and varieties from the gardens at George Washington's Mount Vernon, Thomas Jefferson's Monticello, and Colonial Williamsburg. The result is a traditional four-square plot that she has surrounded with espaliered apple and pear trees. Her plant choices reflect some of the crops grown by Thomas Jefferson at Monticello, including several of his favorite varieties. Because some of these heritage edibles may be difficult to source, more widely available or recent varieties can be substituted.

> A traditional four-square design that takes inspiration from Mount Vernon and Monticello

> Includes heritage varieties of fruits, vegetables, and herbs grown in those historical gardens

> A central cistern or water feature can be used for irrigation

> The garden is edged with a rustic fence that supports espaliered fruit trees

Teresa O'Connor has created a garden that weaves history and food production into an attractive and productive plot ideal for a modern gardener. The garden measures just 20 by 20 feet and is surrounded by a rustic wooden fence that supports a variety of espaliered apple and pear trees. Espaliered fruit trees were admired by colonial gardeners, including George Washington, for their ornamental appearance as well as their fruit. Inside the enclosure she has placed four raised beds and, at the very center, a cistern. Teresa says that a different water feature such as a solar-powered fountain could be used instead of the cistern. "In earlier times, cisterns collected rainwater for irrigating the gardens. This is still a very good idea, considering the frequent droughts across much of the United States," she adds.

Historical spring plantings. The 4- by 4-foot raised beds are the primary production areas of the garden, with each square featuring an assortment of vegetables and herbs that were enjoyed at Mount Vernon, Monticello, or Colonial Williamsburg. Teresa's plant choices come from several sources, including the books *A Rich Spot of Earth* by Peter Hatch and *Vegetable Gardening: The Colonial Williamsburg Way* by Wesley Greene, and reflect the spring planting season.

Teresa's Garden Plan

20' DEEP X 20' WIDE

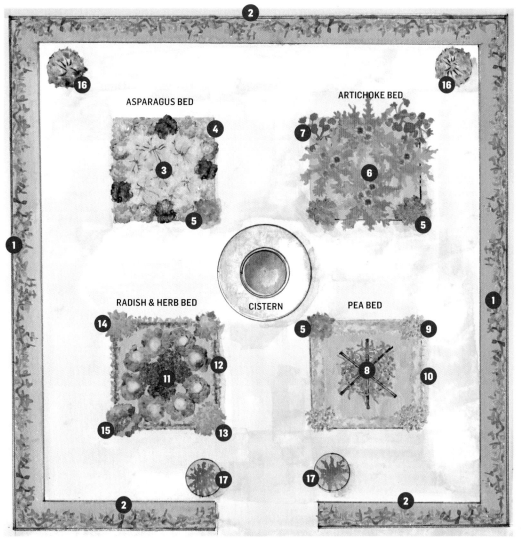

Garden Border

1. **Apples:** 'Newtown Pippin', 'Esopus Spitzenberg', and 'Lady' (espaliered)
2. **Pears:** 'Lawson', 'Bloodgood', and 'Howell' (espaliered)
16. **Pot of lavender**
17. **Rosemary topiary**

Asparagus Bed

3. **Asparagus:** 'Cooper's Pale Green' and 'East India'
4. **Lettuce:** 'Brown Dutch', 'Tennis Ball', and 'Marseilles'
5. **Thyme**

Artichoke Bed

5. **Thyme**
6. **Artichokes:** 'Green Globe'
7. **Nasturtiums:** climbing or 'Empress of India'

Pea Bed

5. **Thyme**
8. **Peas:** 'Prince Albert' and 'Blue Prussian' (on teepee)
9. **Calendulas**
10. **Carrots:** 'Danvers Half Long' and 'St. Valery'

Radish and Herb Bed

11. **Kale and cabbage:** 'Delaware' and 'Malta' kale; 'Choux de Milan' and 'Green Curled Savoy' cabbage
12. **Radishes:** 'Early Scarlet Globe'
13. **Marjoram**
14. **Tarragon**
15. **Parsley**

ASPARAGUS BED

Asparagus, a long-lived perennial vegetable, was a particular favorite of Thomas Jefferson. At Monticello, where the asparagus bed was carefully amended with well-rotted manure, Jefferson grew old varieties including 'Cooper's Pale Green' and 'East India'.

The asparagus is surrounded by an early seeding of lettuce, with a thyme plant tucked into the inside corner facing the cistern. "Lettuce was eaten fresh in salads, steamed like spinach, or cooked for soups," says Teresa. Once spring turns to summer, she recommends replacing the first crop of lettuce with heat-tolerant varieties. "Jefferson grew lettuces even in hot Virginia summers," she says, recommending old or new varieties that can stand up to hot weather, such as 'Black Seeded Simpson' and 'Red Sails'.

ARTICHOKE BED

Teresa has devoted this bed to artichokes and brightly colored nasturtiums, with another thyme plant nestled into the inside corner near the cistern. "Artichokes were a popular gentleman farmer's trophy vegetable, and the mild Virginia climate allowed the perennials to survive with winter support," says Teresa.

Eighteenth-century gardeners had multiple uses for nasturtiums. "Nasturtium seeds were often pickled and used as a substitute for capers in the early Virginia kitchen. A popular 1824 recipe was to cover nasturtium buds with salted boiling water, let them stand a few days, then strain and cover with vinegar and spices," she explains. Gardeners also enjoyed the edible leaves and flowers.

PEA BED

Peas were Thomas Jefferson's favorite crop. "He devoted a great deal of garden space to this cool-season vegetable," Teresa relates. To support the peas, as well as other climbing and vining vegetables, Thomas Jefferson often used teepees constructed from peach tree clippings. Teresa has added such a teepee, although modern gardeners may need to use bamboo or saplings if branches pruned from peach trees aren't readily available.

Surrounding the pea teepee is a border of carrots with clumps of calendula at each corner. Calendula has been a culinary and medicinal herb for centuries. "The petals of calendula were used to dye cheeses and were thrown into stews," Teresa says. "Before 1800, this annual was usually known as 'marygold' by gardeners, and Jefferson planted the cheerful flowers both at his Shadwell boyhood home and also at Monticello." Once the warm weather of summer arrives, she recommends replacing the peas with beans.

RADISH AND HERB BED

This bed is edged with radishes, with a different herb (thyme, marjoram, parsley, and tarragon) at each corner. Teresa notes that all of these were commonly eaten in Jefferson's time, although he reported trouble growing tarragon at Monticello. The middle of the bed is planted with hardy and productive kale and cabbage.

"Cabbage was very popular, providing nutrition especially in the colder months," she says. "Jefferson grew more than 30 types of cabbage, including 'Choux de Milan' and 'Green-Curled Savoy', a variety no longer available." Once the early crops are finished, she suggests replacing the kale and cabbage with tomatoes, peppers, and eggplants — though these vegetables were just starting to win acceptance into the kitchen garden during Jefferson's lifetime, as many gardeners had thought them to be poisonous because of their membership in the often-lethal nightshade family.

CONTINUOUS LETTUCE

Lettuce was often used in cooking. Teresa notes that it was eaten fresh, steamed, or cooked in soup.

Thomas Jefferson wrote, "A thimbleful of lettuce should be sowed every Monday morning, from Feb 1st to Sept 1st."

Terraced Hillside

Trying to grow vegetables and other food plants on a sloped piece of land is difficult and potentially dangerous, depending on how steep the slope is. Water runoff erodes the soil and makes trying to keep the garden irrigated a frustrating experience. In her plan, Barbara Pleasant has created inexpensive raised terraced beds to hold the soil and make gardening on a slope easy and enjoyable.

> This clever design turns an awkward slope into a productive, and beautiful, garden

> Raised beds allow easy planting, weeding, and harvesting without compacting the soil

> Clover pathways reduce weeds and attract pollinators

> Brightly colored clumps of sunflowers, nasturtiums, and zinnias offer blooms for bouquets

Barbara shows that a hillside which receives plenty of plant-loving sunshine can be transformed into a high-yielding vegetable garden by installing a few simple terraces. In her Zone 6 garden, Barbara used untreated, rough-hewn poplar boards (both cost-effective and locally abundant) and rebar stakes to construct several tiers of terraces. "The boards rot in about four years," she says, but notes that repairs are easy to do.

A beautiful living tableau. Terracing a slope is a practical way to put unused space into food production, but with good planning and plant choices you can also create a beautiful place. "Visually, a terraced hillside garden sets up like a tableau — envision a chorus line of plants elevated on risers," says Barbara. "Upright elements exaggerate the stacked effect, so you get double drama from strong verticals like trellised pole beans, sunflowers, and onions."

In Barbara's garden, the level 3-foot-wide beds are easy to manage, and routine chores like planting, weeding, and harvesting can be done without walking on the soil. Two-foot-wide pathways allow easy passage for doing garden chores and moving soil amendments onto the beds.

A carpet of clover. To prevent erosion, Barbara recommends mulching the paths or planting a grass-clover mixture, as she does in her own garden. The clippings from this ground cover can then be applied to the garden beds to reduce weeds and keep the soil moist. Plus the clover flowers will help attract pollinating bees and butterflies to the edible plants, boosting yields.

Well-placed herbs. The four largest beds are planted with a blend of vegetables and annual flowers. Barbara saves the bottom plot for culinary herbs. "You don't want to have to scramble up a slippery hill to get kitchen herbs," she says, "so they get the most accessible space: Front and center." Her top herb picks include basil, sage, oregano, thyme, and parsley. The center of the herb bed contains a large clump of Swiss chard, which can be planted in spring and picked continuously until late autumn. Choose a bright-hued

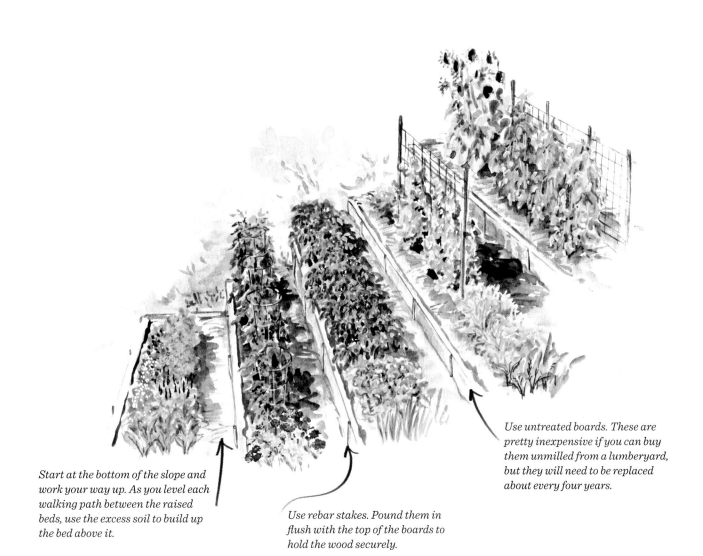

Start at the bottom of the slope and work your way up. As you level each walking path between the raised beds, use the excess soil to build up the bed above it.

Use rebar stakes. Pound them in flush with the top of the boards to hold the wood securely.

Use untreated boards. These are pretty inexpensive if you can buy them unmilled from a lumberyard, but they will need to be replaced about every four years.

Barbara's Garden Plan

23' DEEP X 30' WIDE

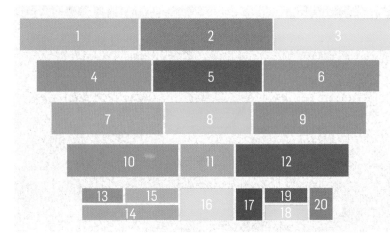

1. Sunflowers and squash
2. Beans (on trellis)
3. Sunflowers and squash
4. Peas (on trellis)
5. Okra and carrots
6. Beets and kohlrabi
7. Spring potatoes and buckwheat
8. Spring lettuce
9. Onions
10. Tomatoes
11. Zinnias (nonedible ornamentals for cutting)
12. Peppers
13. Basil
14. Sweet alyssum (nonedible ornamental for pollinators and beneficial insects)
15. Sage
16. Swiss chard
17. Oregano
18. Thyme
19. Parsley
20. Basil

Barbara's Favorite Varieties

- **Squash:** Butternut or 'Burgess Buttercup' winter; 'Zephyr' and 'Flying Saucers' summer
- **Beans:** 'Spanish Musica' or 'Kentucky Wonder' pole
- **Peas:** 'Mammoth Melting Sugar' snow
- **Carrots:** 'Rainbow Mix' spring
- **Beets:** 'Chioggia' red and 'Touchstone Gold' yellow

- **Kohlrabi:** 'White Vienna' and 'Purple Vienna'
- **Onions:** 'Long Red of Tropea' bulb
- **Tomatoes:** 'Roma'
- **Zinnias:** 'Blue Point Mix' and 'Zowie'
- **Peppers:** 'Lipstick' sweet
- **Swiss chard:** 'Bright Lights', 'Ruby Red', and 'Orange Chiffon'

BARBARA'S SUCCESSION IDEAS

To make her space more productive, Barbara relies on succession planting. Here are a few of her suggestions:

- Replant snow peas with carrots in July.

- Fill the onion bed with arugula in August.

- Replace beets with Asian greens such as baby pak choi, mizuna, or 'Southern Giant Curled' mustard in August.

- In July or August, replant potatoes with 'Georgia' ('Georgia Southern') collards.

- Plant 'Hakurei' turnips in August to replace the spring lettuce.

variety such as 'Bright Lights', 'Ruby Red', or 'Orange Chiffon' for maximum decorative effect.

Reducing the risk of disease. The vigorous squash plants are placed in the top terrace bed because, as Barbara points out with a laugh, you don't always know where they want to go. By situating them at either end of that bed, the vines can trail over the edge of the bed and onto the nearby lawn. She likes to group her plant families in one spot, as soilborne diseases can be a problem. "I keep peppers, tomatoes, and eggplants together, for example," she notes, to simplify the annual rotations that minimize the risk of soilborne diseases. She puts a soaker hose on top of the soil, covering it with a grass-clipping mulch to maintain consistent soil moisture. This simple irrigation system also keeps the leaves of her tomato plants dry, reducing the occurrence of diseases like blight.

Edible Hedge

L ooking for an ornamental or privacy hedge? Forget the privet and give Charlie Nardozzi's hedge a try. His pleasing combination of native and introduced species creates a dense hedge that's both low-maintenance and attractive, with the added bonus of producing tasty fruits like honeyberries, currants, and gooseberries over a long season.

> A beautiful hedge that also bears tasty fruits

> Plants are staggered to create a dense privacy screen

> Includes a hardy blend of native and non-native species

> Thrives in a site with partial shade to full sun

A strong advocate of edible landscaping, Charlie Nardozzi has created a plan for an edible hedge that is both productive and ornamental, reminding us that with a little fresh thinking, we can grow edible plants in unexpected places. "An edible hedge is a great way to accomplish a number of landscaping goals, especially in a small space," he says. "It provides screening from unwanted views, blocks access to your yard, provides habitat for birds and wildlife, and provides delicious berries that may be hard to fit in other places in your yard."

Low-maintenance fruit. His design for a 40- by 12-foot deciduous hedge includes a range of hardy, vigorous plants that were carefully selected for their attractive foliage, form, and flowers — as well as their tasty fruits. Because the plants are arranged in a staggered formation, as they grow they will fill in any open spaces to create a dense hedge. The plan can easily be scaled down to fit a smaller site, or lengthened if space isn't an issue and you want a longer privacy screen. "The beauty of an edible hedge made from native

plants — or plants that are easy to grow in your landscape — is that they don't require a lot of care to produce fruit," Charlie says. Plus, many of Charlie's picks are self-fruitful and require only one bush to yield a decent crop.

Before heading out to your local nursery, Charlie recommends taking a good look around your property to determine your growing conditions. How much sun does your location receive? Is the soil poor? Is it very windy and exposed? He says that most berry shrubs grow best with at least 6 hours of full sun and well-drained soil. Since many berry shrubs are tough and some are native, he adds that part sun and less-than-ideal soil would also work.

Gauge room for growth. While at the nursery, Charlie also advises carefully reading the plant tags, noting how tall and wide the plants will become at maturity. "Make sure you give them room to grow and plenty of space to ensure good air circulation, which reduces the possibility of disease," he says. For a hedge, you will want the plants to grow closely, but you don't want to overcrowd them and allow the branches to intertwine.

During the first season, Charlie suggests watering deeply every few weeks to help the plants establish successfully, but in subsequent years they should need only an annual application of compost. Removing any weeds will reduce competition for water and nutrients, and mulching with a layer of wood or bark chips will help keep weeds at bay. Remember that while the 'Hinnomaki Red' gooseberry may bear fruit the first year, most of the plants take a few years to establish and mature before they begin cropping.

Easy pruning. Pruning can be an intimidating task for many gardeners, but Charlie's plants don't require much fussing. "Pruning mostly consists of removing dead, diseased, broken, or crossing branches in spring," he says. "Most of these shrubs won't require any more extensive pruning."

Charlie's Berry Hedge Favorites

Why plant a strictly ornamental hedge when you can have one that combines beauty with a bounty of berries? The following plants were selected by Charlie for their hardiness, ease of cultivation, attractiveness, and of course — fruits!

'Pink Champagne' currant. A 'Pink Champagne' currant in full crop is truly a sight to behold, with its long chains of translucent berries brushed in soft pink. The bushy shrub will grow to be 3 to 5 feet tall. The plant is very disease-resistant, and because it's self-pollinating, it doesn't need a partner to ensure good fruit set. Use the fine-flavored fruits for jelly, pies, or fresh eating. Hardy in Zones 3 to 8. (May be restricted in some states because they are the alternate host for white pine blister rust.)

'Viking' aronias. 'Viking' is a productive cultivar of the native aronia that bears a late summer harvest of deep violet-black, pea-sized berries. The fruits hang in eye-catching clusters and can be eaten fresh, juiced, or baked into breads, muffins, and pies. The low-maintenance plants, which are self-fertile, grow to be 6 to 8 feet tall with glossy green leaves and a spring show of small white blooms. Hardy to Zones 3 to 8.

'Hinnomaki Red' gooseberry. For sheer productivity and outstanding tangy-sweet flavor, it's hard to beat 'Hinnomaki Red' gooseberry. Small white flowers kick off spring, followed by pretty red fruits and eventually burgundy fall foliage. The compact plants are mildew-resistant and begin fruiting in the first year, making them an excellent choice for impatient gardeners! Eat the ripe berries out of hand, or use them for pies, jams, and jellies. Hardy in Zones 4 to 8. (May be restricted in some states because they are the alternate host for white pine blister rust.)

Nanking (bush) cherries. Nanking or bush cherry is an edible ornamental that tastes as good as it looks. The 8-foot-tall plants are smothered in charming soft pink flowers in late spring, and later bear a good harvest of sweet-tart fruits. Charlie has included two plants to ensure the highest yield. Hardy in Zones 2 to 7.

Honeyberries. In the past few years, honeyberries (also known as Haskap berries) have become a rather trendy plant, quickly selling out at nurseries and garden centers. Each shrub grows to be 4 to 6 feet tall and wide, depending on the variety. Honeyberry is disease- and insect-resistant, very cold hardy, and will thrive in difficult conditions, including moist and shaded sites. The elongated blueberry-like fruits can be eaten fresh or cooked in a variety of dishes. Hardy in Zones 3 to 8.

'Adams' and 'John' elderberries. Elderberry is a shrub native to North America, but the European species is also widely grown for its fruits. Although elderberry is considered to be partially self-fruitful, plant at least two cultivars for optimum yield. Charlie has selected 'Adams' and 'John' for their ease of cultivation and large clusters of tasty blue-black fruits. Each plant will grow to be 8 to 12 feet tall and provide pretty white flowers in the spring. The fruits are commonly used to make juice, jam, jelly, pie, and wine. Hardy in Zones 3 to 9.

Charlie's Garden Plan

12' DEEP X 40' WIDE

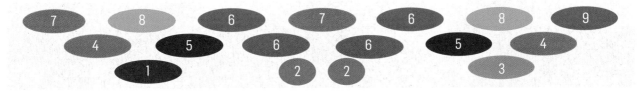

1. 'Pink Champagne' currant
2. 'Viking' aronias
3. 'Hinnomaki Red' gooseberry

4. Nanking (bush) cherries
5. Honeyberries
6. 'Adams' and 'John' elderberries

7. Sea buckthorns
8. 'Regent' saskatoons
9. American cranberrybush viburnum

Sea buckthorns. Sea buckthorn is a Russian species renowned for its juicy orange berries that are rich in vitamin C. It has the agreeable habit of thriving in a range of landscapes and can tolerate poor soil, as well as drought and salt. It will grow to be 6 to 18 feet tall. Because the plants are dioecious (there are separate male and female plants), you will need at least one male and one female plant. Hardy in Zones 3 to 7.

'Regent' saskatoons. Reaching a height of 6 to 10 feet, 'Regent' saskatoon is both decorative and high-yielding. In spring, the show starts with a flush of small white flowers, followed by a generous harvest of sweet, deep purple-black berries. The self-fruitful plants are resistant to diseases and insects, and their foliage turns a bright reddish yellow in autumn. The juicy fruits can be eaten fresh or cooked in jams and pies. Hardy in Zones 3 to 7.

American cranberrybush viburnum. A North American native, the American cranberrybush viburnum is an extremely hardy shrub that grows to be 8 to 12 feet tall. It is a beautiful addition to the landscape for much of the year. Beginning in spring, its white lacecap blooms open, followed by bright red berries in late summer and deep burgundy-purple leaves in autumn. The sour fruits can be used to make jam or cooked into sauces. Hardy in Zones 2 to 8.

Italian Heritage Garden

oug Oster learned from his Italian grandmother-in-law that fresh, flavorful food is central to Italian culture, and to celebrate this fact he created his "Italian Heritage Garden." Doug's plot has nine planting beds separated by generous pathways. Each bed is filled with edibles —tomatoes, basil, garlic, and eggplants — that are central to Italian cuisine. He also shares a unique tomato-staking technique that he learned in Italy, which keeps the rampant growth of vining (indeterminate) tomatoes under control.

> Includes the best plants for making mouth-watering Italian dishes

> An innovative Italian staking technique keeps tomatoes off the ground

> To extend the season, beds are succession planted for a second harvest

> Generous pathways allow easy access for garden maintenance and harvesting

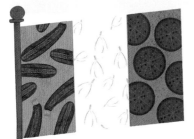

Doug Oster is a self-proclaimed Italian by marriage, yet his own lack of Italian heritage hasn't stopped him from embracing Italian culture — particularly the food. A few years ago, Doug and his wife, Cindy, took a trip to Italy for their 25th wedding anniversary and visited the village where Cindy's grandmother (Tracey) grew up. That trip turned out to be life-changing. "Visiting the country, we were reminded of the importance of fresh produce," recalls Doug. "Food should be picked from the garden right before cooking or serving, just like Tracey used to do."

A parade of Italian favorites. To capture the Mediterranean spirit of fresh, flavorful food, Doug has designed a gourmet Italian garden that provides the longest possible harvest of some of the finest-tasting vegetables and herbs. What would a respectable Italian garden be without a generous harvest of spring greens, versatile garlic, tender zucchini,

cannellini beans, and heirloom tomatoes? By employing careful plant selection and succession planting, Doug keeps the harvest going from early spring to late autumn. Once the initial crops are harvested, he recommends replanting the emptied beds with warm-season vegetables such as cucumbers or zucchini, or quick-growing salad greens, beans, or broccoli raab.

Doug's plan measures a generous 30 by 40 feet, but it can be reduced to fit sites with less space. Novice gardeners may wish to start gradually, beginning with a garden half this size and expanding as they gain confidence in their skills. Most vegetables grow best with ample sunlight, so look for an area that receives at least 6 to 8 hours of direct sun each day.

An old-fashioned tomato. Doug has included a wide range of plants essential to Italian cooking. Like all avid vegetable gardeners, Doug has favorite tomato varieties. He relies

Doug's Garden Plan

30' DEEP X 40' WIDE

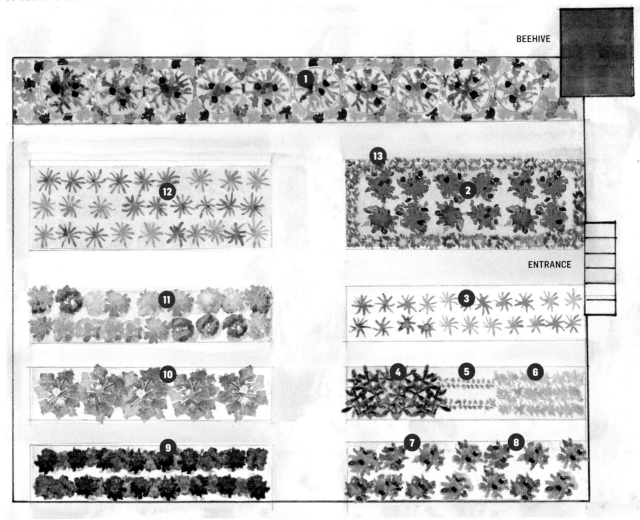

BEEHIVE

ENTRANCE

1. **Tomatoes and greens:** 'Sungold', 'Brandy Boy', and 'Limbaugh Legacy Potato Top' tomatoes underplanted with arugula, leaf lettuce, and endive

2. **Arugula and leaf lettuce:** 'Sylvetta', 'Astro', 'Wasabi', and wild (rustic) arugula; 'Simpson Elite' and 'Amish Deer Tongue' leaf lettuce

3. **Garlic:** 'Music' and 'German White' ('German Extra Hardy') (fall planting)

4. **Beets:** 'Chioggia'

5. **Radishes:** 'Sparkler', 'French Breakfast', and 'Giant of Sicily'

6. **Carrots:** 'Cosmic Purple,' 'Atomic Red', 'Red Cored Chantenay' and 'Scarlet Nantes'

7. **Sweet peppers:** 'Ace', 'Friariello di Napoli', and 'Corno di Toro'

8. **Hot peppers:** 'Super Chili', 'Orange Habanero', 'Ghost Chile' ('Bhut Jolokia'), and 'Long Red Cayenne'

9. **Lettuce and endive:** 'Bronze Arrow' and 'Red Deer Tongue' leaf lettuce; 'Salad King' endive

10. **Zucchini:** 'Tondo di Toscana'

11. **Assorted herbs:** 'Italian Large Leaf', 'Lettuce Leaf', and 'Genovese' basil, rosemary, thyme, cilantro, fennel, and oregano

12. **Garlic:** 'Chesnok Red' and 'Georgian Fire' (fall planting)

13. **Italian dandelions**

on these year after year, but he is also open to trialing any and all varieties and hybrids, with a focus on the diverse selection of heirloom tomatoes now available through seed companies. One of his top picks is a heritage variety called 'Limbaugh Legacy Potato Top', whose seeds were sent to him by the late Fred Limbaugh of Robinson, Pennsylvania — a reader of his newspaper column. The plants bear large 1- to 2-pound pink fruits that are exceptionally sweet and fruity. "It has an old-fashioned flavor that is unmatched," notes Doug.

Tomatoes can be determinate or indeterminate in their growth. Determinate tomatoes are often called bush types, as they grow to a certain height — usually a compact 3 to 4 feet — and set all their fruits at about the same time, which is ideal for those who want to preserve the harvest. Indeterminate varieties, on the other hand, will continue to grow and bear fruit until the plants are killed by frost. Sometimes called vining types, they can grow taller than 6 feet and require sturdy staking. Many of the heirloom varieties are indeterminate.

Italian tomato tents. To support his tomato plants, Doug often depends on cages, but he also uses a method he discovered while traveling in Italy. "They used 8-foot bamboo stakes pounded into the center of the bed," he says. "Then, strings are run like a tent on either side of the stake so that four plants can climb up the strings." This keeps the plants off the ground, discourages disease, increases air circulation around the plants, and makes harvesting easy. As the vines grow, Doug gently wraps the string around the stems.

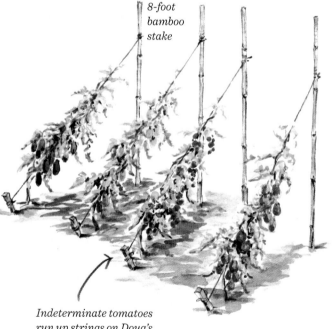

8-foot bamboo stake

Indeterminate tomatoes run up strings on Doug's Italian tomato tent.

SECOND HELPINGS

As an intensive gardener, Doug doesn't like to waste garden space. Therefore, when yield declines or a crop has finished producing, he quickly replants the bed with fresh seeds or seedlings to ensure the longest possible harvest. Some of his favorite successive crops include the following:

- 'Black Beauty' and 'Listada de Gandia' eggplants in place of spent arugula and lettuce

- Broccoli raab, 'Italian Large Leaf' basil, and 'Lingot' cannellini beans planted after the garlic is harvested

- 'Green Curled Ruffec' endive after beets and radishes

- 'Cetriolo Piccolo di Parigi' cucumbers after the lettuce has bolted

Community Plot

N o room to garden? No excuse! With the rapid rise in the number of community gardens, those who wish to grow food are discovering that these organizations offer more than a simple patch of earth — they also provide support, encouragement, and advice. In his "Community Plot" plan, Michael Nolan relies on the square-foot gardening method to produce an intensive crop of favorite vegetables and herbs in a compact 4- by 10-foot bed.

> Reflects the size and shape of many community garden plots

> Organized using the square foot gardening method to maximize yield

> Pea and bean netting provides vertical space for vining crops

> Includes an assortment of tasty vegetables and herbs to cut grocery costs

Michael notes that community gardens offer more than just space to grow plants. "I have seen friendships and symbiotic relationships form and flourish because of community gardens, and I have seen food bank shelves filled with fresh food because communities came together to make a difference." Community gardens also promote active living and a healthy lifestyle. Equally important, they add much-needed plant diversity to our neighborhoods, which encourages native pollinators, beneficial insects, birds, and butterflies.

Typically, each member of a community garden is given an individual plot, where they can tend their choice of vegetables, herbs, flowers, and even fruits. The dimensions of each garden depend on a wide number of factors, including available space and the amount of plots. For this design, Michael has crafted an average-sized single community plot that measures 4 by 10 feet. This may not sound large, but Michael notes that even a small space can be used to grow a surprisingly large amount of food when planted thoughtfully.

Square-foot gardening. Using the method pioneered by Mel Bartholomew, Michael's plan divides each garden bed into square-foot sections that are each intensively planted to ensure a sizable harvest. For example, in just one square foot of space 16 carrots, 9 onions, or 4 Swiss chard plants can be cultivated. Square-foot gardening is easy to learn and maintain and yields more food in a smaller footprint, making it an excellent fit for community garden plots, which can be relatively small.

Stake out your site. For those new to the square-foot method, Michael recommends laying a grid on top of the bed to help keep the space well organized. A grid can quickly be added to a raised bed with wooden sides using twine and nails, and to an inground garden using twine and stakes. Some gardeners prefer a sturdier grid made from wooden slats, which lasts for several seasons.

Trellised cukes. Another way to increase productivity in a small plot is to take advantage of vertical space by growing climbing vegetables up trellises, posts hung with pea and bean netting, or walls. In Michael's design, four cucumber plants are trained up a simple trellis. This makes harvesting a snap, allows the fruits to grow clean and straight, and helps prevent disease. Other vegetables that can be grown vertically include tomatoes, pole beans, and climbing 'Trombocino' squash.

As Michael points out, success of a certain variety can depend on location; what grows well in the American South won't necessarily thrive in Vancouver. That said, Michael encourages gardeners to seek out heirloom varieties of tomatoes that thrive in their region; he harbors an obsession for heirloom tomatoes and herbs, growing all that he can find!

Michael's Garden Plan

4' DEEP X 10' WIDE

1. **Carrots:** 'Touchon' (16)
2. **Parsnips:** 'Hollow Crown' (16)
3. **Garlic:** Elephant and 'California Early White' (4–6)
4. **Onions:** 'Exhibition' and 'Red Candy' (9)
5. **Parsley:** Italian flat (1)
6. **Sage:** 'Tricolor' (1)
7. **Rosemary** (1)
8. **Thyme:** Lemon (1)
9. **Pepper:** 'Purple Beauty' sweet or 'Early Jalapeño' hot (1)
10. **Kale:** 'Lacinato' and 'Red Russian' (2)
11. **Swiss chard:** 'Bright Lights' (4)
12. **Marigolds** (4)
13. **Pole beans:** 'Kentucky Wonder' (9)
14. **Spinach:** 'Tyee' and 'Bloomsdale' (4)
15. **Turnips:** 'Hakurei' (4)
16. **Tomato, marigolds, and lettuce:** 'Red Brandywine' tomato (1) underplanted with marigolds (2) and leaf lettuce (2)
17. **Tomato and lettuce:** 'Amish Paste' tomato (1) underplanted with leaf lettuce (4)
18. **Basil:** 'Genovese' (1)
19. **Oregano:** 'Greek' (1)
20. **Mint in pot**
21. **Dill:** 'Mammoth' (1)
22. **Nasturtium:** 'Alaska Mix' (1)
23. **Celery:** 'Tango' (1)
24. **Cucumbers:** 'Straight Eight' (4)

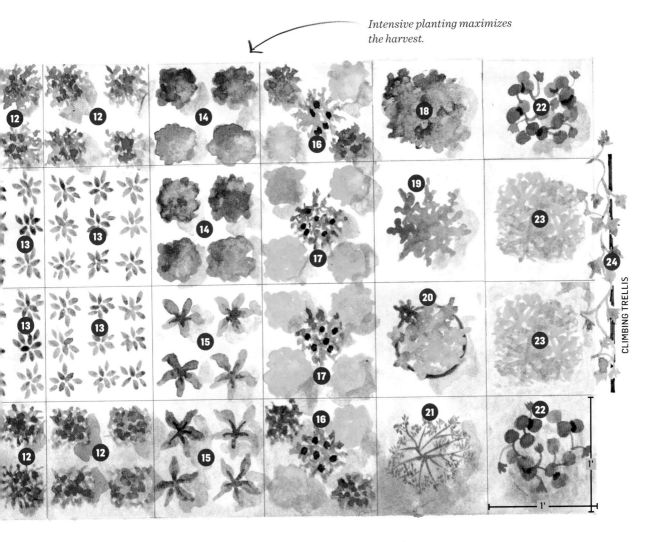

Intensive planting maximizes the harvest.

CLIMBING TRELLIS

THE BASICS OF SQUARE-FOOT GARDENING

Developed by Mel Bartholomew, square-foot gardening is a method of growing food that focuses on intensive planting in tidy 1-foot-square blocks. For example, a 4- by 4-foot bed is divided into 16 squares by a grid of wooden slats or twine. Each square is then planted with 1, 4, 9, or 16 plants, depending on the size of the chosen crop. For example, 1 broccoli, 4 corn, 9 beets, or 16 carrots will fit in 1 square foot.

The square-foot method also advises growing in raised beds, as these make it easier to divide the garden into squares and allow for permanent pathways between the beds. Once a square has been harvested, compost is added to the soil and fresh seeds or seedlings are planted.

Edible Cutting Garden

Proving that an edible plot can be as stylish as any ornamental garden, Debra Prinzing's plan brings pizzazz to a sunny patio. Fruits, vegetables, herbs, and edible flowers are arranged in a stunning sunburst pattern around a small flagstone terrace, with a grape arbor at the open end.

> Produces a delicious combination of fruit trees, berries, vegetables, herbs, and edible flowers

> Use your harvest to impress guests with stunning edible arrangements

> Charming stepping-stone pathways divide the half-circle garden into three main beds

This garden was inspired by Debra's research on the emerging "slow flower" movement, which introduced her to many of the flower farmers and floral designers across the country, an experience she has found incredibly inspiring. "There is something quite alluring when edibles show up in the vase — from pea tendrils to cherry tomatoes still on the vine," she says. She has brought the fruits of her research together in her edible cutting garden. "The edible plants for this new design are widely grown by cut-flower farmers and eagerly snatched up by florists wishing for uncommon design ingredients."

Plants circle a patio. Her half-circle plan is based on the design that she created and installed behind the Seattle home where she and her family lived from 1998 to 2006, but re-imagined to include edibles. "I love the feeling of a half-circle patio," she says, noting that they used tumbled bluestone for their 12- by 6-foot patio. Surrounding the stone patio is a 6-foot-deep crescent-shaped border planted with a diverse but carefully chosen selection of vegetables, herbs, fruits, edible flowers, and ornamental plants. Stepping-stone pathways subdivide the plot into three sections.

A NEW KIND OF HORS D'OEUVRE

When entertaining, Debra recommends impressing your guests by gathering edible flowers and food from her garden plan to craft a simple, but unique, *amuse-bouche.* "The guests can snack on the centerpiece before the main meal is served — but only if your garden is organic!" she advises.

Debra's Garden Plan

12' DEEP X 24' WIDE

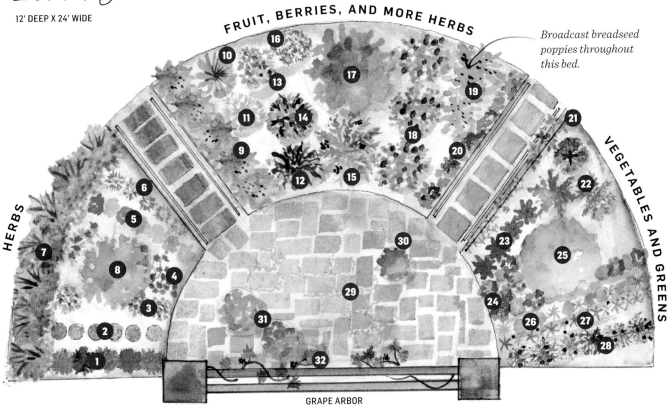

FRUIT, BERRIES, AND MORE HERBS

Broadcast breadseed poppies throughout this bed.

HERBS

VEGETABLES AND GREENS

GRAPE ARBOR

Herbs

1. **Basil:** Common alternated with purple or Thai

2. **Mint:** Spearmint and variegated (in pots sunk in the ground)

3. **Geraniums and salvias:** Apple, rose, and mint-scented geraniums (nonedible ornamentals) alternating with 'Tricolor' sage and other salvias

4. **Edible flowers:** Nasturtiums, calendulas, marigolds, chives, or borage

5. **Ornamental oreganos:** 'Kent Beauty', 'Norton Gold', and 'Showy Pink'

6. **Catmint** (nonedible ornamental)

7. **Lavender hedge:** 'Hidcote' and/or 'Grosso' (7 plants)

8. **Fig:** 'Black Jack' or 'Lattarula'

Fruit, Berries, and More Herbs

9. **Blueberry hedge:** 'Misty', 'Olympia', and 'Top Hat'

10. **Rosemary:** 'Tuscan Blue'

11. **Lemon verbena**

12. **Flowering or fruiting quince**

13. **Anise hyssop**

14. **Bee balm**

15. **American elderberry**

16. **Chamomile**

17. **Plum tree:** 'Damson' or 'Satsuma'

18. **Rose:** Rosa moyesii, 'Nootka', and 'Hedgehog'

19. **Raspberries:** 'Anne' (yellow) and 'Brandywine' (purple)

20. **Strawberries:** 'Alexandra' and 'White Soul' alpine

Vegetables and Greens

21. **Peas and beans:** Sweet and edible peas; scarlet runner beans (on trellis)

22. **Artichoke** (1), **rhubarb** (1), and **cardoon** (1) (planted in a triangle)

23. **Artichokes**

24. **Chard and kale:** 'Rainbow' chard and 'Lacinato' ('Nero di Toscana') kale

25. **Crab apple tree:** 'Prairifire'

26. **Colorful carrots, heirloom lettuces, and shiso**

27. **Leeks and ornamental alliums**

28. **Tomatoes:** Cherry and vining (indeterminate)

Interior Patio Plants

29. **Mint:** Corsican (between stepping stones)

30. **Bay** (in container)

31. **Dwarf lemon and lime** (in containers)

32. **Grapes:** 'Purpurea' (on arbor)

"The two paths branch out on either side, like arms reaching toward the rest of the garden," she says.

Herb portion. The leftmost section of the garden is devoted to culinary and aromatic herbs such as basil, mint, ornamental oregano, and scented geraniums. In the middle of the bed, a fig tree supplies vertical interest as well as luscious fruits. In colder climates, the fig can be planted in a pot so it can easily be moved to a sheltered location for overwintering. The lavender hedge along the outside edge yields edible flowers for scones or shortbread cookies, adds fragrance, and attracts bees and other pollinators to the garden. Alongside the path, a row of low-growing catmint spills onto the stones, softening the hardscape. Though not edible, catmint is beautiful as an "edging," it's great for attracting pollinators, and its soft blue flowers blend well with all other colors in flower arrangements.

Fruit portion. The middle segment of the garden, the largest planting area, is devoted to fruiting trees and shrubs, berries, and additional herbs. When the blueberries are in fruit, Debra advises cutting some of the boughs to make an unusual edible arrangement. Fruiting shrubs include raspberries, flowering quince, and elderberry, and three different roses for decorative and edible hips. In among the taller plants she has tucked rosemary and ornamental anise hyssop, bee balm, and feverfew. "Broadcast breadseed poppies throughout this bed," suggests Debra. "You can save the seeds from year to year, and the dried seed heads are beautiful in floral arrangements."

Vegetable portion. In the last segment of the crescent-shaped garden, Debra celebrates beautiful vegetables and greens. Rhubarb, cardoon, and artichoke (included because their leaves are so dramatic in arrangements) are planted in a triangle to give them the extra space they need. A dwarf crab apple tree balances out the other small trees in the garden; when in full bloom or laden with fruit, its elegant branches can be cut and used in arrangements. A 5-foot-tall trellis lends support to the vining runner beans and peas. It can also (and should!) be used to grow fragrant sweet peas for summer bouquets.

Fragrant, soft ground cover. Spreading clumps of edible creeping thyme are tucked among the stepping stones set along the two pathways, making a soft cushion for wandering feet. In the crevices between the tumbled bluestone on the patio, Debra has put in low-growing Corsican mint, which releases a strong minty fragrance when trod upon.

Pots of dwarf citrus and a bay tree have also been placed on the patio. "You can use the flowering branches and the fruit of the citrus trees" in arrangements, says Debra, "and they can all be brought indoors in winter, if needed." An arbor makes a picturesque entrance to the garden from a deck or back door, depending on the existing features of the site, while offering sturdy support to a purple-leaved 'Purpurea' grapevine.

Biodynamic Farm

Biodynamics is a farming method that focuses on building the soil by adding to it organic matter, green manure crops, and compost, and by rotating crops. This plan for a small-scale biodynamic farm is based on the design at the Pfeiffer Center in New York. The half-acre vegetable garden is divided into 4 main planting areas, which are further subdivided into 68 manageable beds to provide a steady harvest of organic food from early spring through late autumn.

> A large-scale sustainable design that encourages gardeners to concentrate on soil building

> To nourish soil, crops are rotated and beds are regularly planted with cover crops

> A bountiful harvest comes from succession planting spring through autumn

The Pfeiffer Center occupies about $5^1/_2$ acres of land in total, with 3 acres reserved for pasturing two draft horses, 1 acre for field vegetables, $^1/_2$ acre for vegetable garden production, $^1/_2$ acre for herbs and flowers in the Healing Plant Garden, and $^1/_2$ acre for the greenhouse, orchard, and other smaller gardens. Because diversity is a key element in biodynamics, the center also includes composting areas, an apiary, berry production, a wood-fired bread oven, raised beds for growing herbs for teas, perennial gardens for bee forage, and a dyers' garden for fiber crafts.

Compost and diversity are key. Compost plays a large role in biodynamics. "Ideally, the compost is made from materials from the farm, such as manure from your own animals, leaves from your property, and so on," explains Program Director Mac Mead. Having a diverse range of crops is also a cornerstone of biodynamics, and it's beneficial to the bees as well as other pollinating and beneficial insects.

The soil at the Pfeiffer Center is handworked, which means that most of the gardening is done by hand or with simple hand tools. "It is important in training interns that they learn basic handwork methods first before moving on to more mechanized techniques," notes Mac.

Resting the land. To maintain and support soil health, the vegetable beds at the Pfeiffer Center are rotated regularly so that they are not in constant production. "Our goal is to rest one-quarter of the garden in order to really nourish the land," says Megan Durney, the head gardener. The soil can become tired or depleted from constant production, but by growing regenerative crops like legumes and grasses, it can quickly be brought back to health. To organize the space and ensure the garden is properly rotated, the main $^1/_2$-acre vegetable garden is separated into 4 large planting areas that are further subdivided into 68 smaller raised beds.

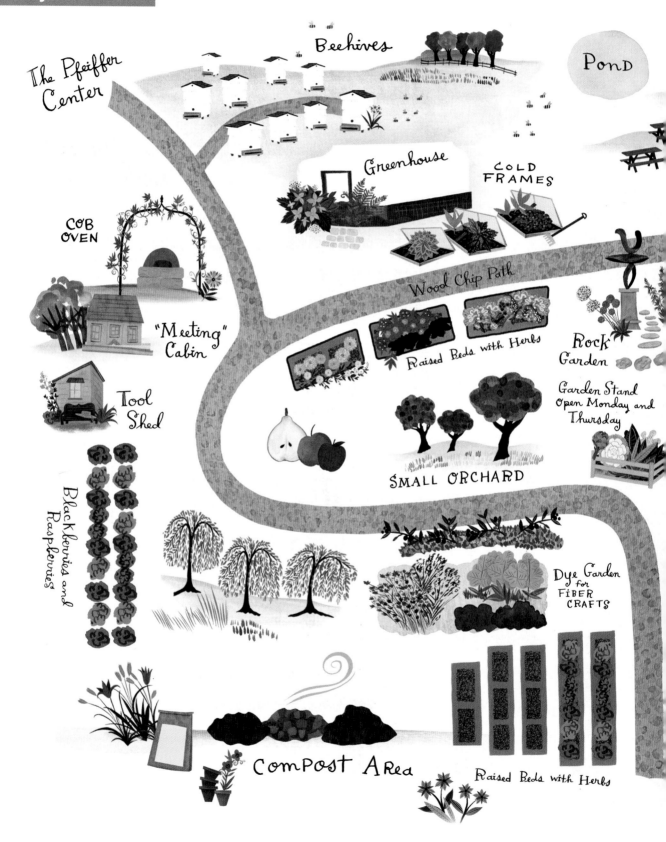

The Pfeiffer Center

Beehives

Pond

Greenhouse

COLD FRAMES

COB OVEN

"Meeting" Cabin

Wood Chip Path

Raised Beds with Herbs

Rock Garden

Tool Shed

Garden Stand Open Monday and Thursday

Blackberries and Raspberries

SMALL ORCHARD

Dye Garden for FIBER CRAFTS

COMPOST AREA

Raised Beds with Herbs

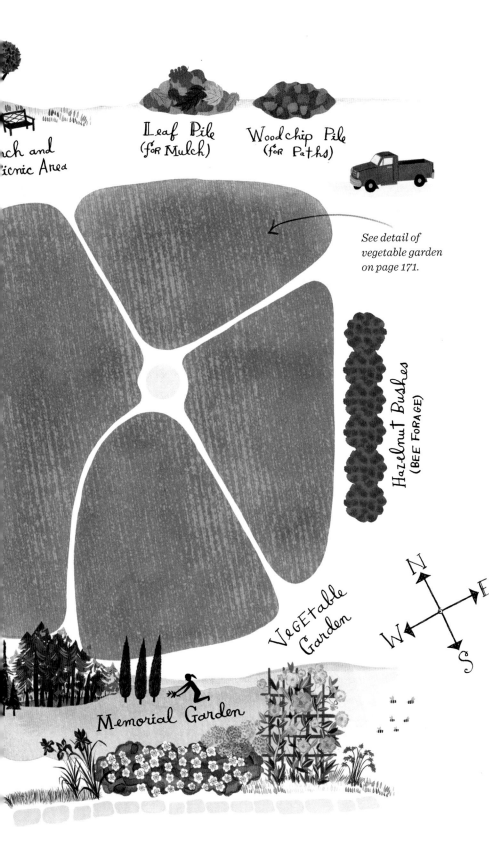

Leaf Pile
(for Mulch)

Woodchip Pile
(for Paths)

~ch and
~icnic Area

*See detail of
vegetable garden
on page 171.*

Hazelnut Bushes
(BEE FORAGE)

VeGEtable
Garden

N
E
W
S

Memorial Garden

WHAT IS BIODYNAMICS?

According to Pfeiffer Center Program Director Mac Mead, biodynamics means "life energy." The concept of biodynamic gardening was introduced in 1924 by Rudolf Steiner in a series of lectures on agriculture. This approach to gardening and farming seeks ways to bring a rich vitality to the soil and plants, thus enhancing the quality of the produce and revitalizing the earth at the same time. "Like the human being," Mac says, "the earth when cared for properly can be healthy and dynamic."

Raised-bed veggies. Planted in the raised beds are "a diverse array of annual vegetables and some perennial vegetables, accompanied by a variety of perennial and annual flowers — specifically focused on bee forage," says Megan. The harvested vegetables are sold at a local café, a garden stand, and the local co-op; those not sold are donated to a food bank.

A large rock sculpture at the center of the four main garden beds holds water for birds and honeybees. It is surrounded by a ring of pollinator-friendly perennials including roses, lavender, catmint, and sage.

At the Pfeiffer Center, planting begins early in the season. "The first sowings happen from early spring to midsummer, and the second and third sowings are planted roughly from midsummer to early autumn," says Megan. Succession planting is key to a bountiful harvest, so quick-growing vegetables like lettuce are sown every two weeks beginning in early spring for a steady supply.

Selecting successive crops. As the first round of vegetables is harvested and removed, some of the beds are replanted with more food crops. Others are sown with cover crops such as rye, peas, oats, buckwheat, and vetch mix. The cover crop chosen will depend on what was previously grown in the soil and when and what crops will be next planted.

"For instance, if a bed had just grown a long-season brassica like fall cabbage, which tends to gobble up fertility, we want to plant a cover crop like peas, an early legume that will nourish the soil with nitrogen-fixing bacteria." explains Megan.

Scattered among the tidy vegetable beds, rows of chamomile, calendulas, signet marigolds and other herbs and flowers support the pollinator populations and provide edible blooms for salads, garnishes, and teas. In the northeast corner of the garden, one bed contains perennial vegetables Turkish rocket and sea kale — a sizable plant grown for its edible leaves, shoots, and flowerbuds, providing a reliable annual harvest.

Pfeiffer Center's Garden Plan

Rows 1–5: Valerian, rhubarb, dye flowers (cosmos; nonedible), asparagus

Rows 6–10: Basil; mixed rows of tomatoes, marigolds, and basil; parsley

Rows 11–15: Mixed rows of tomatoes and marigolds; lettuce

Rows 16–20: Carrots; strawberries; mixed row of peas and spinach

Rows 21–25: Lettuce, Swiss chard, kale, perennial scallions (bunching onions)

Rows 26–30: Summer squash, 'Sugar Snap' snap peas, assorted greens, trellised cucumbers

Rows 31 & 42: Perennial flowers (bee forage focus) and perennial vegetables (sea kale and Turkish rocket)

Rows 45–50: Calendulas, Florence (bulb) fennel, beans, kale, zucchini, chamomile

Rows 51–56: Zucchini; beets; baby greens; tomatoes; peas; mixed row of yarrow and anise hyssop

Rows 57–60: Holy basil, trellised cucumbers, peas, chamomile

Row 62: Beans

Rows 65–68: Lettuce; cabbage; mixed row of turnips and parsnips; Swiss chard

Resting beds: 4, 11, 20, 22, 32–41, 43, 44, 61, 63, 64

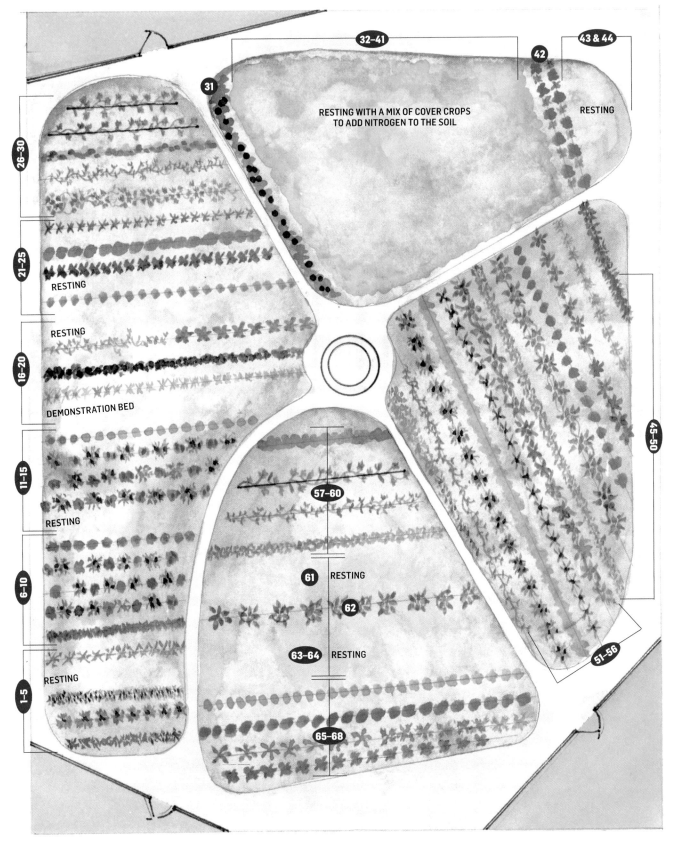

RESTING WITH A MIX OF COVER CROPS
TO ADD NITROGEN TO THE SOIL

32–41

42

43 & 44

RESTING

31

26–30

21–25

RESTING

RESTING

16–20

DEMONSTRATION BED

11–15

RESTING

6–10

1–5

RESTING

45–50

51–56

57–60

61   RESTING

62

63–64   RESTING

65–68

Garlic Sampler

Liz Primeau's small garden showcases the range of flavors found among the many varieties of garlic. One of the easiest crops to grow, garlic demands little in the way of maintenance and is virtually pest- and disease-free. Even deer tend to ignore this vegetable! Between her tidy rows of garlic, Liz has added clumps of low-growing thyme, hens and chicks, and creeping Jenny to create a colorful carpet and suppress weed growth.

> A small but productive space

> Includes eight varieties of aromatic and easy-to-grow garlic, ranging in flavor from mild to strong

> Low-growing perennials tucked between the garlic plants provide color and control weeds

> Grows enough garlic to keep your pantry stocked into the winter months

Any serious cook will tell you that garlic is an essential ingredient in the kitchen. There is nothing quite like the flavor of homegrown garlic, which is fresher, richer, and more aromatic than anything you can buy at the supermarket. As Liz's plan demonstrates, you don't need a huge site to grow good garlic. Just be sure to find a spot with decent soil and at least 6 hours of sun, so your plants produce the largest bulbs possible.

Hardy hardneck. In the north, hardneck garlic is the predominant type and is valued for its hardiness and cold resistance. The cloves of this type are arranged around a central flower stalk or scape that emerges in early summer; typically it's removed so the plant's energy is directed toward producing large bulbs and not flowers. Many gardeners consider the scapes a gourmet treat, turning them into gourmet pestos or chopping and sprinkling them into quiches, scrambled eggs, or pastas. Hardneck garlic needs to be planted "pointy side up" and so is reserved for small-scale farming operations and backyards.

Plain hardneck garlic is divided into three true groups that produce a flower scape:

- **Rocambole.** Among the most popular of hardnecks, Rocambole types have large, easy-to-peel cloves with a delicious, robust flavor. Storage life is up to six months. Varieties include 'Spanish Roja', 'Russian Red', and 'Killarney Red'.

- **Purple Stripe.** Purple Stripe bulbs have striking purple-streaked wrappers and up to a dozen very flavorful cloves per bulb. Glazed and Marbled are usually classified as subtypes of Purple Stripe. Varieties include 'Chesnok Red', 'Shatili', 'Brown Tempest', and 'Metechi'.

- **Porcelain.** If you're looking for big bulbs with large cloves, Porcelain garlic varieties should be at the top of your list. Each bulb bears about 4 to 6 sizable cloves with excellent strong flavor. Varieties include 'Music', 'Majestic', 'Rosewood', and 'Northern Quebec'.

Liz's Garden Plan

8' DEEP X 6' WIDE

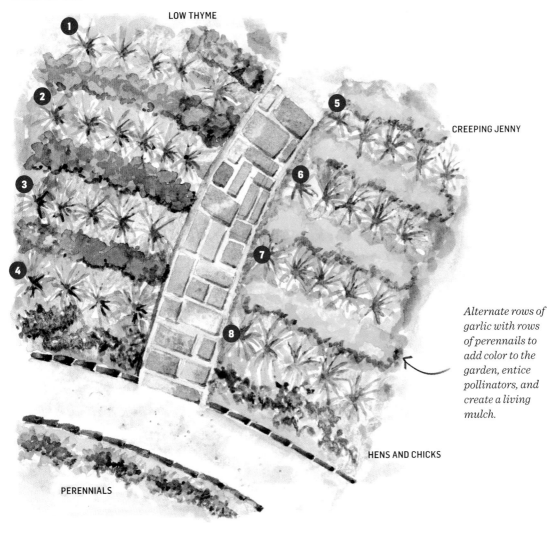

LOW THYME

CREEPING JENNY

Alternate rows of garlic with rows of perennials to add color to the garden, entice pollinators, and create a living mulch.

HENS AND CHICKS

PERENNIALS

1. **'Music'.** A high-producing, mild Porcelain type with white skins blushed in pink. The big cloves are easy to peel, and the bulbs will store for about nine months. This garden favorite is widely available.

2. **'Spanish Roja'.** This heirloom Rocambole type is a standout in northern gardens with a flavor often described as "true garlic." The bulbs have purplish brown skins and will store for six to nine months.

3. **'Rose de Lautrec'.** Most likely a Creole type, 'Rose de Lautrec' is the signature ingredient in the classic French soup Soup a l'Ail Rose de Lautrec. The bulbs have a mild and earthy flavor. This rare variety is prized among garlic lovers.

4. **'Russian Red'.** A Rocambole garlic, 'Russian Red' has a rich, garlicky flavor and easy-to-peel cloves. This is an excellent table garlic and each bulb will yield six to eight cloves.

5. **'Chesnok Red'.** This is a Purple Stripe type that originally hails from Georgia in the former USSR. It gets its name from the striking bulbs whose white papery skin is striped in purple. The flavor is commonly described as "bold," and the bulbs will store for up to six months.

6. **'Majestic'.** This Porcelain type produces strong plants with good-size bulbs. Expect to harvest 4 to 5 large cloves per bulb, covered with a satiny white wrapper.

7. **'Lorz Italian'.** This is a softneck heirloom garlic that was brought to the United States from Italy in the middle of the nineteenth century. The large cloves have a strong, bold flavor and form sizable heads. The plants adapt easily to hot summers.

8. **'Rosewood'.** This is another Porcelain garlic with a mild flavor that is rich but not overwhelming. The plump cloves are easy to peel, with 4 to 5 per bulb.

Braidable softneck. Softneck garlic is favored in milder climates and if grown in cold regions may bolt in spring, diminishing the eventual size of the bulb. Unlike hardneck garlic, softneck types don't typically produce a hard central stalk, so they are easier to plait into decorative braids. Softneck garlic can also be mechanically planted and is therefore the predominant type found at supermarkets.

Plain softneck garlic is divided into two main groups:

- Silverskin. Named for their white papery wrappers, Silverskin varieties are excellent for long-term storage and braid easily. Varieties include 'Silver White', 'Rose du Var', and 'Nootka Rose'.

- Artichoke. Named for their layers of overlapping cloves, Artichoke varieties produce large bulbs that store very well. Varieties include 'Early Red Italian', 'Chet's Italian Red', and 'Corsican Red'.

The setting. Inspired by Liz's actual garlic garden, this compact plan combines some of her favorite varieties — one softneck and seven hardneck — in a very ornamental setting. Liz has tucked the garlic garden into the middle of her extensive perennial garden, but it could also be sited off a deck or near a back door, where it's only a short stroll from the kitchen to the garlic patch.

Storing the stink. More or fewer garlic plants or varieties could be grown, depending on one's garlic

needs. "This garden gives me enough garlic to keep me 'til just before Christmas," she says. Hardneck garlic, once cured and property stored, will keep for about six months. Softneck garlic, on the other hand, will keep up to a year when stored in a cool, ventilated room with a temperature between 60 and 65°F (15 to 18°C). The eight varieties shown here were chosen for their various flavors that range from mild to strong.

Between each row of garlic, Liz has planted a narrow strip of a low-growing perennial, either creeping Jenny, various thymes, or hens and chicks. These add bright color to the garden, entice pollinators, and also create a living mulch to keep weeds at bay. Liz chose to include compact perennials between her garlic rows because they don't cast shade on the all-important garlic plants, which have few leaves and need all of the sun they can get.

It's a big garlic world. Liz admits that her garlic choices vary from year to year, and that as a garlic lover she enjoys experimenting with new varieties in her garden. She often finds them at garlic festivals and fairs across North America and Europe. "All of these varieties are pretty strong in flavor, except for the famed 'Rose de Lautrec', which is milder and earthier than the others," she notes. "There are nuances in flavor, but all of the varieties still have that distinctive garlic taste."

HARDNECK OR SOFTNECK?

These three groups of minor hardnecks may produce a minimal scape, sometimes appearing as softneck.

- **Creole.** Often considered a softneck garlic, Creole will form a flower stalk when grown in the north, but the sweet bulbs will be small. Varieties include 'Rose de Lautrec' and 'Creole Red'.

- **Asiatic.** This weakly bolting garlic produces compact plants that usually bear a floppy scape when planted in northern regions. Tight skins make the cloves hard to peel. Varieties include 'Chinese Purple' and 'Korean Red'.

- **Turban.** Another weakly bolting garlic, this type will also form flower stalks in the north, but they tend to droop. Cloves are easy to peel, and bulbs will last for up to five months. Varieties include 'Early Portugese' and 'Thai Fire'.

Rooftop Farm

*I**n urban areas with little open land,*** gardeners are turning to rooftops to grow food. Colin McCrate and Hilary Dahl have transformed a barren rooftop into an urban oasis with room for a variety of potted and raised-bed crops, as well as a pergola-covered seating area topped by a hops vine.

> Raised beds and half-barrel planters provide plenty of growing space for crops

> A hop-covered pergola creates a cozy spot for outdoor gatherings and meals

> Beehives ensure pollination of the fruiting crops and supply homegrown honey

The folks at the Seattle Urban Farm Company, founded by Colin McCrate and Brad Halm, want to see more rooftops put into food production. "Rooftops are an incredibly underutilized resource," says Colin. "Creating food-producing green spaces seems like a great way to get more value from our urban land." He cites many benefits of rooftop farming, including reducing storm water runoff, lowering energy bills, and cooling the environment. A big benefit is the satisfaction of creating a space that is relaxing yet able to produce a surprisingly large volume of food. "Whether it is a community garden on an apartment building, a production garden for a restaurant, or a market garden, thousands of pounds of produce can be grown right above our homes and offices," he says.

Overcoming difficult conditions. Gardening on an exposed rooftop does offer its share of challenges, however. "Rooftops can be much windier and have more extreme temperatures (hotter and colder) than at ground level," warns Colin. Because containers and beds have limited soil depth on rooftops, the soil needs to be consistently amended with high-quality composts and fertilizers. Colin also notes that it is easy to over- or underfertilize crops in containers, and he recommends yearly pH and soil nutrient tests.

Planting in barrels. Colin and Hilary have included nine half-barrel planters for edibles and annual flowers, as well as six cedar-framed raised beds measuring 4 by 6 feet. They recommend that the beds be at least 10 to 12 inches deep to preserve moisture and make it easier to maintain adequate nutrient levels. The two dwarf

COLIN'S TIPS FOR SUCCESS ON A ROOFTOP

- **Look into access.** Make sure that you have easy access to the roof space (to transport materials up and down).

- **Consult with the building engineer.** Check that the roof can support the weight of the garden (and the gardeners!). Also make sure that the garden construction and management will not damage the roof membrane.

- **Find a water source.** Use an automatic watering system to cut down on the work you need to do. Rooftop beds can dry out quickly, and during the hottest parts of the year may need water two to three times a day. Your garden has a much better chance of success if it receives regular, timely irrigation.

- **Use sturdy materials and secure them well.** Rooftop gardens need to withstand high winds and extreme temperatures. Wind-blown materials could present a serious danger.

- **Use appropriately sized containers for the crops you want to grow.** We like to use a half-wine-barrel planter for dwarf trees like columnar apples, Meyer lemons, and bay laurel, and shrubs like blueberries. Half a wine barrel holds around 30 gallons (4 cubic feet) of potting soil.

- **Pick the right planting medium.** Seattle Urban Farm Company uses a pre-mixed organic potting soil for rooftop crops that are planted in containers and raised beds. It's lighter than typical garden soil and it won't compact over time. They amend soil with organic fertilizers before planting.

- **Look for a storage space.** You'll need it to keep fertilizers, extra bags of compost, tools, and other supplies organized and handy.

- **Consider your crop choices.** Grow the right plants at the right time and in the right place. Certain crops, like salad greens, benefit from some shading in summer, but they also thrive in the spring and fall garden. If growing tall, trellised crops like pole beans, tomatoes, and cucumbers, make sure your supports are adequate and the plants are sheltered from the wind.

fruit trees should also be planted in half-barrel planters or containers of a similar size. Columnar apples stay small with minimal pruning and thrive in containers.

To make the most of limited space, Colin recommends succession planting, amending the soil and sowing another crop as soon as the initial crop has been harvested. He advises adding a small amount of compost and organic fertilizers to each bed between crops and occasionally boosting crops with compost tea or a liquid organic fertilizer.

Lush sanctuary. Colin and Hilary's plan was to grow edible crops, but also to create a small sanctuary in the middle of the city. They have included a cozy seating area, which is tucked in a corner of the garden under the shelter of a hop-covered pergola. "The hops are a deciduous vine and will provide a break from the heat in the summer, while allowing for a nice sunny spot during the cooler months," says Colin.

Help for urban bees. A rooftop is also a great place for urban bees, and Colin and Hilary have included three hives in this plan. "Rooftops are out-of-the-way, sunny locations, so they provide an opportunity to increase the number of urban bees while keeping stinging hazards on ground level to a minimum," Colin says. With the decline in bee populations, Colin says that many urbanites are setting up hives to help bolster the populations, with the bonus of collecting honey.

Colin & Hilary's Garden Plan

15' DEEP X 20' WIDE

A hops-covered arbor creates a cozy seating area.

STAIRWAY FROM GROUND

SMALL STAIRCASE OVER PARAPET

A rooftop is a great location for bees.

Half-barrel containers are perfect for dwarf fruit trees, potatoes, and annual flowers.

4' × 6' CEDAR-SIDED RAISED BEDS

BEEHIVES

For Raised Beds

1. **Assorted greens:** 'Deer Tongue', 'Nancy', 'Winter Density', and 'Breen' lettuce; 'Surrey' and 'Roquette' arugula; 'Calypso' and 'Santo' cilantro

2. **Beets:** 'Napoli', 'Scarlet Nantes', and 'Purple Haze' carrots; 'Early Wonder', 'Chioggia', and 'Touchstone Gold'

3. **Onions:** 'Red Rezan', 'Polish White', and 'French Pink' garlic; 'Ailsa Craig', 'Prince', and 'Ruby Ring'

4. **Perennial herbs:** Italian oregano, 'Aureum' golden oregano, Greek oregano, common (English) or 'French' thyme, peppermint, and rosemary

5. **Kale, broccoli, and Swiss chard:** 'Toscano', 'Rainbow Lacinato', and 'White Russian' kale; 'Bay Meadows' and 'Arcadia' broccoli; 'Bright Lights' Swiss chard

6. **Strawberries:** 'Seascape'

For Half-Barrel Containers

7. **Hot peppers:** 'Thai Hot', 'Early Jalapeño', 'Ancho', and 'Fish'

8. **Dwarf fruit trees:** 'North Pole' and 'Golden Sentinel' columnar apples (need two different apple cultivars with corresponding blooming times to ensure pollination)

9. **Annual flowers:** Good choices to support the bee population include calendulas and nasturtiums (edible flowers), anise hyssop (edible leaves), and sweet alyssum and lobelia (nonedible ornamentals)

10. **Squash:** 'Zephyr' and 'Gentry' summer squash; 'Jackpot' zucchini

11. **Potatoes:** 'Yukon Gold', 'All Blue', and 'Colorado Rose'

For Trellis/Arbor

12. **Tomatoes:** 'Black Prince', 'Pineapple', 'Sungold', 'Black Cherry', 'San Marzano', and 'Brandywine' (trellised)

13. **Hops:** 'Cascade', 'Centennial', or 'Willamette'

14. **Cucumbers:** 'Marketmore 76', 'Suyo Long', and 'Lemon' (trellised)

15. **Pole beans:** 'Fortex' (trellised)

RENEE SHEPHERD & BETH BENJAMIN'S

Gourmet Containers

Growing a garden in containers on a sunny deck, balcony, or patio is an easy way to keep aromatic herbs and ripe vegetables within easy reach of the kitchen. If you're going to the trouble of growing edible plants in pots, you'll want to pick the best-tasting varieties. In their garden plan, which measures less than 50 square feet, Renee Shepherd and Beth Benjamin feature over a dozen varieties of attractive edibles, all with outstanding flavor, and most bred specifically for container culture.

> ❯ Easier to care for than an in-ground garden
>
> ❯ Ideal for decks, patios, and balconies
>
> ❯ Specially selected plant varieties grow well in pots, have outstanding flavor, and produce well

For would-be vegetable gardeners without room for an in-ground plot, or whose yards are steeped in shade, container gardening makes it possible to grow food. The containers can be placed on cramped city balconies, high-rise rooftops, backyard decks and patios, or anywhere else with a flat surface and some sunshine. Those with sore knees, bad backs, or other physical limitations may prefer the ease of gardening in elevated pots, which reduces the need to bend and stoop.

A focus on quality. With a little planning, virtually any type of vegetable or herb may be grown in containers. As it's difficult to duplicate the productivity of an in-ground plot, Renee and Beth recommend gardening for quality rather than quantity, choosing gourmet varieties based on their flavor and vigor. Their plan for a potted kitchen garden includes well-tested vegetables and herbs that thrive when grown in containers, such as 'Astia' zucchini, 'Garden Babies' lettuce, and 'Super Bush' tomato. Renee notes that container-specific varieties can be compact plants with full-size fruits, or they can be truly miniature in stature with baby fruits.

Multitalented plants. When container gardens are located in outdoor living spaces where you will be entertaining or relaxing, it's nice to have plants that taste *and* look good. With the belief that a food garden can also be a beautiful place, Renee and Beth's gourmet plant choices are based on several criteria: they must be visually pleasing, they must have outstanding taste, and they must produce over an extended period of time, ensuring the longest possible harvest. Even the salad greens that are included in this plan are bolt-resistant, attractive, and long-standing varieties that will provide months of fresh greens for salad, stir-fries, and sandwiches.

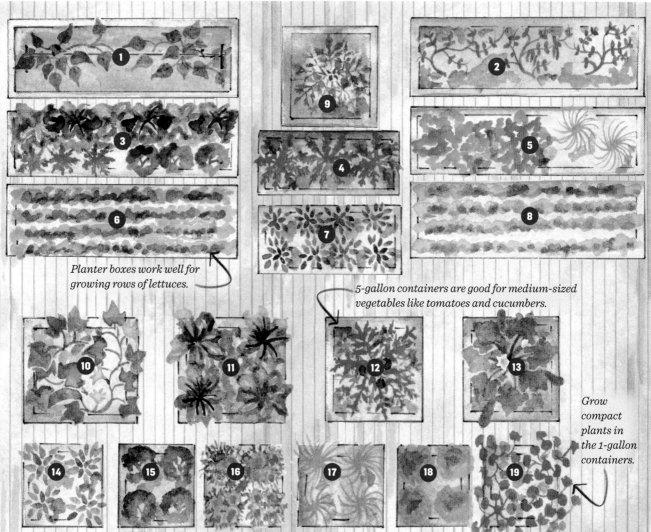

Planter boxes work well for growing rows of lettuces.

5-gallon containers are good for medium-sized vegetables like tomatoes and cucumbers.

Grow compact plants in the 1-gallon containers.

1-GALLON CONTAINERS

Renee & Beth's Garden Plan

For Long Planter Boxes

1. **Pole beans:** 'Emerite' (on trellis)
2. **Peas:** 'Sugar Snap' (on trellis)
3. **Swiss chard, arugula, and parsley:** 'Rainbow' Swiss chard; 'Rustic' arugula; flat-leaved (Italian) parsley
4. **Parsley:** flat-leaved (Italian)
5. **Chives and kale:** Portugese (sea) kale
6. **Lettuce:** 'Monet's Garden' cutting mix
7. **Basil:** 'Italian Cameo' or 'Windowbox' bush (4 to 8)
8. **Mesclun:** 'Wine Country'

For 5-Gallon Containers

9. **Tomato:** 'Sungold' (1, caged)
10. **Cucumber:** 'Bush Slicer' (1)
11. **Swiss chard:** 'Rainbow' (3 or 4)
12. **Tomato:** 'Super Bush' (1)
13. **Zucchini:** 'Astia' (1)

For 1-Gallon Containers

14. **Basil:** 'Cameo' (4)
15. **Parsley:** flat-leaved (Italian) or curly (3 or 4)
16. **Marigold:** 'Summer Splash' (1 to 3)
17. **Chives** (3 or 4)
18. **Lettuce:** 'Garden Babies' (4)
19. **Nasturtium:** 'Empress of India' (4)

Keeping containers looking fresh. To boost production and ensure the garden "will always look good," Beth recommends seeding a fresh pot of greens and other quick-growing vegetables partway through the season, while the older plants are still going strong. When the first crop has peaked it can be switched out for the fresh container filled with plants almost ready for harvest.

Sizing up. Renee cautions you to read your seed packet carefully before planting, and to choose the right size container to save yourself time and frustration. Most crops in Renee and Beth's plan are grown in long planter boxes and 1- or 5-gallon containers; the small pots are reserved for the most compact crops, including basil, marigolds, and 'Garden Babies' lettuce. Leave at least 1 foot of space between pots to ensure adequate air circulation and room for the plants to grow.

To get your edible container garden off to a good start, fill your pots with a high-quality potting mix and be sure to water and fertilize your crops consistently. Potted vegetables and herbs need more water than plants in in-ground gardens, and their moisture levels should be checked daily.

Trellising with containers. At the back of the garden, Renee and Beth include several trellises to lend support to vining 'Sugar Snap' peas and 'Emerite' pole beans. Growing vegetables vertically is a smart way to use space, and also it leads to larger yields per square foot and makes harvesting easier (less need to bend). If nosy neighbors are closer than you'd like, use trellised crops to create a living privacy screen. Edibles that can be grown vertically include small pumpkins, cucumbers, squash, tomatoes, beans, and peas. Ornamental gourds and flowering vines are other options for privacy trellises.

RENEE'S TOP 6 REASONS TO GROW A GOURMET CONTAINER GARDEN

1. To overcome a lack of ideal in-ground garden space.

2. To shorten your trips to the garden. Grow the plants that you're going to eat close to the house for easy harvest — especially when you're busy in the kitchen!

3. To simplify gardening in extreme climates. When it's very hot, you can provide shade by moving the containers beneath trees or into the shade cast by the house. Where it's too cold, simply place your pots in the warmest parts of the property.

4. To put plants at a convenient level for those with bad backs or physical limitations

5. To enjoy exceptionally flavored vegetable and herbs that are not easily found (or too expensive) at local supermarkets

6. To have your kale and eat it too. Because many of these plant choices are both delicious and attractive, it's a clever way to beautify a deck or patio.

Cocktail Garden

C *ocktails anyone?* After a long day at the office, a great way to relax and unwind is with a homegrown cocktail like The Herbarium or The Farmers' Market (see page 184 for recipes), especially if you enjoy them in the garden surrounded by the plants that provided the just-picked ingredients. This "Cocktail Garden" provides plenty of space for a range of cocktail-themed plants, cocktail accessories, and cozy seating for enjoying your just-mixed botanical beverages.

> Selected plants are used in both standard and unusual cocktails

> Containers of varying height, size, and color provide visual interest

> Vertical shelves and wall planters boost yield

Amy Stewart is a writer who, when tackling a new project, immerses herself wholeheartedly in her research. She notes that the research for her latest project, *The Drunken Botanist,* involved "an in-depth exploration of the dizzying array of plants that humans have, through ingenuity, inspiration, and sheer desperation, contrived to transform into alcohol." Part of her fieldwork required rigorous testing of dozens (and dozens) of recipes for a range of mixed drinks, which necessitated easy access to fresh ingredients like mint, strawberries, basil, and cucumbers. "This cocktail-themed garden got its start as a messy collection of plants in plastic pots arranged around my kitchen door," recalls Amy.

Amy's potpourri of cocktail-friendly plants soon expanded as more unusual specimens — black currants, sloe berries, hops, and elderflowers — found their way onto her doorstep. "That's when I realized I needed a garden devoted exclusively to cocktail-friendly plants!" she exclaims. "I had two requirements: it had to be right off the kitchen, and it had to be a fun place to hang out."

Fun setting. Amy enlisted the help of landscape designer Susan Morrison, who was able to envision the narrow strip next to her house — the majority of which is just 7 feet wide — as a place for both fun and functionality. For fun, she included decorative elements (mirrors and glass terrariums), a bar for crafting cocktails, and plenty of seating for party guests. "But it's also a functional garden that accommodates my growing collection of edible mixers and garnishes," adds Amy.

Designing with color. For the patio, Susan chose a concrete surface, edging it with narrow raised beds and an assortment of round and square pots. Before any materials were purchased, Susan and Amy set the color palette to keep the garden cohesive. "The majority of the containers are made from unfinished wood which is then painted, making it easy to repeat the blue-green color scheme throughout the space," explains Susan.

Designing with shapes. Many of the pots are tall and narrow, which is ideal in a garden like Amy's, as their slim profile means the plants in the containers won't spill into the pathway and restrict foot traffic. Susan recommends that containers be at least 28 inches tall and 14 inches wide to allow plenty of room for roots to grow.

The larger pots on the patio are home to the more sizable plants like the columnar apple trees, which could be substituted with dwarf varieties if the site offered more in-ground space. In *The Drunken Botanist*, Amy points out that the first alcoholic concoction to come from apples was cider.

Planting on shelves. With the blank wall, Susan saw an opportunity to grow more plants for garnishes and mixers, as well as a convenient spot to display decorative pieces like mirrors, artwork, and vintage windows. "Mirrors and 'windows' can help make a space seem larger," says Susan. "Planters on the walls add additional growing space and are perfect for shallow-rooting edibles such

as herbs and strawberries." In fact, Amy prefers to grow strawberries vertically, so that the berries won't turn to mush on the ground. Nearby shelving offers additional space for Amy's potted plants, decorative piece, or "cocktail accoutrements," laughs Susan, who notes that Amy added drainage holes to the shelves so they can be easily hosed down.

The majority of Amy's botanical beverage plants are easily grown in pots. Some are obvious choices — mint, celery, lemon verbena — while calendula, cilantro, and lavender are slightly less conventional. Calendula, for example, has pretty petals that can be sprinkled into glasses as a garnish, adding a jolt of color to mixed drinks. "The advantage of calendula is that it isn't colorfast — so the bright orange hue will actually seep into vodka or simple syrup," says Amy.

When buying seedlings to use as mixers or garnishes, look for plants that were grown organically. Of course, you can also start your own from seed.

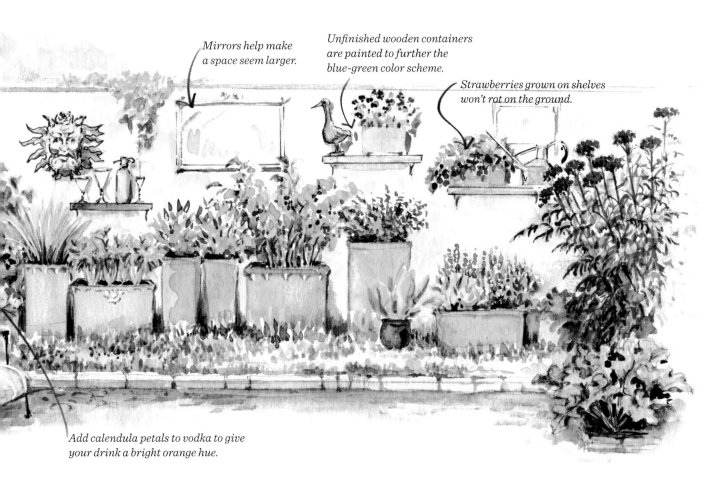

Mirrors help make a space seem larger.

Unfinished wooden containers are painted to further the blue-green color scheme.

Strawberries grown on shelves won't rot on the ground.

Add calendula petals to vodka to give your drink a bright orange hue.

AMY'S FAVORITE COCKTAIL GARDEN PLANTS

Veggies and Fruits

'Jelly Bean' and 'Peach Sorbet' dwarf blueberries

Black currant

Sloe (blackthorn, *Prunus spinosa*)

Calamondin citrus tree

'Lemon' and 'Mexican Sour Gherkin' cucumbers

Strawberries

'Redventure' celery

Chile peppers

'Raspberry Shortcake' dwarf raspberry

Rhubarb

Apple

Cherry

Plum

Blackberries

Tomatillos

Watermelons

Herbs

Pineapple sage

Thyme

Winter savory

Oregano

Rosemary

Fennel

Dill

Lavender

Lemongrass

Thai basil

Cilantro

Parsley

Mint

Summer savory

Sichuan buttons (*Acmella oleracea*)

Ornamentals

'Black Lace' elderberry (flowers and fruits are edible)

Scented geranium (edible foliage)

Rugosa rose (edible flowers and hips)

Fuchsia (edible flowers and fruits)

Calendula (edible flowers and edible, but not palatable, foliage)

Johnny jump ups (edible flowers and foliage)

DRINKING THE HARVEST

Here are a couple of Amy's killer cocktails. Pick a few vegetables and herbs, combine them with some spirits, and sip comfortably in your garden.

The Herbarium

¼ lemon
1.5 ounces Hendrick's Gin
0.5 ounce St. Germain elderflower liqueur
3–4 chunks 'Lemon' cucumber
2–3 sprigs basil
ice
club soda
borage blossom or basil leaf for garnish

Squeeze lemon into cocktail shaker and add the gin and elderflower liqueur. Muddle cucumber and basil and add to shaker. Add ice, shake, and strain into a tall, skinny Collins glass filled with ice. Top with club soda and garnish.

The Farmers' Market

1.5 ounces vodka (try Glacier potato vodka from Idaho)
2–3 'Mexican Sour Gherkin' cucumbers
1–2 stalks 'Redventure' celery
2–3 sprigs cilantro
2–3 slices small spicy or mild chile peppers
6 cherry tomatoes or 1–2 slices large tomato
dash of Worcestershire sauce (try Annie's for a vegetarian version)
ice
3–4 ounces Q or Fever Tree tonic water

Reserve a celery stalk, cherry tomato, or cucumber for garnish. Combine the vodka, cucumbers, celery, cilantro, peppers, tomatoes, and Worcestershire sauce in a cocktail shaker. Gently crush the vegetables and herbs, making sure to release the juice from the tomatoes. Add ice, shake, and strain into a tumbler filled with ice. Top with tonic water and add garnish.

Chicago Hot-Dog Garden

Who says gardening is all work and no play? Certainly not Chicago resident Amanda Thomsen, who has created a quirky garden plan that celebrates the quintessential Chicago-style hot dog: beef frankfurter on a poppyseed bun topped with pickle, onion, neon green relish, tomatoes, 'Sport' hot peppers, mustard, and celery salt. The 20-foot-long, 10-foot-wide garden bed is shaped like a well-topped hot dog and planted with edibles and flowers that can be used to create your own perfect dog.

❯ Includes all the necessary toppings for an authentic Chicago hot dog

❯ Unusual shape of garden is a fun way to encourage kids to eat their veggies!

❯ Plus, a bonus design — a mini portable hot-dog garden

To create the perfect hot dog outline, use a garden hose or rope to form the shape of the bed, and remove it once you've dug the basic outline. A border of flexible landscape edging, stones, or bricks will emphasize the contours of the hot dog and prevent weeds from encroaching. If you prefer, you can grow your plants in a more traditional or existing vegetable garden. But if you have the space, why not go for the full meal deal and create an unforgettable garden plot?

Garden-fresh toppings. In the spirit of creating an authentic dog, Amanda has included all the toppings that you'll need. In most regions, the celery, peppers, and tomatoes should be planted as seedlings bought from a local garden center, or started indoors in early spring. The mustards, poppies, and cucumbers can be direct-seeded into the garden. The onions should be planted from purchased sets or seedlings. Amanda suggests applying a layer of straw mulch on the "bun" of the hot-dog garden to keep weeds down and the soil cool and moist. Plus, the golden brown hue of the straw matches that of a well-baked bun!

In the middle of the garden, a wide swath of breadseed poppies form the "meat" of the hot dog, while the onion, white mustard, and pepper beds are arranged as the toppings. A wooden A-frame trellis will support the vigorous cucumber vines. The tomato plants should also be supported with cages or stakes, inserted at the time of planting.

No ketchup here. If you don't want to feel the wrath of Amanda, you will not put ketchup on your Chicago-style hot dog. "It isn't allowed on a dog, unless you're under 12," she admonishes. "The object of the game is to layer up the traditional toppings until it takes your full attention to eat it, both for stability and sanitation."

Amanda's Garden Plan

10' DEEP X 20' WIDE

Mustard — never ketchup — sits atop a Chicago-style hot dog.

HOT-DOG-CART GARDEN

"If you're a hot-dog lover on the go, you can repurpose an old hot-dog cart and push it where the sun shines!" says Amanda. Train cucumbers to scale the umbrella pole, grow peppers in the bin drawer, and watch tomatoes grow up the front of the cart.

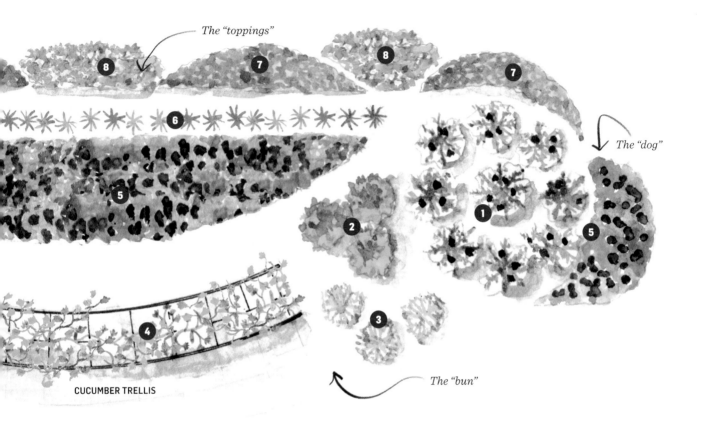

The "toppings"

The "dog"

The "bun"

CUCUMBER TRELLIS

For the "Bun"

1. **Tomatoes.** A proper dog should be topped with wedges of your homegrown, vine-ripened tomatoes. "I'm not going to get too fussy here," says Amanda. "I will reserve my fussiness for the peppers, but you need a tomato that is red and baseball sized."

2. **Celery.** Described by Amanda as "magical hot doggity pixie dust," celery salt is the ingredient that brings the whole Chicago-style hot-dog experience together. You can make your own by putting celery seeds or bits of dried celery in a blender with coarse sea salt and blending it like crazy. "Jar it up and enjoy!" she says.

3. **Dill.** Since you're going to make your own pickles for your hot dog, Amanda advises growing your own dill, which is easy to start from seed. "It's really the gift that keeps on giving!" she says.

4. **'Straight Eight' or 'Marketmore 76' cucumbers.** Next come the cucumbers, which do double duty as a pickle wedge and as neon green relish.

For the "Hot Dog"

5. **Breadseed poppies.** Sure they're pretty, but also the seeds of breadseed poppies are a must-have on your homemade buns. "They're weirdly easy to grow and harvest," says Amanda.

For the Toppings

6. **White onions.** Onions are a must, and the row of white onions will supply more than enough bulbs for dicing.

7. **White mustard.** "Yes, you can make your own yellow mustard" by combining the ground mustard seeds with vinegar and spices declares Amanda. Buy seeds of white mustard (its seeds are yellow to beige-colored), which is very quick-growing from seed. Not only will you be able to turn the eventual seeds into homemade gourmet mustard for your hot dog, but also you can enjoy the spicy leaves in salads and stir-fries.

8. **'Sport' hot peppers.** According to Amanda, here is where things get a bit weird, as the 'Sport' pepper is the only acceptable pepper for a Chicago-style hot dog. Unfortunately, it won't be easy to find the plants or seeds at a local garden center, so she suggests ordering them through an online seed company. Use extra 'Sport' peppers to make giardiniera, a pickled pepper mixture that Chicagoans eat on Italian beef.

Upcycled Edible Patio

*S*ure, you can grow food plants in conventional plastic pots or wooden planters. But with a little creative thinking you can also turn old, outdated, or unusual items into one-of-a-kind containers for your vegetables and herbs. Jean Ann Van Krevelen is always on the lookout for unique objects to "upcycle" into pots (no old toilets, thank you), a trend that is reflected in her "Upcycled Edible Patio" plan.

> Creates a truly unique garden with low-cost "upcycled" items like baskets, buckets, and crates

> Vegetables and herbs are selected for their ornamental and edible value

> Vertical vining crops like tomatoes and pole beans offer privacy and increased yields

When it comes to selecting pots, Jean Ann likes to seek unorthodox containers from thrift stores or yard sales to reflect her fun-loving and eclectic personality. "I've used bicycle baskets, galvanized tin tubs, wooden crates, and more," she says. When evaluating an item for use as a possible container, consider its material and size. Metal articles like milk jugs, old tool boxes, colanders, and galvanized pails will quickly heat up on a sunny day, damaging plants and drying out quickly. To counter this, line your metal containers with a similarly shaped and sized fiber or plastic pot, or shield the metal from the sun by layering containers in front.

Adapting containers. Shallow, wide items like vintage suitcases, dresser drawers, or wicker baskets can also be put into patio food production, but these will benefit from a plastic liner. In the case of wood, the issue isn't overheating but rot. Loosely woven baskets can also leak soil and dry out quickly, making a liner a low-maintenance solution. For these upcycled items, opt for shallow-rooted salad and root vegetables such as leaf lettuce, baby chard, spinach, baby beets, turnips, and radishes.

Whatever types of pots you choose, remember that adequate drainage is a must, so poke or drill holes in the bottom. And — sorry, boys — size matters. Plants, especially vegetables, should be matched to the proper-sized pot so there is plenty of root room for each plant, and so plants won't need to compete for nutrients, moisture, and light. Even carrots can be grown in pots — just be sure to choose a container at least 12 inches deep to allow adequate room for root development. Jean Ann likes to combine 'Lunar White' and purple 'Black Knight' carrots in one pot, and place the tender, crisp roots of 'Little Finger' in another.

Crops grown in pots will also require a little more TLC than those grown in a traditional in-ground garden. Water twice a day when it's hot, and use a good slow-release fertilizer when potting up the containers. Supplement with a foliar fertilizer like fish emulsion every few weeks to keep production high and plants healthy.

An old bicycle basket gets a new life as a planter for kale.

UPCYCLED CONTAINER COMBINATIONS

- **Use an old metal horse trough** as a fabulous pot for trellised veggies. Try four to six Scarlet runner beans on a twig teepee or an assortment of espaliered tomatoes: 'Black Krim', 'Indigo Rose', 'Green Grape', and 'Green Zebra'. Don't forget to add drainage holes!

- **Drill some holes in your old, broken-down wheelbarrow** and fill it with 'Bleu de Solaize' leeks, 'Redventure' celery, and white sweet alyssum (nonedible).

- **Turn an old wire supermarket shopping basket** into a show-stopping veggie and flower basket. Try planting 'Graffiti' purple cauliflower and white or purple sweet alyssum (nonedible), or 'Bleu de Solaize' leeks and purple sweet alyssum.

- **Pick up some old wooden bushel baskets** at a farm stand or farmers' market. Plant 'Red Russian' kale, 'Forellenschluss' lettuce, and 'Superbells Blackberry Punch' million bells (nonedible) in them.

- **Use a ladder** to create a vertical support for small and medium-sized pots and planters. Pot up your favorite compact veggies (such as mesclun mix and 'Tristar' strawberries), herbs, and edible flowers in paint-splattered buckets for an extra punch of color!

- **When your kids outgrow their rainboots,** attach the worn-out boots to a fence or shed. Poke a hole in the bottom for drainage and fill the boots with herbs like ginger mint, 'Genovese' basil, and 'Red Rubin' purple basil.

Feast for the eyes. In keeping with the notion that edibles can be beautiful, Jean Ann chooses crops that are both pretty and productive. With its blistery texture and strappy, blue-green leaves, 'Lacinato' kale is a favorite ornamental edible, but Jean Ann also appreciates the deep purple-maroon pods of 'Royal Burgundy' bush beans that invite picking as they dangle within the deep green foliage.

Jean Ann also likes to pair her favorite edibles with colorful annuals such as million bells, alyssum, and petunias. She combines 'Red Russian' kale with 'Forellenschluss' red-speckled romaine lettuce and 'Superbells Blackberry Punch' to produce a dynamite blend of plant sizes, leaf textures, bold foliage color, and pretty blooms. The combination provides months of eye candy on the patio as well as fresh greens for gourmet salads.

Espaliered tomatoes. Jean Ann likes to use a large planter box to hold some of her favorite heirloom tomatoes. She suggests espaliering the indeterminate (vining) types. This pruning technique improves air circulation around the plants, helping to prevent disease, and it also allows ample sunlight to reach the foliage, boosting production. Jean Ann's top tomato picks are 'Black Krim', 'Indigo Rose', 'Green Grape', and 'Green Zebra'.

Jean Ann also suggests including a vertical element like a garden arch, which can be used to allow passage from a patio or deck to the rest of the landscape. The arch could support the vigorous vines of 'Celebration' and 'Delicata' winter squash. Other delicious and decorative climbing vegetables, like scarlet runner beans or cucumbers, can scale structures such as bamboo teepees, obelisks, or twig trellises. Vertically grown plants can be situated to creating a living screen for exposed decks and patios, reducing strong winds and boosting privacy. Even compact crops can be grown vertically; Jean Ann suggests using a small shelving unit or a chest of drawers to grow layers of luscious strawberries and salad greens.

Patio apples. Columnar apple trees provide a modest harvest of full-size apples when grown in pots. Each single-stemmed tree grows just 8 to 10 feet tall and 2 feet wide at maturity, making these narrow plants a good choice for a deck or patio of any size. Keep in mind that two varieties of apple are needed for cross-pollination.

JEAN ANN'S DOS AND DON'TS

Do Use:

- Bicycle baskets
- Wooden wine crates
- Radio Flyer wagons
- Vintage tool/tackle boxes
- Birdbaths/fountains

Don't Use:

- Old hiking boots
- Undergarments
- Toilets
- Kiddie pools
- Jeans or jean shorts

Pallet Garden

Pallet gardening is popular, and for good reason! With a little time and even less money, gardeners can turn an old pallet into a handy vertical garden. An upcycled pallet, mounted on a wall or fence — preferably just outside the kitchen — makes a handy planter for compact crops like curly parsley, leaf lettuce, and Swiss chard, and even dwarf tomatoes and nasturtiums.

> A fun and easy project for kids or DIY-types

> Can be mounted on a wall or fence for a no-space garden

> A great way to grow aromatic herbs and compact crops

Joe Lamp'l is passionate about getting people to grow more food — even in tiny urban lots and concrete balconies — and he has embraced the concept of a pallet garden for its incredible versatility. Pioneered by Fern Richardson in her blog *Life on the Balcony*, pallet gardens are typically mounted to a wall, fence, or other structure, but handy gardeners can also make "feet" or a stand so that pallets can be freestanding on decks and patios. Plus, an edible pallet garden is very low-maintenance, requiring little ongoing care aside from regular watering and an occasional dose of liquid organic fertilizer.

A pallet garden is a great project for do-it-yourself types, as well as those on a tight budget. Two people can assemble and plant a pallet garden in about an hour if all materials are gathered beforehand.

Picking the right pallet. Sourcing a pallet should be easy — many businesses are happy to share their used pallets at little to no cost — but Joe says to "look for pallets made of untreated wood and also seek out pallets marked HT, which stands for heat treated, as a safe alternative for treating pests." He also suggests inspecting the pallet for splintered wood or stray nails. Once you've found one that makes the grade, give it a good hosing off to remove dirt and grime.

The best plants for a pallet. When choosing plants for an edible pallet garden, Joe advises looking for dwarf or bush types of vegetables and herbs, as well as compact fruits like strawberries. In his plan he includes a wide selection of favorite edibles: salad greens, zucchini, cucumbers, peppers, and tomatoes. "Peppers and tomatoes will need to go in the top section because they are the tallest and will need room to grow and possibly staking," says Joe. "The big thing is to work with compact and determinate tomato varieties wherever possible." He also suggests tucking nasturtium seedlings throughout the pallet garden for a "punch of edible color." Other options include a pallet filled with culinary herbs or salad greens.

Joe's Garden Plan

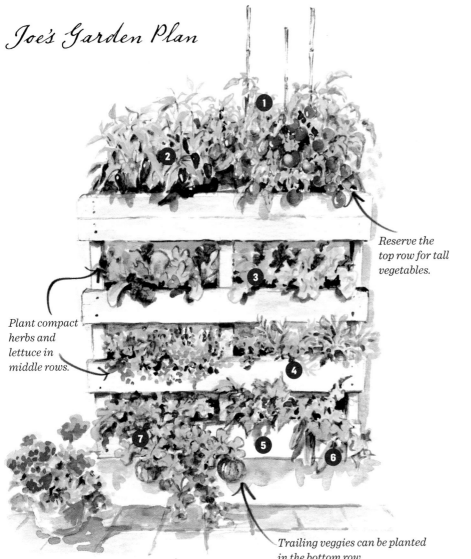

Reserve the top row for tall vegetables.

Plant compact herbs and lettuce in middle rows.

Trailing veggies can be planted in the bottom row.

Simple L-brackets are used to mount the planted pallet garden to the side of a house, fence, shed or other vertical surface.

Top Row

1. **Tomatoes:** 'Celebrity', 'Fresh Salsa', or 'SuperTasty' (determinate)

2. **Peppers:** 'Sweet Heat', 'Great Stuff', or 'Baby Belle'

Middle Rows

3. **Lettuce mix:** 'Healing Hands', 'Alfresco', or 'City Garden Mix'

4. **Herbs:** 'Red Rubin' or 'Genovese' basil, sage, spearmint, rosemary, oregano, thyme, and cilantro

Lowest Row

5. **Summer squash:** 'Saffron' or 'Dwarf Summer Crookneck'

6. **Cucumbers:** 'Bush Champion', 'Salad Bush', or 'Spacemaster'

7. **Watermelons:** 'Bush Sugar Baby' or 'Golden Midget'

HOW TO MAKE JOE'S PALLET GARDEN

MATERIALS

- 1 untreated shipping pallet, hosed clean
- 4 mounting L-brackets, one for each corner of the pallet

Weather-resistant screws

Roofing nails or staples

Landscape (weed barrier) fabric

Plastic sheet or other waterproofing material (optional)

Thin plywood, cut to the size of the pallet

Potting soil

Plants

TOOLS

Hammer or staple gun

Drill

Level

Eye protection (always a good idea when working with tools)

1. With the help of a friend, position your pallet against the wall or fence where you want it mounted and use your level to make sure it's straight. Using a pencil, mark on the fence or wall where you would like to install each of the four L-brackets. Situate the top left and right L-brackets so they'll be about 2 inches from the top of the pallet, while the bottom two L-brackets should be about 6 inches from the bottom of the pallet. Once you've marked their positions, move your pallet to the side.

2. Drill pilot holes slightly smaller than the diameter of your screws into the supporting fence or wall. Using your drill, screw the L-brackets into place on the fence. (It's much easier to install the brackets *before* the pallet is filled with soil and plants. Then, once you're ready to hang it, all you'll need to do is slide it into place and secure it with the screws.)

3. Move the pallet to a flat surface and lay it down so that the side with the largest openings is facing up. This is the side that will be mounted against the wall.

4. Cover the back and bottom of the pallet with the landscape fabric, cutting it to size. This will prevent the soil from falling out. Pull the fabric tight and secure with roofing nails or staples, placing one nail or staple every 2 to 3 inches around the perimeter of the pallet as well as down the center beams. If you want a layer of plastic or another waterproofing material between the pallet and the support, add it now. This additional layer will protect the side of the house or wall from moisture and grime from the pallet garden.

5. Attach the thin sheet of plywood to the cloth-covered back of the pallet and secure with nails every 6 inches.

6. Flip over the pallet and fill the rows with premoistened potting soil. Tilt the pallet so that it's almost vertical to let the soil settle a bit, then add more soil until the rows are full.

7. Now it's time for the fun stuff! Grab your plants and start packing them into the rows between the slats.

8. Mount the pallet. Have your friend help you position the pallet between the pre-installed brackets. (Aren't you glad you mounted those already?) Using your drill, screw the brackets to the pallet.

9. Check for settled soil, filling where necessary, and water well. Take a few minutes to admire your new space-saving, high-producing vertical pallet garden!

"Good Bug" Garden

With more gardeners — both ornamental and edible — becoming aware of just how important pollinating and beneficial insects are to our gardens, the demand for pollinator-friendly plants is beginning to rise. Encouraging high populations of "good" bugs such as ladybugs is a cornerstone of organic gardening and one of the best ways to keep damage from "bad" bugs (like aphids) to a minimum. In this innovative design, beneficial bug expert Jessica Walliser has created a biologically diverse environment that provides a bounty of homegrown vegetables and herbs, as well as the basic essentials required by beneficial and pollinating insects.

> A permanent center bed features perennial herbs like thyme and sage

> Four outer beds contain a biologically diverse selection of edible and ornamental plants

> Supplies nectar and pollen, and has a water source for "good bugs"

Use underplantings like sweet alyssum below tomatoes to attract beneficial insects to your edibles.

Jessica's plan is modeled after her own garden, which is 20 by 30 feet. The diamond-shaped central bed is a permanent section of the garden, where perennial herbs like thyme, sage, and mint can grow undisturbed from year to year. The outer beds are filled with a carefully chosen selection of annual vegetables, herbs, and flowers that Jessica has matched to the needs of pollinating and beneficial insects.

Floral architecture. "Many species of beneficial insects have mouthparts that are not specialized for delving into deep, tubular flowers, but rather prefer to source pollen and nectar from flowers with shallow, more exposed nectaries," Jessica says, adding that many beneficials need to have nectar and/or pollen in their diets in order to thrive and reproduce. Jessica has also included plants with diverse floral architecture, which appeal to a wider number of insects.

Super sunflowers. The annual flowering sunflowers, sweet alyssum, and zinnias can be purchased as plants or grown directly from seed sown in the late spring garden. Sunflowers are among the richest food sources for beneficial insects. "Not only do they have readily accessible pollen (unless you're growing pollenless varieties, which as far as good bugs go is not a good idea), but they also produce extrafloral nectar from nectary glands on the undersides of their leaves," says Jessica. Extrafloral nectar is an excellent source of carbohydrates and is produced by many different plants as a reward to the various species of beneficial insects that help protect them from pests. "Zinnias are not quite as good at this, as they don't produce extrafloral nectar, but they are long-blooming and provide habitat for beneficials," Jessica says.

Jessica's Garden Plan

20' DEEP X 30' WIDE

1. **Cucumbers** (on netting strung between poles)
2. **Zinnias:** 'Pinwheel' (nonedible ornamental)
3. **Onions:** 'Big Daddy', 'Walla Walla', and 'Ruby Ring'
4. **Carrots:** 'Purple Haze', 'Scarlet Nantes', and 'Romeo'
5. **Lettuce:** 'Deer Tongue', 'Little Gem', and 'Merlot'
6. **Sweet alyssum** (nonedible ornamental)
7. **Chamomile**
8. **Chervil**
9. **Mustard greens:** 'Osaka Purple'
10. **Squash:** 'Black Beauty' zucchini; 'Yellow Crookneck' summer
11. **Tomatoes:** 'Pineapple' and 'Persimmon'; 'Snow White' cherry (underplanted with sweet alyssum)
12. **Pole beans** (on trellis against fence)
13. **Snap peas** (on netting strung between poles)
14. **Eggplants:** 'Fairy Tale', 'Millionaire', and 'Rosa Bianca'
15. **Broccoli:** 'Veronica' and 'Belstar'
16. **Cabbage:** 'Ruby Ball' and 'Quick Start'
17. **Oregano**
18. **Cosmos** (nonedible ornamental)
19. **Basil**
20. **Beets:** 'Chioggia', 'Golden', and 'Red Ace'
21. **Peppers:** 'Anaheim' and 'Cherry Bomb' hot; 'Crème Brulée', and 'Yum Yum Gold' sweet
22. **Beans:** 'Provider' and yellow wax bush
23. **Sunflowers** (avoid pollenless cultivars)
24. **Thyme**
25. **Horsemint** (*Monarda punctata*)
26. **Dill**
27. **Parsley**
28. **Fennel**
29. **Sage**

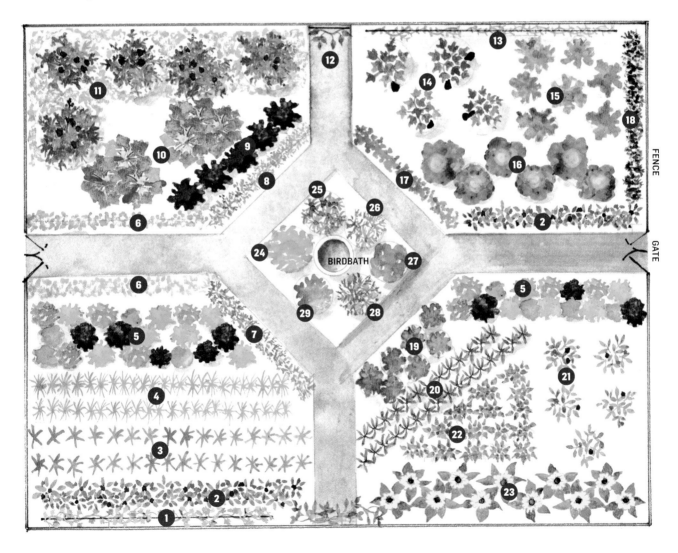

JESSICA'S FIVE FAVORITE BENEFICIAL INSECTS

- **Parasitic wasps.** Nearly all of the thousands of different species of parasitic wasps use other insects as hosts for their young, laying eggs singly or in groups on, or inside of, a host insect. The larvae then hatch and develop inside of the host. Parasitic wasps attack almost every group of insects, including aphids, beetles, flies, scales, true bugs, and caterpillars of every sort.

- **Tachinid flies.** This large and diverse family of parasitoids participates in some of the most fascinating interactions of the insect world. Adult tachinids feed on pollen, nectar, and honeydew and are important pollinators. All species of tachinids use various insects at different life stages — from caterpillars to adults and larval beetles — as larval hosts.

- **Syrphid flies.** Members of this very important group of flies are frequently found hovering around flowers on bright, sunny days. While the adults feed on nectar and pollen, their larvae are busy chowing down on various soft-bodied insects, including aphids, thrips, leafhoppers, scales, caterpillars, and others. Each maggot can consume several hundred insects during its three larval instars (life stages between molts).

- **Minute pirate bugs.** Because of their tiny size (adults measure a mere 0.08 to 0.2 inches [2 to 5 mm] in length), gardeners seldom see minute pirate bugs, though they are among the most common predators in our yards and gardens. Despite their minuscule stature, minute pirate bugs are wicked predators, consuming 30 or more pests such as thrips, spider mites, insect eggs, aphids, small caterpillars, corn earworms, leafhopper nymphs, psyllids, scale crawlers, and whiteflies per day.

- **Damsel bugs.** This true predator has front legs that are raptorial (much like a miniature version of a preying mantid). The many victims of damsel bugs include insect eggs, aphids, small caterpillars, corn earworms, cabbageworms, corn borers, leafhoppers, larval sawflies, mites, plant bugs, asparagus beetles, and Colorado potato beetles.

Underplanting with flowers. A sneaky way to bump up your good bug populations is to partner your edible crops with flowers like sweet alyssum. "Underplanting the tomatoes with sweet alyssum lures the parasitoidal wasps that control aphids, tomato and tobacco hornworms, whiteflies, and other common tomato pests," observes Jessica.

In spring the herbs can be harvested moderately, but once summer arrives, reduce harvesting on some plants to allow them to bear flowers. "If allowed to bloom, they'll serve as nectar and pollen sources for pollinators and predatory insects," Jessica says. Any unharvested broccoli or uneaten mustard greens can also be allowed to flower to support the good bug populations. After flowering, the seed of any open-pollinated herbs, flowers, and vegetables can be collected for future crops.

Bath and perch. At the center of the garden, tucked among the herbs, a birdbath serves as both an architectural element and an attraction for bug-eating birds. If sticks or rocks are added to a section of the birdbath, visiting bees and butterflies can also perch and enjoy a quick drink on a hot day.

For ease of cultivation and maintenance, Jessica suggests making the walkways at least 2 to 3 feet wide. For a natural pathway, plant grass or white Dutch clover, a low-growing plant that will also nourish pollinating and beneficial insects.

Elizabethan Garden

If you traveled back through time to the age of Shakespeare, chances are rather good that your daily meals would include rampion, scorzonera, salsify, or skirret. At that time, these were common garden crops, yet, over the centuries, these vegetables have become all but forgotten. Stephen Westcott-Gratton reintroduces gardeners to these unusual edibles and their unique flavors that he so enjoys.

> Historical edibles such as rampion, skirret, and cardoon are delicious and easy to grow

> Several plants are very compact and fit nicely into tight spaces

> A birdbath entices local birds to dine on garden pests

Stephen Westcott-Gratton likes to explore the historical and often curious side of garden edibles. He began growing traditional vegetables, but when family and friends started giving him their seasonal glut, his interest "turned to more obscure offerings, primarily vegetables that had been mainstream in the past but are now all but forgotten," he says. "It started as curiosity, but blossomed into true love and a vastly extended palate."

According to Stephen, the five vegetables included in his garden were all cultivated in Elizabethan England, introduced by gardeners from the Continent — principally from France and Italy. "They are still grown there in greater numbers than they ever have been in North America," he says. "Cardoon is known as *cardoni* in Italy and is still a popular vegetable, and you can buy canned salsify everywhere in the Netherlands!"

Hidden potential. As to why these edibles fell out of favor, Stephen points to the fact that some, such as cardoon, are prickly and take up a lot of space.

Others, such as skirret, don't look all that inviting. "The thin, branched roots are wrinkled and don't look terrifically appetizing at first glance," says Stephen, adding that we shouldn't be so quick to judge, as they actually have firm, aromatically sweet flesh.

Like most edibles, Stephen's unique vegetables will grow best in a sunny location with rich, well-drained soil. He recommends including a path between garden beds that is wide enough to allow easy access for a wheelbarrow, and he suggests having a birdbath because birds keep undesirable insects at bay.

Garden beauties. These vegetables are worth growing even if you don't plan to harvest heavily from your plot, as they are also very ornamental in appearance. "All five vegetables also sport lovely flowers if you forget to harvest them," he laughs. For additional color, edge the garden with 'Gem' series Signet marigolds, whose flowers are edible. "Their citrusy flavor partners well with these neglected old vegetables," he says.

Stephen's Elizabethan Favorites

RAMPION

This unusual edible is deeply rooted in the fairy tale Rapunzel. When Rapunzel's mother was pregnant, she was overtaken by a craving for the lush rampion (*Campanula rapunculus*) plants growing so enticingly in the witch's garden next door. The witch caught her picking the plant and, as punishment, demanded her first-born baby, so Rapunzel was handed over after her birth.

In the kitchen. Rampion was, and still is, prized for its sweet, turnip-like roots that can be eaten raw when young, or boiled until tender when mature. Stephen advocates blanching the shoots and eating them like asparagus. The leaves can also be enjoyed as a salad green from spring through autumn, or cooked like spinach. If allowed to flower, the small blue blooms are rather graceful.

In the garden. As rampion is a biennial, the root will be diminished in size if plants are allowed to bloom. Sow seed directly in the garden in mid-spring, eventually thinning to 12 inches on center.

SALSIFY

Commonly called vegetable oyster, salsify (*Tragopogon porrifolius*) is an ancient root vegetable that was foraged by the Greeks and Romans. Eventually it became a cultivated crop grown for its bumpy, beige parsniplike roots.

In the kitchen. The roots should be eaten soon after harvest, as quality and flavor fade quickly. "Salsify can be baked, made into a delicious cream soup, or steamed and served with a mustard-cheese sauce," Stephen advises.

In the garden. The foliage is very grassy, so it can easily be mistaken for a weed when young. If allowed to overwinter, this biennial plant produces pretty purple flowers in the second summer, eventually producing seeds. "Songbirds go crazy for the seed heads of salsify!" says Stephen. The roots will grow about 8 to 10 inches long and 1 inch in diameter. Like most roots crops, it is best grown directly from seed that is planted in early spring. Thin to 12 inches on center once the seedlings are growing well.

SCORZONERA

Because of their similar growth habits, scorzonera (*Scorzonera hispanica*) is often grown alongside salsify. It too is a root crop with grassy foliage, but its long, slender roots have dark brownish charcoal skin. If allowed to flower in its second year, scorzonera will produce bright yellow blossoms.

In the kitchen. The roots have a stronger oyster taste than salsify. "Cooked scorzonera is fantastic with salt, pepper, and butter," says Stephen, who recommends leaving the black skin on the roots. "Or serve it cool with a hearty vinaigrette dressing."

In the garden. For a late-season harvest, the plants can be mulched with shredded leaves or straw and the 8- to 12-inch-long roots dug into winter. Direct-seed in early spring, thinning to 12 inches on center.

SKIRRET

Like scorzonera and salsify, skirret (*Sium sisarum*) is an ancient root vegetable beloved in ancient Rome and throughout Europe (although it's thought to hail from China). But unlike those vegetables, the roots of skirret are not single taproots but clusters that resemble chubby gray fingers. The perennial plants are a member of the carrot family.

In the kitchen. The flavor is sweet; the name "skirret" originates from the Dutch *zuikerwortel,* which means "sugar root." "I like it grated raw in salads, and it's fantastic when baked (like parsnips) or creamed," says Stephen. "The blanched roots are especially good when battered and deep fried, then served with a warm, sweet, and fruity relish."

In the garden. Skirret can be grown from seed or by replanting the root offsets after the plants are dug for harvest. Set the plants on 24-inch centers to allow the 3- to 4-foot-tall plants enough room to produce their fleshy roots.

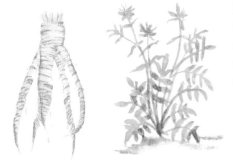

CARDOON

A member of the aster family, cardoon (*Cynara cardunculus*) is closely related to artichokes. North of Zone 7, cardoon is an annual and won't overwinter reliably. In dry climates, it can become invasive if allowed to produce seed, so grow it with caution in hot, dry regions. Even if you don't intend to eat your cardoon, the plants are extremely decorative, forming a silvery green rosette of sharply toothed leaves that grows 3 to 4 feet tall and 2 feet wide.

In the kitchen. Cardoon is grown for its stalks, which are usually blanched. Once harvested, the central midrib (or leaf stalk) is peeled and often steamed or baked. "The blanched stalks taste like a cross between celery and artichokes," he says. "They can be braised in sauce, breaded and deep-fried, and added to soups or potato salad."

In the garden. In cold climates, start seed indoors, transplanting the seedlings to the garden six to eight weeks later on 3- to 4-foot centers. It's a water pig, so irrigate often and deeply if there has been no rain. "Three or four weeks before the first frosts are expected, the leaves should be bunched together with string and covered with a breathable material to exclude light," says Stephen, adding that he cuts up large paper bags for this.

COOKING WITH CARDOON

Stephen says the best way to eat cardoon is to go Italian and make *bagna cauda* (hot anchcovy sauce). It's sort of an Italian fondue from the Piedmont region, but diners dunk vegetables instead of bread, and cardoon is traditional for this. Blanch stems in boiling water (2 minutes), then bread and fry. Serve hot with melted cheese and hot anchovy sauce (or tuna for the faint of heart). There are many variations — all delicious — of *bagna cauda.*

An Easy Way to Expand Your Existing Garden

OVER THE YEARS, AS HELEN YOEST EXPANDED HER GARDEN BEDS to reduce the amount of lawn she needed to tend, she often struggled over what to plant in the new areas. Helen, an award-winning freelance garden writer and stylist, wanted something besides the common ground covers. She knew that most edges are filled with low-growing plants, so when deciding on plant choices for the extended garden, she realized that she could make an edible edge out of strawberries. Helen says that with their vibrant green leaves, pretty white blooms, and sweet fruits, strawberries make a wonderful low-maintenance ground cover. Plus, strawberry plants are often sold in bundles of 25, making them cost-effective for covering a large area.

The best time to plant a strawberry ground cover is in the spring, when there is ample moisture to establish the plants. Strawberries will grow best in a site that offers at least 8 hours of full sun each day and has soil that is slightly acidic (with a pH between 5.5 and 6.8). Before planting, loosen the earth and amend with compost or aged manure. Because strawberry plants will rot if planted too deeply, Helen says to set the crown of each plant (where the leaves emerge) at soil level. She recommends a spacing of 18 inches to leave room for the daughter plants. "If initially it seems like you are looking at a lot of ground, don't despair," she advises. "After bearing fruit, strawberries produce runners, giving you even more plants!" Within a few weeks, the area will be filled in.

A hardy perennial in most areas, the plants will die back in winter and appear again in spring when the soil warms up. After a few years, production may decrease, and any declining plants can be popped out and replaced with fresh ones.

Helen recommends using three different strawberry cultivars, preferably a mixture of June-bearing and everbearing types, for the longest possible harvest season. June-bearing strawberries "bear fruit all at once — typically over a three-week period," she says. Everbearing strawberries, on the other hand, "produce a big crop from spring flowers, but also set fruit throughout the summer, although lightly," Helen explains. "Come fall, they bloom and bear again well into the late summer and fall." In her garden, she planted the June-bearing varieties 'Tennessee Beauty' and 'Cardinal'. Her remaining plants are the everbearing strawberries 'Sequoia', 'Ozark Beauty', and 'Quinault'.

Forager's Garden

A forager's garden may seem rather contradictory, since foraging involves hunting for wild food plants, but Ellen Zachos points out that many forage-able plants also make excellent, low-maintenance garden plants. Her kidney-shaped bed combines native selections with nonnatives to make foraging at home a snap!

> Provides fruits, tubers, berries, and buds to forage on

> Uses low-maintenance and drought-tolerant plants

> The large, kidney-shaped bed is intensively planted and has a pergola for vigorous groundnuts

Foraging for wild edibles is becoming a popular pursuit for many who appreciate the range of edible plants found in the natural world. Those who don't have the opportunity to forage in the wild, or who don't live near desirable plant populations, can grow many of those delicious and unusual edibles in their gardens. Although not all of the plants included in Ellen's design are native to North America, all have edible parts and make excellent garden plants. When foraging in the wild or selecting wild plants for your edible garden, there are two important considerations. First, if you're not sure what plants or plant parts are edible, always refer to a comprehensive field guide or talk to an expert before you taste. Second, always obtain the permission of the landowner before you begin collecting.

Unique and delicious flavors. Ellen's plan for a forager's garden is based on the planting in her backyard, where she grows a range of wild plants, as well as cultivated varieties of wild plants, in a kidney-shaped garden. Her bed measures approximately 16 by 16 feet and is densely planted with trees, shrubs, and perennials grown for their fruits, flowers or buds, tubers, leaves, and stolons. "These are plants that I've enjoyed foraging for in the wild," she notes. "They have unique tastes that are unlike anything you've ever tried before, and if they weren't delicious, I wouldn't grow them."

Because half of Ellen's garden is shaded by a neighbor's large oak tree, she has tucked shade-tolerant plants at the back of the bed, leaving the sun lovers near the front. If shade isn't an issue, this plan will also work in a full-sun location.

Protein-packed groundnut. The serviceberry trees at the back of the garden create a living privacy screen, blocking out undesirable views, while a sturdy wooden pergola at the front of the garden adds vertical interest and support for the vigorous growth of the groundnut, which can grow up to 20 feet long. This native legume was a staple in the diet of Native Americans, who enjoyed the tubers. Like potatoes, groundnut tubers are high in starch, but they're also incredibly rich in protein, containing about three times as much protein as a regular potato.

While Ellen enjoys foraging for wild edibles, she doesn't advocate digging up entire plants to bring them back to your kitchen or garden. All of the plants included in her plan are available at nurseries or through mail order. When foraging in the wild for edibles, Ellen offers some advice on harvesting. "A general rule among foragers," she says, "is to take no more than a third of the crop, to leave some for wildlife and other foragers, and to allow the species to continue to propagate."

Low-maintenance plants. Growing perennial native or cultivated varieties of native plants is also a simple way to enjoy homegrown food with little work and ongoing maintenance. Ellen considers herself a "lazy, lazy gardener," and she appreciates the drought tolerance and low grooming demands of these plants (no daily deadheading). Her native plant selections come together to form an attractive, low-maintenance, and productive garden that will support the local populations of bees, butterflies, and birds who rely on pollen and nectar from native plants for food.

1. **Spicebush** (*Lindera benzoin*). Grown for its berries. Include 1 male and 1 female plant. "It's hard to describe the taste of the berries in terms of other tastes; I find it somewhat peppery but also like it in desserts," says Ellen. "Some people compare it to allspice, and it blends well with the wild ginger stolons in pies and rubs (for meat)."

2. **Cornelian cherry.** Grown for its fruit, this is not a true cherry but a relative of flowering dogwood. Only one is needed to produce fruit. Many varieties are "too tart for most people to enjoy plain," but "this fruit has tons of pectin and makes an easy jelly," notes Ellen.

3. **'Tiger Eyes' cutleaf staghorn sumac.** Grown for its berries, 'Tiger Eyes' is a better-behaved member of the sumac family, a species well known for vigorous suckering. If you're worried about this small shrub becoming invasive, plant it in a container. Use the berries to make sumac lemonade or sumac-elderberry jelly.

4. **Rugosa roses.** Grown for their hips. "Rose hip soup!" laughs Ellen. Three plants are included here to make a nice clump.

5. **Orange daylilies.** Grown for their unopened buds and tubers. "Sauté the buds in olive oil and garlic — they're better than green beans!" Ellen says. "The tubers can be roasted like potatoes." Ellen also says that the young shoots and mature flower petals are edible, but she finds them less remarkable.

6. **Bee balm.** Grown for its flowers and leaves. Ellen notes that red-flowering cultivars lend eye-catching color to homemade vinegars and that the flowers and leaves of bee balm make excellent substitutes for oregano.

7. **Sedums** (a low-growing type such as *Sedum cauticola* [*Hylotephium cauticola*], *S. rupestre*, or *S. sieboldii*). Grown for their leaves. "Add a few leaves to your salad for a succulent crunch," Ellen suggests.

8. **Groundnuts** (*Apios americana*). Grown for their tubers. Two of these plants are trained to trail over the pergola. "The taste is like a dry, nutty potato, and they can be roasted, boiled, or pan-fried," says Ellen.

9. **Flowering (Japanese) quince.** Grown for its fruit. "The fruits are too hard and tart to eat plain, but they make an excellent jelly (lots of pectin)," she says. "I also love them for membrillo (a quince paste) and poached in red wine."

10. **Elderberries.** Grown for their flowers and fruit. In the garden, Ellen prefers a black foliage cultivar, such as 'Black Lace', for its ornamental and edible qualities, using it to make elderflower "champagne" as well as elderberry jelly and wine. She notes that the black foliage cultivars are slightly less productive than their green-leafed counterparts.

11. **Jerusalem artichokes.** Grown for their tubers. "I like them best very thinly sliced raw in salads, but they're also tasty baked, boiled, and pureed," she says.

12. **Serviceberries, shadbush.** Grown for their berries. Ellen emphasizes that the berries should only be picked when fully ripe and dark purple in color. "If you harvest red or reddish blue fruit, you'll be disappointed, since the fruit won't be fully sweet," she says.

13. **Mayapples.** Grown for their fruit. "All parts of the mayapple are poisonous except for the ripe fruit, which are yellow and slightly soft to the touch," says Ellen. "You may read that unripe fruit can be harvested and allowed to ripen on the windowsill, but I don't recommend it, as the superb, tropical flavor doesn't fully develop this way." She adds that if you must pick the fruit before they are fully ripe, make sure they are showing at least some sign of yellow because completely green fruit will never ripen to be delicious.

14. **Canada wild ginger.** Grown for its underground stolons. "I dig up several clumps in the fall, snip the stolons that connect the clumps, then replant the clumps," says Ellen. "No harm done to the plants, and the stolons are an unusual and versatile spice." Use them fresh or dried with apples, pears, and pork.

Ellen's Garden Plan

16' DEEP X 16' WIDE

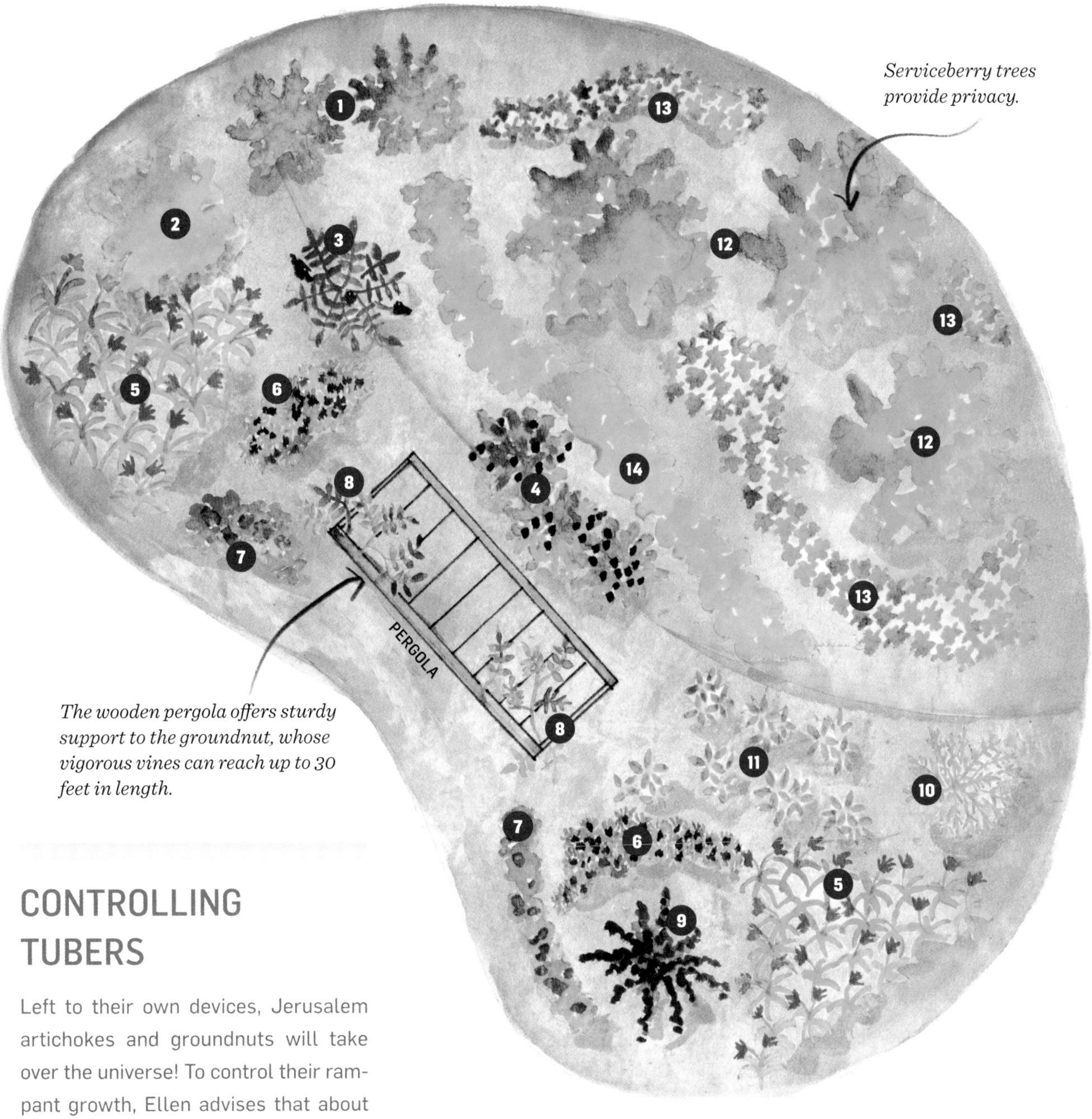

Serviceberry trees provide privacy.

PERGOLA

The wooden pergola offers sturdy support to the groundnut, whose vigorous vines can reach up to 30 feet in length.

CONTROLLING TUBERS

Left to their own devices, Jerusalem artichokes and groundnuts will take over the universe! To control their rampant growth, Ellen advises that about half to one-third of the tubers should be dug up each year in autumn and stored for eating. The rest can be left in the ground for future crops.

Water-Wise Herbs & More

A California native who lives in arid San Diego, Nan Sterman has grown up gardening with little water. Her stylish design boasts three levels that lead to a slab stone bench tucked beneath an espaliered fig. To grow food where there is little water, Nan relies on drought-tolerant edible plants — figs, artichokes, and herbs — combined with an efficient drip irrigation system.

> Showcases the variety of water-wise ornamental and edible plants available to hot climate gardeners

> Uses targeted and efficient irrigation methods

> Potted bay trees underplanted with oregano provide a stately entrance

Each year, rains fall in San Diego from November through March. Then it's hot and dry until the following autumn. To avoid wasting water, Nan concentrates on plants that are adapted to her dry climate, rather than growing plants native to wetter regions that would require regular and frequent irrigation. "My philosophy is that if we are going to spend water, let's spend it on something that feeds us, but we should still use as little water as possible," she says.

Nan has designed a beautiful, productive garden in which to grow low-water-use edibles managed with water-wise techniques like mulching and smart irrigation. The plot measures approximately 24 feet long by 20 feet wide and gently slopes uphill. She divided the garden into three terraced levels, with the entry at the lowest point. "Each level is a single step above the lower one, and the central path terminates at a slab stone bench beneath an espaliered fig," explains Nan. The terraces add visual interest to the garden, but they don't affect the water-wise aspect. Nan recommends using a light-colored, stabilized decomposed granite for the pathway and upper landing. Install aluminum edging to keep the material in place and out of the beds. (Sure-loc makes a good aluminum edging.) "Set it flush to the surface of the walkway so that it is basically invisible," she advises.

Water-wise pots. Two large, blood red ceramic pots (22 inches wide and 27 inches tall) surrounded by white-flowering yarrow flank the entrance to the garden, with each containing a multi-trunk bay laurel. Nan suggests choosing bay trees that are about 3½ feet tall. They're underplanted with dittany of Crete, an ornamental variety of oregano with fuzzy, silvery leaves and large pinkish flower bracts. She notes that the oregano cascades beautifully over the sides of pots. Pots are topped with ⅜-inch rounded gravel. To keep the plants watered, each pot contains a cylinder of DriWater, which holds a water-retaining gel composed of common food-grade ingredients. The DriWater helps keep the plants moist over a period of time without additional watering, and the cylinders only need to be replaced approximately every three months or so, depending on the season and weather.

Mediterranean diet. There isn't a wide selection of water-wise edibles, which Nan says often surprises people. She points out that most water-wise edibles originate from Mediterranean climates, where rainfall is extremely limited. This multitiered garden includes figs and grapes, as well as artichokes. Oregano, lemongrass, thyme, rosemary, and peppermint geraniums provide seasonings and fragrance. In the oregano beds, flagstone stepping stones lead to the grapevines, allowing easy access for maintenance and harvesting. Each plant was carefully selected by Nan for its drought tolerance, and once established, needs very little water. "Yarrow, for example is native across the Northern Hemisphere, including California — where it is extremely drought tolerant," she says. "Only the lemongrass is on the thirsty side, but I find it gets along just fine with far less water than its Asian heritage would suggest."

Smart irrigation technology. Because water-wise gardening involves more than just picking the most drought-tolerant plants, Nan also relies on smart infrastructure. "Irrigation technology and irrigation management are just as important as a good layer of mulch," she remarks. "Drip irrigation puts water into the soil where the roots live, and as each drop is released, it is absorbed directly into the ground," Nan explains, noting that the efficiency rate is 90 percent or higher. She prefers drip irrigation

to overhead spray systems, which spray water into the air, wasting 50 percent to evaporation or misdirection. In-line drip, also called dripperline, is hands-down the most efficient of irrigation technologies" Dripperline is $1/4$- or $1/2$-inch-diameter polyethylene tubes with water emitters embedded *inside* the tubes; when the emitter releases water, it drips out the holes.

Once the irrigation lines are in place, the planting beds are topped with a 3-inch layer of mulch over the dripperline, further reducing water loss. "The need to irrigate [above and beyond the water delivered by the drip system] goes down to almost zero," she says. "This garden needs little to no fertilizer, and only the grapes and fig require pruning."

Nan's Dry-Climate Plants

VEGGIES AND FRUITS

'Panache fig. The espaliered fig forms the back "wall" of Nan's garden. She advises pruning it to a broad espalier about 6 feet wide and 18 inches deep (front to back), training it into a wide and multi-trunked tree. This variety produces figs with green and yellow stripes. "The flesh is strawberry red and very sweet," adds Nan. (Zones 6 to 11)

Grape. The grapevines will form the side "walls" of the garden and are trained on two horizontal cordons.

Nan advises checking with your local Cooperative Extension Service for variety suggestions because grapes are highly region-specific. She adds that there are four types of grapes (wine, juice, fresh-eating, and raisin) to choose from, and many colors of fruits (red, gold, green, white, and purple) within those groups.

'Violetta' artichoke. In Nan's region, artichokes are a perennial plant, but in colder regions, they are grown as annuals. " 'Violetta' is an Italian heirloom variety with purple blush buds," she says. "The buds are harvested starting when they are ping-pong-size all the way up to softball-size." (Zones 7 to 11)

HERBS

Bay. Planted in tall ceramic pots at the garden entrance, bay adds a note of formality to this garden plan. It is an evergreen Mediterranean tree with a slightly conical shape and aromatic glossy green leaves. It adds flavor to pasta sauces, soups, and other dishes. (Zones 8 to 11)

Dittany of Crete oregano. This tender perennial is tucked at the feet of the bay laurel trees so it will spill over the edges of the large pots. The silvery green, velvety leaves invite touch as one enters the garden, while attractive pink flower bracts attract beneficial and pollinating insects. (Zones 7 to 11)

Dwarf or 'Dwarf Greek' oregano. These low-growing oreganos quickly form a carpet of deep green foliage, brightened by white or purple flowers. 'Dwarf Greek' has a more pronounced flavor, if you're looking to use this in cooking. Nan advises starting with plants in 4-inch pots. (Zones 5 to 11)

'Tuscan Blue' rosemary. Rosemary is beloved for its extremely aromatic needlelike foliage and flowers, typically soft or deep blue, but sometimes white or pink. "To form the front and rear 'walls' of the garden, lightly prune the rosemary to 3 or 4 feet tall by 4 feet wide," says Nan. Generously sprinkle homegrown rosemary over roasted potatoes or homemade focaccia. (Zones 8 to 11)

Lemongrass. Easy to grow, lemongrass forms attractive grassy clumps with pale green leaves that smell of fresh lemons. Use the white stalks in Asian dishes, and steep the green parts in boiled water for tea. (Zones 8 to 11)

Common (English) thyme. Nan designed water-wise thyme under and around the stone bench so it can release its fragrance when stepped on. Thyme also edges the top tier of the garden, tumbling over the stone wall. The spreading plants grow to be about 1 foot tall and produce tiny pink flowers. (Zones 5 to 11)

ORNAMENTALS

Peppermint-scented geranium. There are so many reasons to love this plant: it has soft fuzzy leaves, a minty aroma, and delicate white and pink flowers, plus it's easy to maintain. Peppermint geranium grows to be 2 feet tall and 4 feet wide at maturity. Nan used it at the base of the rosemary and fig, so people sitting on the bench brush against the leaves and release the delightful aroma. (Zones 10 to 11)

'Otto Quast' Spanish lavender. Planted as a low hedge at the base of the grape vines, 'Otto Quast' Spanish lavender is a low-maintenance perennial with showy deep purple flower spikes that attract pollinators and butterflies. (Zones 7 to 9)

Yarrow. A hardy perennial that tolerates drought, yarrow has ferny foliage and flat-topped flowers that are extremely effective at attracting beneficial insects. Nan chose a white-flowering variety to ring the base of each potted bay tree. (Zones 3 to 11)

IRRIGATION DETAILS

Nan has divided her garden into two water zones based on her plants' needs (see diagram on next page). Zone H1 has subsurface drips (placed 4 to 6 inches below the surface), and zone H2 has on-surface drips. Both are covered in mulch, and she recommends using an inline dripper line (such as Techline CV available from Netafim), with drippers spaced every 12 inches. The lines are best set 12 inches apart in parallel lines.

Select a drip rate appropriate to your soil type. For plants in heavy clay soil, choose a slower drip rate such as 0.26 gallons per hour (GPH). Plants in well-draining sandy soils do better with a drip rate of 0.6 GPH, while plants in loamy soils that hold water, yet drain well, do best with a drip rate of 0.4 GPH. For plants in the coarsest soils, try a drip line that delivers water at 0.9 GPH.

Nan's Garden Plan

24' DEEP X 20' WIDE

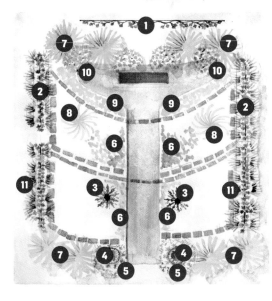

1. 'Panache' fig
2. Grape
3. 'Violetta' artichoke
4. Bay and dittany of Crete oregano
5. Yarrow
6. Dwarf or 'Dwarf Greek' oregano
7. 'Tuscan Blue' rosemary
8. Lemongrass
9. Common (English) thyme
10. Peppermint-scented geranium
11. 'Otto Quast' Spanish lavender

NAN'S IRRIGATION ZONES

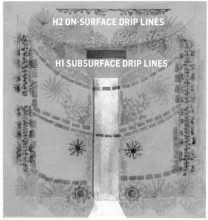

H2 ON-SURFACE DRIP LINES

H1 SUBSURFACE DRIP LINES

Beat the Grocery Bill

Choosing to grow high-cost, quick-spoiling foods like raspberries, tomatoes, or gourmet salad greens is a smart way to save some money on your weekly food bill. In his "Beat the Grocery Bill" garden, Mark Cullen has laid out an attractive plot that will supply a steady harvest of high-value organic fruits and vegetables from spring through autumn.

> Concentrates on high-value organic fruits, berries, vegetables, and herbs

> Plants are low-maintenance and will produce for three seasons

> Narrow beds are easy to care for and contain space-saving vertical structures

"Soil preparation is the #1 key to success — invest in good soil!" says Mark Cullen.

Mark's plan is based on his own garden, which feeds his family of six and produces a surplus that he donates to a food bank. His garden will supply a nonstop parade of organic food from late spring through late autumn, which will help reduce your weekly grocery bill.

The plan requires a sunny, preferably flat space that is just 22 by 27 feet. "If possible, plant vegetables in a south-facing location," advises Mark. "If that isn't possible, choose a southeastern or southwestern exposure, because most vegetables and herbs require no fewer than 6 hours of sunlight each day."

Well-planned beds. Three long beds for vegetable and cut-flower production run in a north-south direction to capture maximum sunlight. The two vegetable beds each measure 2 by 18 feet and are separated by 2-foot pathways. Several crops (peas, cucumbers, and tomatoes) are grown vertically on supports to maximize production in a small space. Mark favors metal spirals to support his tomato plants, such as his favorite heirloom variety 'Mountain

Princess'. "Lattice frames for the cucumbers allow the plants to grow up the frame, and the fruits can hang through holes," says Mark. "It's easy picking and keeps the cucumbers off the ground, which reduces rotting."

The Swiss chard, mesclun salad greens mix, and carrots can be sown in early spring and replanted once the initial crop begins to decline. Swiss chard is one of Mark's favorite edibles for its high production, ornamental appearance, and outstanding taste. To get a jump on his spring crop, he sows seed in one of his cold frames in late winter, moving the young plants to the garden in May.

Flower border. The nearby 1- by 18-foot flower bed will yield plenty of pretty blooms for the vase, and it will also entice pollinating and beneficial insects to the garden. Mark suggests planting a mixture of annual flowers such as zinnias, cosmos, cleome, dwarf sunflowers, sweet alyssum, and calendulas in a single row along the length of the narrow bed.

Apples inspired by Monet. Organic apples are expensive to buy at the supermarket. To offset this

Mark's Garden Plan

27' DEEP X 22' WIDE

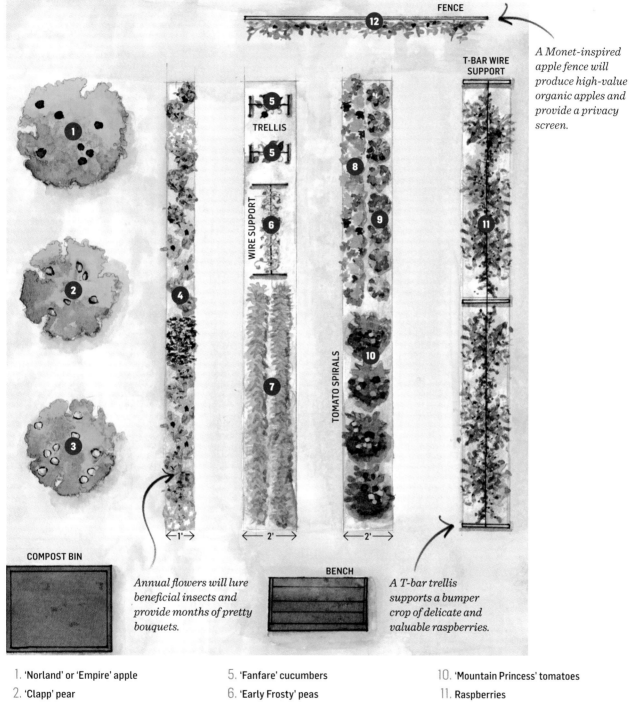

FENCE

A Monet-inspired apple fence will produce high-value organic apples and provide a privacy screen.

T-BAR WIRE SUPPORT

TRELLIS

WIRE SUPPORT

TOMATO SPIRALS

←1'→   ← 2' →   ← 2' →

COMPOST BIN

Annual flowers will lure beneficial insects and provide months of pretty bouquets.

BENCH

A T-bar trellis supports a bumper crop of delicate and valuable raspberries.

1. 'Norland' or 'Empire' apple
2. 'Clapp' pear
3. 'Luscious' pear
4. **Annual flowers:** zinnias, cosmos, cleome, dwarf sunflowers, sweet alyssum, and calendulas

5. 'Fanfare' cucumbers
6. 'Early Frosty' peas
7. 'Scarlet Nantes' carrots
8. Lettuce and/or mesclun mix
9. 'Bright Lights' Swiss chard

10. 'Mountain Princess' tomatoes
11. Raspberries
12. 'Honeycrisp' apple (espaliered)

cost, Mark has included an espaliered apple fence along the north side of the garden to supply an annual harvest of crisp, homegrown fruit. Mark first glimpsed an espalier apple fence at Monet's Garden in Giverny, France. "Monet was a pioneer in this growing technique and in the 1920s planted his living apple fence," writes Mark in his blog.

In Mark's plan, the apple espalier, which is comprised of two trees, also creates a screen that can be located strategically to block neighbors, nearby traffic, or an unsightly view.

To ensure good pollination and fruit set, Mark has added another apple tree on the west side of the garden. This specimen should be a different variety than the apple fence, but to be a good pollinating partner it needs to bloom at the same time. Two pear trees, which should also be two different varieties for cross-pollination purposes, have been placed near the apple tree.

Raspberries trained to a trellis. The 18-foot-long raspberry patch, which runs along the eastern side of the garden, will save you from having

to buy this high-value crop at the market. To keep the rampant plants under control and prevent them from flopping on the ground, Mark recommends using a wire support system. In his standard T-bar trellis, there are three 5-foot-tall wooden stakes with 3-foot wooden crossbars spaced 9 feet apart. Wire is then fastened to the ends of the crossbars and runs the entire length of the raspberry patch to support the rambling plants. Choose a mix of summer- and fall-bearing cultivars for the longest season of harvest.

FEEDING MORE THAN BELLIES

Food is beautiful. Am I the only one who thinks that a garden filled with edible bounty is a thing of pure beauty? It is not that I love to cook: I don't. I love what a food garden represents. Sustenance for a hungry world, the miracle of nutrition from the most powerful combination on earth: seed, soil and water. These are the things that make my back ache in the nicest possible way each planting season. And then again during harvest. — Mark Cullen

Fall & Winter Vegetables

People think I'm crazy when I tell them that we have a winter vegetable garden. "But you live in Canada," they say. True, it does get rather cold here in the winter, but that doesn't mean I can't still enjoy a cold-season harvest of vegetables such as leeks, kale, carrots, beets, parsley, and cold-tolerant salad greens. The key is to grow the right plants, to sow them at the right time, and to protect them with the right season extenders.

> ❯ Extends the harvest season to year-round production
>
> ❯ Focuses on cool- and cold-season veggies and herbs
>
> ❯ Blueberry shrubs anchor the corners of the garden and provide sweet summer fruits

There are many benefits to a winter vegetable garden. First and foremost, it's extremely low maintenance, requiring little work (aside from harvesting!) from November through March. During these dark and cold months, I don't need to water or vent the structures, tasks which can be put aside until the return of spring. And it allows us to harvest homegrown organic food 365 days a year. As well, many of our winter vegetables have a superior flavor to their summer-grown counterparts. Carrots, kale, beets, and parsnips, for example, boast higher sugar content in winter, resulting in a sweeter flavor. Plus common garden pests like rabbits and deer can't reach our winter-covered crops, and there are no more spring and summer slugs or snails to foil my tender salad greens.

In my plan for a 20- by 30-foot fall and winter vegetable garden, I've arranged the space as permanent beds (raised or at soil level). A 3-foot-wide bed runs around the perimeter of the garden, with space left at one end for an entrance topped by a grape-smothered arbor. In the middle of the garden, the four 3- by 8-foot beds can be quickly covered with mini hoop tunnels for extending the harvest. On the north end of the plan, two 3- by 6-foot south-facing cold frames shelter a range of cold-season vegetables. And in each of the four corners of the garden there is a highbush blueberry plant that will bear sweet summer fruit.

Top cold-season crops. I've picked my favorite cold-season cast of characters, — celeriac, leeks, spinach, carrots, and kale — as well as numerous leafy greens for a non-stop supply of gourmet salads. Many of these crops (kale, leeks, celeriac, parsnips, and carrots) are planted in early summer to midsummer. Others are seeded from late summer through early autumn, for example, Asian greens and salad greens such as endive, spinach, and lettuce.

To figure out the planting date for your chosen fall and winter crops, you need two pieces of information: 1) your estimated first hard frost date (October 20 in my region; check with your local Cooperative Extension Service or a member of your local garden club), and 2) the days to maturity for your selected vegetable (check your seed packet or seed catalog). Here's how to put that information to use: 'Marathon' broccoli takes approximately 68 days to mature from transplanting, or 90 days if direct-seeded, but because short autumn days slow down growth, I tack on an extra week or two to ensure maturity. So let's say transplanted 'Marathon' broccoli will take 80 days to mature (direct-seeded 100 days). To get my transplanting date I count 80 days back from October 20, to August 1, while for direct seeding, I count 100 days back from October 20, to July 12. Therefore, to have a good fall and winter crop I have to transplant my seedlings in mid-summer.

A parade of techniques. I have included a range of season extenders, from a basic layer of mulch (shredded leaves or straw) to cold frames to mini hoop tunnels. These simple techniques and devices will allow you to harvest during winter and to overwinter crops for an extra-early spring harvest. A 1-foot-deep layer of shredded leaves or straw is the easiest way to stretch the harvest season of crops like leeks, or root vegetables like carrots, beets, parsnips, daikon radishes, and celeriac.

Finding beds in snow. We top our mulch with an old row cover or bedsheet secured well with rocks or weights to ensure it doesn't blow away in winter winds. I also place a color-coded bamboo post next to each bed (orange for carrots, and so on) so I know where to find my vegetables when the garden is covered in snow. (It took me years to figure that out!)

If limited to only one season extender, I would choose a cold frame. Cold frames are bottomless boxes with clear tops that form a microclimate around your vegetables, blocking inclement weather and cold winds and capturing solar energy. Our cold frames are made from local 2-inch-thick untreated hemlock boards and topped with Lexan, a twinwall polycarbonate that won't break and does a better job of insulating than a single layer of glass. Temporary cold frames can be made from straw bales arranged to form the sides of the box and covered with an old door or window.

Experiment! I recommend planting a wide assortment of cool- and cold-season vegetables and herbs in the cold frames. Don't be afraid to try new-to-you vegetables. Who knows, you may find some new family favorites!

MINI HOOP TUNNELS

The mini hoop tunnels in the middle beds can be constructed in mere minutes from ½-inch-diameter PVC pipe. Just bend each length over the bed, slipping the ends over 1-foot-long rebar stakes pounded into the ground, and space the hoops 3 to 4 feet apart. In the spring and fall garden, I don't bother with a center support. But for winter snow shedding, I add an 8-foot length of 1 × 2 wood along the top of the mini hoop tunnel, securing the wood to each hoop with a screw. Mini hoop tunnels are great for sheltering tall crops such as kale, collard greens, and leeks, although I also use them to overwinter fall-planted spinach, endive, and Asian greens for a super-early March and April harvest.

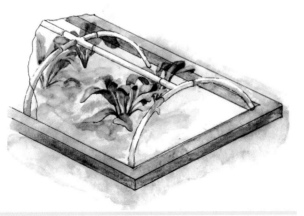

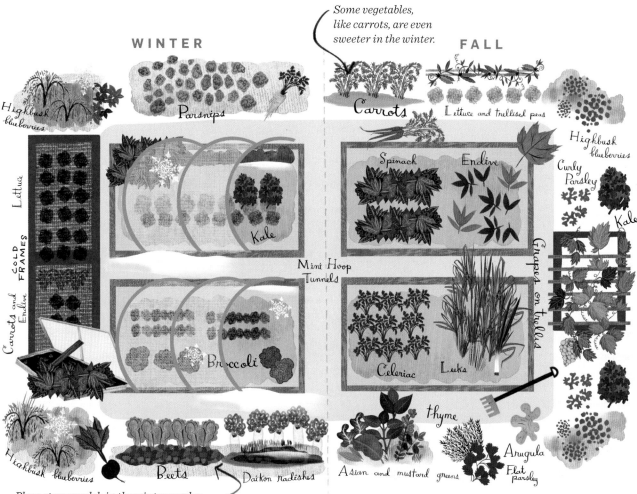

Some vegetables, like carrots, are even sweeter in the winter.

WINTER

FALL

Highbush blueberries

Parsnips

Carrots

Lettuce and trellised peas

Highbush blueberries

Lettuce

Curly Parsley

Kale

COLD FRAMES

Spinach

Endive

Kale

Carrots and Endive

Mini Hoop Tunnels

Grapes on trellis

Broccoli

Celeriac

Leeks

thyme

Highbush blueberries

Beets

Daikon radishes

Asian and mustard greens

Arugula

Flat parsley

Place straw mulch in the winter garden.

Niki's Favorite Cold-Season Varieties

FRUITS

- **Blueberries:** 'Bluecrop', 'Bluegold', and 'Patriot' highbush
- **Grapes:** 'L'Acadie Blanc' and 'Frontenac' (wine) and 'Swenson Red' (eating)

GREENS

- **Arugula:** 'Astro', 'Sylvetta', and 'Wasabi'
- **Mustard greens:** 'Red Giant', 'Purple Osaka', and 'Green Wave'
- **Asian greens:** Mizuna and mibuna

- **Lettuce:** 'Tom Thumb', 'Red Salad Bowl', 'Winter Density', 'Winter Marvel', and 'Rouge d'Hiver'
- **Kale:** 'Winterbor', 'Redbor', 'Red Russian', 'Lacinato', and 'Rainbow Lacinato'
- **Spinach:** 'Tyee', 'Winter Bloomsdale', and 'Winter Giant' (to be overwintered)
- **Endive:** 'Bianca Riccia' and 'Green Curled Ruffec' (to be overwintered)

ROOT & OTHER VEGGIES

- **Daikon radishes:** 'Miyashige' and 'April Cross'
- **Beets:** 'Lutz Green Leaf' ('Lutz Winter Keeper'), 'Detroit Dark Red', and 'Bull's Blood' (for salad greens, rather than roots)
- **Carrots:** 'Napoli' and 'Yaya'
- **Parsnips:** 'Hollow Crown'
- **Leeks:** 'Tadorna' and 'Bandit'
- **Celeriac:** 'Diamant'
- **Broccoli:** 'Marathon' and 'Arcadia'

52 Weeks of Salad

A garden doesn't have to be large to be productive, as demonstrated by Michelle Chapman's modest 4- by 8-foot plot that provides a steady supply of leafy crops for every week of the year. Michelle matches her crops to the season, opting for heat-tolerant salad ingredients in summer and cold-resistant ones in winter. Even on those days when driving rain or plunging temperatures keep you indoors, your salad bowl shouldn't be empty. Michelle's solution? Microgreens or sprouts!

> ❯ Takes up little room but offers year-round production

> ❯ The best crops are selected for each season

> ❯ A large container to the side of the garden grows more salad fixin's

In late 2011, award-winning garden blogger Michelle Chapman turned her attention to a new project: The 52-Week Salad Challenge. She and many other bloggers and gardeners from around the world decided to try to encourage more people to grow some of their own food. As the year progressed, they regularly shared their successes and failures on their blogs. "The main idea was that we all would grow and/or forage some salad leaves to eat every week that year," she says. The types of greens that were cultivated varied by gardener, since crop selection depends on location, taste preference, skill level, and available garden space.

Never go greens-less. To celebrate the spirit of the 52-week challenge, Michelle has created a salad plot that measures just 4 by 8 feet but yields a continuous parade of favorite salad crops, supplemented by Michelle's foraging suggestions and a few potted salad essentials like cherry tomatoes, herbs, and edible flowers.

Winter tunnel. For winter protection, a simple mini hoop tunnel or tunnel cloche can be erected over the bed in late autumn, before the hard frosts. Use ½-inch PVC pipe for the hoops and cover with a clear polycarbonate material, securing well with clips or weighting down with rocks, logs, or bags of soil. To harvest in winter, simply lift the plastic cover and take what you need.

Michelle's Garden Plan

4' DEEP X 8' WIDE

SPRING BED

'Red Russian' and other kale varieties will winter over, producing tender spring foliage.

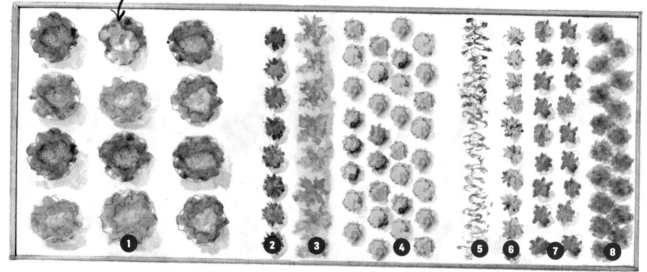

1. **Kale**. When the plants bolt in late spring, the broccoli-like flower buds can be gathered and eaten raw or lightly cooked. If the buds are allowed to open, the cheerful yellow blooms can be tossed in salads. Michelle suggests sowing a few quick-growing root crops such as radishes or beets around the kale in early spring.

2 and 3. **Asian greens.** In Zones 5 and above, the leaves of the Asian greens from winter will still be growing strong in early spring but will soon bolt, so Michelle suggests sowing a fresh batch of mizuna.

4. **Lettuce.** Start seeds indoors in February in flats or pots and move the plants to the garden in early spring. Protect them with a row cover or cloche, and you'll be harvesting by April. Try planting them in a grid pattern to get the most out of your space.

5. **Pea shoots.** "They add a lovely, fresh pea taste in early spring and crop relatively quickly," says Michelle, adding that they can also be grown indoors in pots over the winter.

6. **French (garden) sorrel.** A small planting of sorrel will add a punch of lemon flavor to your salads. "I love the shape of 'Buckler Leaf' sorrel, and red-veined sorrel adds pleasing color to the salad bowl," Michelle says.

7. **Spinach.** Spinach grows well in the cool, damp weather of spring. "I grow baby leaves rather than full-grown, and I particularly like 'Apollo'," Michelle says. "Another is 'Bordeaux', which has lately been renamed 'Red Cardinal' and has lovely crimson stems and leaf veins."

8. **Arugula.** "I prefer wild arugula for its more peppery flavor and longer cropping," notes Michelle. Once the plants bolt, she adds the flowers to salads.

On the side. Supplement with a large pot of violas, whose flowers add color to salads, and forage for young dandelion leaves and hairy bittercress. "They add interesting flavors to a salad," says Michelle.

SUMMER BED

To avoid a gap between spring and summer crops, start your summer lettuce indoors, moving seedlings to the garden when the spring crops are waning.

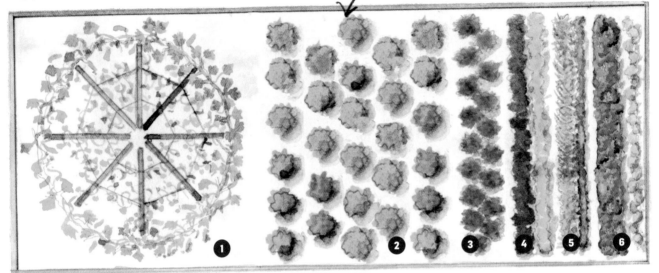

1. **Cucumbers and snow peas.** Two 'Marketmore 76' cucumbers (which "will probably spill over the allotted space!") are planted around the base of a teepee of 'Oregon Sugar Pod' or 'Shiraz' snow peas ("a fab new purple-podded variety"). Michelle suggests winding the plants around the teepee as they grow. Other cucumber varieties she enjoys include 'Diva', 'Crystal Apple', and 'Cornichon de Paris'.

2. **Lettuce.** Some of Michelle's favorites include 'Little Gem', 'Red Salad Bowl', 'Freckles', 'Lolla Rossa', and 'Lollo Bionda'. When you pick leaf lettuces, harvest the outside leaves, leaving the central core to grow, she advises. "This allows the lettuces to crop over many months without running to seed."

3. **Arugula.** Also called rocket or *roquette* for its rapid growth, arugula is very easy to grow and ready to harvest after just 30 days, depending on the variety. Quick-growing regular garden arugula has deep green, strappy leaves with a peppery zip, while wild types like 'Sylvetta' are slower-growing with smaller, finely cut foliage.

4–6. **Various herbs.** Michelle's favorite salad herbs are basil ("I particularly like Greek basil — it has smaller leaves which can be snipped into salads"), an anise-flavored herb such as fennel or chervil, and cilantro, which she allows to go to seed at the end of the season to produce coriander.

On the side. Supplement with a large pot of nasturtiums, which have edible leaves, flowers, and seeds, and a pleasing watercress-like flavor. "If space is tight, nasturtiums can be grown vertically and left to trail down," she says. She favors 'Empress of India' (mounding) or 'Jewel of Africa' (trailing).

Michelle also recommends a big pot planted with cherry tomatoes. "My favorites are 'Gardener's Delight' and 'Sungold', but 'Tumbler' is great for a hanging basket," she says.

AUTUMN BED

When the cucumber finishes producing, replace it with kale.

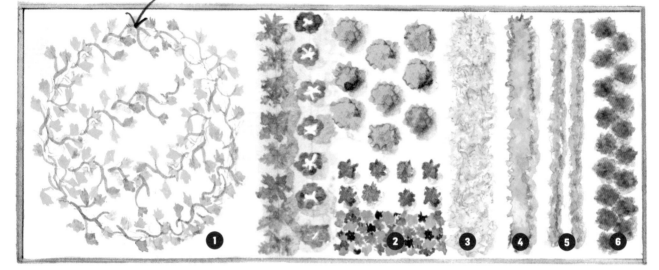

1. **Cucumber followed by kale.** "The cucumber from the summer will keep going until the first frosts, though the last fruits will be smaller," warns Michelle. "Replace it with kale plants started in flats or pots."

2. **Lettuce, spinach, and Asian greens.** Harvest the summer lettuce until it bolts to seed or turns bitter. As this happens, those rows can be cleaned out and sown with quick-growing, heat-tolerant Asian greens such as pak choi. Once the summer heat fades you can start sowing spinach. In early autumn, sow Asian mustard greens and mizuna for winter harvest.

3. **Fennel.** "I love bulb fennel at this time of the year," raves Michelle, who says that she has better success with late sowings of bulb fennel than the standard May planting. "The thinnings, the leafy fronds, and the bulb itself are all good in salads, and I particularly like 'Zefa Tardo'." 'Colossal' is a variety that Michelle often sows at the end of August for good-sized bulbs by late October.

4. **Cilantro.** For the longest-lasting harvest, stick to bolt-resistant types like 'Confetti' or 'Slow-bolt'. In the autumn, "I can usually manage a quick crop of cilantro if the weather stays warm like it has done in the past few years," she says.

5. **Chervil.** This hardy herb will winter over with a little protection in Zones 5 and above. For colder zones, Michelle suggests cold-tolerant claytonia (winter purslane) as an alternative.

6. **Arugula.** Choose a wild type like 'Sylvetta', which is slower to bolt than regular arugula.

On the side. Michelle keeps a big pot of parsley handy in winter, preferring the flat-leaved type. "This can be moved indoors toward the end of autumn for continued cropping," she says. To provide carrot leaves and roots for autumn and winter, she sows seed in a pot in late summer. "Carrot leaves can be used as another mild-tasting leaf for salads," adds Michelle. "A friend also makes a great carrot-top pesto, just as you would with basil!"

WINTER BED

Mâche, or lamb's lettuce, is a winter stalwart.

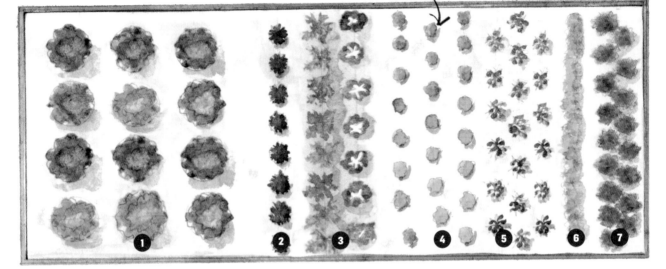

1. **Kale.** Michelle grows 'Red Russian' kale, which winters over in many areas of the United States, Canada, and the United Kingdom. As an alternative to 'Red Russian', you can grow the heirloom kale 'Lacinato' ('Nero di Toscana') for use in salads, but Michelle recommends picking it when small for the highest-quality greens. Gardeners in Zones 4 and below need to protect their winter kale and other greens with a mini hoop tunnel.

2 and 3. **Asian greens.** Mizuna is a favorite for its mild taste and lacy texture, and mustards such as 'Green Frills' and 'Red Giant' add a nice hot flavor. "I'm also trying tatsoi and komatsuna (Japanese mustard spinach) for the first time this year," she says. Michelle likes to sow the seed indoors in long, thin styrofoam trays for later transplanting to the garden.

4. **Mâche.** Also known as lamb's lettuce or corn salad, Michelle says lamb's lettuce was "the first of my winter stalwarts!" Michelle uses it as a "salad-building agent" and advises adding flavorful Asian mustards or land cress to the salad bowl to liven up the lamb's lettuce. She says "the leaves are rather small, hence the slightly larger area devoted to this crop."

5. **Land cress.** Also known as American cress, land cress is Michelle's "absolute winter favorite," she raves. "I love its peppery taste and almost indestructibility in winter."

6. **Claytonia.** Also known as miner's lettuce or winter purslane, claytonia is a North American native. It is an extremely cold-tolerant salad crop with a spinachlike flavor and succulent leaves. In late winter, tiny edible flowers will emerge and can be tossed in salads for added interest.

7. **Arugula.** For a winter crop, stick to the hardiest types of arugula. These include 'Sylvetta', 'Ice-Bred', and 'Astro'.

PERK UP YOUR WINTER SALAD

For a nutritional punch, Michelle recommends planting some sprouts (germinated seeds) and microgreens (tiny forms of young edible greens) indoors on a south-facing windowsill. "They crop in just days, so they are a great emergency standby, and the seeds add crunch, and the microgreens intense bursts of flavor," she says.

For sprouting, she suggests mung beans (bean sprouts), chick peas, and alfalfa. For flavorful microgreens she proposes radish, leeks, and coriander.

Edible School Garden

A school garden can be as simple as a few pots of plants or as elaborate as Benjamin Eichorn's "Edible School Garden," which includes a range of gardens, a chicken coop, a pizza oven, and a sheltered ramada for outdoor lessons. Benjamin's garden is meant for a warm region, but even cold-climate gardeners can find inspiration in his detailed design, adapting it by substituting suitable plants for their area.

> Offers plenty of inspiration and ideas to schools and other institutions

> Includes a range of plants and elements like a chicken coop, a pizza oven, and a greenhouse

> A central ramada shelters the outdoor classroom

Benjamin is a passionate supporter of edible school gardens — gardens that give children of all ages a chance to get their hands dirty planting seeds, tending crops, and eventually harvesting and eating the fruits of their labors. "Edible school gardens connect people to place, to food, to each other, and to the cycles of matter and energy on planet Earth," says Benjamin. "Eating from a garden that you helped to nurture is a most affirming experience." He notes that even if a school doesn't have the space or budget for a large garden, students can still grow food in large pots or half-barrel planters.

Site-specific. This plan for an edible school garden is based on a design Benjamin created for a specific school in the warm Californian climate. He cautions that each garden will need to be customized to the site, as well as to the goal and budget of the project. "We have built gardens that are made up of a few raised beds on a rooftop, and others that have over 2 acres and more than 100 fruit trees," he says. Yet with each design, he tries to include a handful of essential elements: a central meeting place, vegetable beds, fruit trees, plants for pollinators, a compost area, a greenhouse, and a tool shed. This garden, which is about 35 feet by 110 feet, contains many of these components. Benjamin has also added a pizza oven, a butterfly garden, herb beds, an area for native and drought-resistant plants, and a chicken coop that will house up to 10 hens for egg laying.

Pizza as motivation. The pizza oven is located on the west side of the garden and is an important educational tool. Benjamin admits that while getting young children excited about gardening is easy, once they enter their teens, it becomes more difficult as their curiosity and interest in vegetable cultivation dwindles. One good motivation is food — like pizza, which can be topped with school-grown ingredients.

In cooler regions, the olive orchard, mixed citrus, and fig and pomegranate plantings should be replaced with hardier fruit or nut trees.

Edible School Garden

"Edible school gardens help us remember who we are and where we come from. As Americans, this is a most necessary experience, as many of our communities are fragmented and desperately need to be (re-)woven together. The garden is the needle and food is the thread," says Benjamin Eichorn.

Benjamin's Garden Plan

Espaliered fruit tree

Compost bins

Tool Shed

Olive orchard

Grapes on trellis

Pizza oven

Pizza garden

Greenhouse

Mixed fruit trees

Chicken Coop

Benjamin's Favorite School Garden Plants

- **Mixed fruit trees:** Apples, Asian pears, peaches, Asian and European plums, and persimmons
- **Annual vegetables:** Tomatoes, cucumbers, summer squash, carrots, beets, and salad greens
- **Ramada vines:** 'Hayward' and 'Tormuri' kiwi
- **Mixed citrus:** 'Meyer' lemons and limes

- **Fig and pomegranate orchard:** 'Brown Turkey' and 'Black Mission' figs; 'Ambrosia' and 'Wonderful' pomegranates
- **Olive orchard:** 'Mission' and 'Manzanillo' olive trees
- **Native and drought-resistant flowering plants:** California poppy, island alum root, yarrow, and salvia
- **Butterfly garden:** Milkweed, angelica,

borage, zinnias, yarrow, and catmint
- **Herb garden:** Parsley, rosemary, tarragon, Greek oregano, sage, and thyme
- **Pizza garden:** 'Genovese' basil, 'Inchelium Red' garlic, and 'Tiny Tiger' heirloom tomato
- **Grapes:** 'Thompson Seedless'
- **Espaliered fruit trees:** Dwarf apples, pears, or other hardy fruit trees

With the cafeteria next to the garden, kids can learn how to prepare what they harvest!

School

Birdbath

Herbs

Butterfly garden

Mixed Citrus trees

Kiwi on ramada

Annual vegetables

Fig and pomegranate orchard

Native and drought-resistant flowering plants

Olive orchard

In cooler regions, replace the olive, citrus, fig, and pomegranate trees with apple, pear, and nut trees.

KIWI RAMADA

At the center of the garden Benjamin has placed a circular ramada — a semi-sheltered structure — to give teachers and students a place to meet, learn, and share information. Fruiting vines or other climbers should be planted and trained to scale the ramada, casting shade and enhancing the lesson space. Benjamin chose kiwi vines to scale the circular enclosure, which is surrounded with beds of annual vegetables.

If you decide to grow kiwis in your own garden, be sure to include at least two vines — a male and a female — to ensure pollination.

Backyard Brewer's

I n her plan for a brewer's garden, Rebecca Kneen takes hops production from the "back forty" to the backyard. Armchair brewers daydreaming about crafting their own microbrews can now rise from their seats and start growing the ingredients for their custom ales and lagers: organic hops, flavoring flowers and herbs, fruits, and more. Rebecca demonstrates how easy it is to transform an average-size backyard into a small-scale hops operation with a design that's both productive and beautiful.

❯ A beautiful backyard landscape that supplies hops and brewing plants for custom beer

❯ A large hop-covered pergola provides summer shelter for outdoor meals

❯ Diverse plant collection includes fruits, berries, flowers, vegetables, herbs, and grains

Because hops are an essential ingredient in beer brewing, giving flavor and aroma to the finished product, they take center stage in Rebecca's garden. The dominant element of the landscape is the 9- by 12-foot wooden pergola that lends its sturdy support to 10 rampant hops vines while creating a shady retreat for al fresco meals. "Hops growing requires infrastructure," says Rebecca. "They are huge plants that are tall and wide, and you need to allow 12 to 18 feet in height for each plant and 3 to 5 feet in width." She also notes that a spot with full sun and good soil is a must, and she recommends digging in generous amounts of compost each year.

Managing hops vines. At the base of the hops vines, Rebecca has planted mostly annual plants including Thai basil, cilantro, and barley. The hops rhizomes need to be dug up each spring and pruned back — a process that could damage perennial plants or bulbs. "Some large mature crowns can produce 20 to 30 rhizomes per plant, and if such exuberant growth is left unchecked, the plants will soon cover the entire acreage with a solid mass of plant material!" warns Rebecca. The pruned rhizomes can be used to expand production or be shared with fellow brewers. The two small patches of barley are included mostly for show. "But it could also be used for home malting experiments or to make smoked grains for specialty beers," Rebecca suggests.

Another patch of hops vines lines the north side of the garden, with the fast-growing plants supported on tall posts, preferably made of cedar because of its durability. The posts should be at least 10 to 12 feet tall and spaced 3 to 5 feet apart. "A heavy wire (12-gauge high-tensile wire is ideal) or aircraft cable should run between the posts," says Rebecca, adding that each year, heavy-duty string, sisal twine, coir, or paper twine should be tied to the cable for the hops to climb up.

Tasty and practical mulch. At the base of these post-supported hops,

Rebecca's Garden Plan

30' DEEP X 40' WIDE

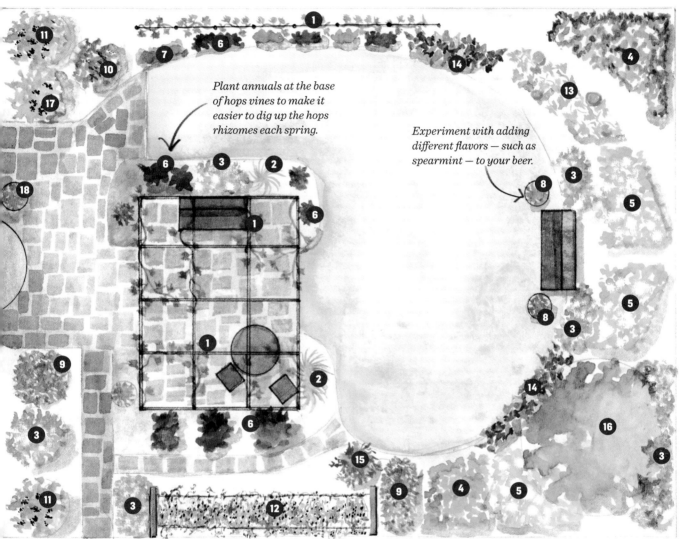

Plant annuals at the base of hops vines to make it easier to dig up the hops rhizomes each spring.

Experiment with adding different flavors — such as spearmint — to your beer.

Main Ingredients

1. Hops
2. Barley

Bittering Agents

3. Yarrow
4. Meadowsweet
5. Angelica

Brewing Adjuncts

6. Thai basil
7. Cilantro
8. Spearmint (in pots)
9. Bee balm
10. Red currant
11. Black currant
12. Raspberries
13. 'Red Kuri' winter squash, pie pumpkins, or giant pumpkins
14. Potatoes
15. Juniper
16. 'Adams' crab apple
17. Jostaberry
18. Lemon in pot

more cilantro and Thai basil, as well as potatoes, are planted to create a living mulch. "You can cook the potatoes and eat them with the beer, or you can use them in the beer as a starch source, much like rolled oats or flake barley," says Rebecca. She suggests that the cilantro be used in homemade salsas to accompany the beer and some homemade potato chips. Cilantro seeds, better known as coriander, can be collected to make spiced winter ales or wheat beers. The Thai basil, on the other hand, adds anise notes to beer; the flowering tops can also be used to flavor vinegar, turning it a soft pink.

Thanks to a suggestion by Rebecca's partner, Brian MacIsaac, she has included several pots of aromatic spearmint — another brewing herb that can be used fresh in beer. Brian also suggests a juniper for making sahti (a traditional beer from Finland); juniper berries and branches can be included "either in the brew or as a strainer for hot wort to make an easy version," Rebecca says.

Using flowers. Throughout summer, the tall flowers in this plan— meadowsweet, angelica, yarrow, and bee balm — provide long-lasting color to the garden. "All of these flowers are used for bittering beer," says Rebecca. "Bittering in beer is important because without it the malty, grainy flavors would lack structure and backbone, creating a very soft, flabby, and sweet flavor." She points out that all of the herbs and flowers used in brewing also have medicinal uses, which makes beer both flavorful and healthful.

If space and local by-laws allow, Rebecca suggests including a beehive in the garden, perhaps tucking it behind the pumpkins or beneath the crabapple. The honey could be used as an additional source of sugar in various beers, or used to make mead.

The small selection of fruiting trees and shrubs serves several purposes. These plants add an important visual element because they provide year-round structure to the garden. They also yield juicy fruits that can be used to flavor homebrews, or eaten right off the bush! A row of raspberries are supported on a T-bar wire trellis. Jostaberries are a cross between a black currant and a gooseberry; these vigorous plants can grow over 6 feet tall. A crab apple (for cider or beer) anchors one corner, and red and black currants anchor another.

Pumpkin ale. The northeast corner of the garden is home to pumpkins or winter squash, which can be used for pies or pumpkin ale, and the big ones as casks. "[They] also make a good base plant for the hops vines, as the pumpkins would only be shading the vines late in the season when it doesn't matter," says Rebecca.

SELECTING THE RIGHT HOPS

Pick your hops varieties carefully based on what you intend to make from them. "Any grower of hops must be very familiar with the uses of hops and the desired acid and oil profiles for any given variety," says Rebecca. Another reason to choose wisely: the plants will stick around for a while. "Hops crowns live for up to 25 years in good conditions, and each vine will produce up to 2 pounds (0.8 kg) of hops a year," says Rebecca.

- **'Goldings' and 'Challenger'.** Used primarily as aroma hops by brewers, these are lovely hops for many English and Irish-style ales.

- **'Mt Hood'.** An American cultivar of a Hallertauer hop, this can be used to make lagers and pilsners.

- **'Cascade'.** Used only to make American-style IPA or Pale Ale.

- **'Willamette'.** An American cultivar of Fuggle hops, it's hardy and very useful for the classic English mild ale.

- **'Magnum'.** An excellent bittering hop.

TOBY ADAMS & ANNIE NOVAK'S

OTTO Pizza Garden

ere's a quick way to engage children in the garden: First, find out their favorite food (Answer: pizza); second, plant a pizza garden! Everyone loves a piping hot pizza. If you tell children this pizza-shaped plan is all about their toppings, they'll thoroughly enjoy growing their own oregano, sweet peppers, onions, and eggplants. Who knows, they may even learn to like their vegetables!

❯ Engages children in growing their own food by appealing to their soft spot: pizza!

❯ Popular toppings such as tomatoes, oregano, basil, and peppers grow in giant "slices"

❯ A portion of the "crust" is wheat, demonstrating the plant used to make flour

One of the most popular plots in the Ruth Rea Howell Family Garden, the centerpiece of the Edible Academy at the New York Botanical Garden, is the pizza plot. "The shape of this garden goes a long way to establish the relationship between the food we eat — sometimes maybe too often, like a slice of pizza — and the plants these foods are made from," observes Director Toby Adams. "It is an awesome combination of factors for us: to see the pizza shape, to smell the aroma of fresh oregano, to taste a fresh basil leaf, and to feel the resistance of a swollen onion as it's tugged out of the ground by its leaves."

Variations on the theme. The pizza garden was sponsored by the famed OTTO pizzeria and designed by Toby Adams and Manager Annie Novak. "The garden has six slices that are arranged to resemble a pie and measures 15 feet in diameter," notes Toby. A smaller pizza could be constructed in a compact backyard. Or, if space is truly at a premium, the plan can also be applied to a large circular container, like a half-barrel, to create a pizza pot.

Making the "crust." To make the pizza garden as authentic as possible, Toby and Annie included a stand of wheat as part of the "crust" or outer border of the beds. "We allocate about 1 foot for the wheat on three of our slices and use oregano (used to spice most pizza tomato sauces) to form the outside or 'crust' of our other three slices," says Toby.

Two-foot-wide paths separate the triangular beds and allow easy access for garden chores, harvesting, and inspecting the plots for pests or other problems. To keep the paths clean and weed-free, a mulch of bark, grass clippings, shredded leaves, or straw can be laid between each slice. Stones, bricks, or untreated wood planks can be used to edge the slice-shaped beds if desired.

Selecting toppings. Each slice-shaped bed is planted with a mixture of traditional pizza toppings: tomatoes, sweet peppers, eggplants, onions, basil, and pepperoni (just kidding). If preferred, each bed could instead be dedicated to a single topping. "We always seek out varieties of plants that boast outstanding flavor, and balance that with productivity whenever possible, due to the volume of visitors at the New York Botanical Garden that we share the harvest with," says Toby. "Where possible, Annie and I made an extra effort to include Italian varieties of the plants, such as 'Rosa Bianca' eggplant or 'Marconi Red' sweet pepper."

Versatile tomatoes. Tomatoes do double-duty as a topping and as a star ingredient in pizza sauce. "The tomatoes we selected, also Italian heirlooms, are all varieties best used for saucing," Toby notes. Other areas of the Ruth Rea Howell Family Garden are planted with varieties that are best eaten fresh. If you want a steady

supply of tomatoes to top your pies, consider including a cherry tomato variety such as 'Sungold', 'Ildi', or 'Black Cherry' in your pizza plot. The clumps of aromatic basil and oregano growing in the garden can be clipped and added to the tomato sauce as well as liberally sprinkled on top of the pizza itself.

OTHER TOPPING IDEAS

Spice up your pizza garden with these additional topping plants:

Artichokes. Start seeds indoors in late winter, moving plants to the garden once all risk of frost has passed in late spring. Try 'Imperial Star', a variety that will produce tender artichokes the first season and can even be grown in Zone 5.

Arugula. Add a handful of just-picked arugula to the top of a pizza as soon it comes out of the oven for a tasty treat! Any arugula will do, but 'Astro' is particularly reliable.

Asparagus. As a perennial vegetable, asparagus is very easy to grow, but it does require a good site. Look for full sun and well-drained soil, and amend with plenty of compost or aged manure before planting. Give the plants three years to establish and then enjoy an eight-week harvest period each spring. Opt for high-producing male cultivars like 'Jersey Giant' or 'Jersey Knight'.

Spicy peppers. For those who prefer their food with a little heat, include some hot peppers such as 'Early Jalapeño' or 'Hot Banana', a heavy-yielding hybrid that produces 6-inch-long sunny yellow fruits.

Toby and Annie's Garden Plan

15' DIAMETER

Two-foot-wide mulched paths make it easy to access the beds.

Many plants, like oregano, do double-duty as ingredients in the sauce and as pizza toppings.

For the "Crust"

1. **Spring wheat:** 'Glenn Hard Red' (1 planting in spring and 1 in midsummer)

2. **Greek oregano**

For the Pie Center

3. **Onions:** 'Red Zeppelin' and 'Walla Walla'

4. **Basil:** 'Mostruoso', 'Finissimo', 'Genovese', and 'Purple Ruffles'

5. **Tomatoes:** 'Amish Paste', 'Rosso Sicilian', and 'Martino's Roma'

6. **Eggplants:** 'Rosa Bianca', 'Galine', and 'Nubia'

7. **Sweet peppers:** 'Marconi Red', 'King of the North', 'Jimmy Nardello', and 'Tolli's Sweet Italian'

Year-Round Front-Yard Garden

If you're planning on growing food in the front yard, why not make the landscaping visually pleasing while you're at it? Rebecca Sweet's stunning front-yard garden shows you how. At the heart of her garden, a curved flagstone pathway meanders through three triangular beds that are surrounded by an extensive collection of edible and ornamental plants including 'Kaleidoscope' abelias, oakleaf hydrangeas, 'Hidcote' lavenders, and 'Sunshine Blue' blueberries.

> A "California fusion" style garden that blends decorative plants with fruits, vegetables, and herbs

> Berms around the vegetable beds add height to the flat space

> Compact and well-mannered edibles were chosen to keep the garden tidy

Garden designer and writer Rebecca Sweet enjoys creating gardens — often front-yard landscapes — in her signature "California fusion" style that blends the personal goals of her clients with regionally appropriate, often native plants. "The result is a garden that is layered, lush, and environmentally friendly," says Rebecca.

Rebecca's design for a front-yard garden is highly productive — supplying a selection of fresh herbs, vegetables, and fruits 12 months of the year — but it is also beautiful. It includes ornamental shrubs, perennials, and grasses for additional interest, texture, and color. "This year-round garden was designed to be enjoyed by the homeowners as well as the neighbors," says Rebecca. "It consists of colorful low-water, low-maintenance, and evergreen shrubs and perennials, as well as well-behaved edibles." Her high-performance food plants include evergreen herbs like creeping thyme, sage, and rosemary, plus long-performing blueberries and citrus plants.

The appeal of berms. Unlike traditional vegetable gardens planted in straight rows or raised beds, Rebecca's garden boasts a slight berm along the front, which adds to its ornamental appearance. A berm, which is much less expensive than a retaining wall, is constructed from one or more low mounds of soil. If these are formed into slightly undulating hills, they will blend in naturally with the surrounding garden. "Subtle berms surround the vegetable beds to add much-needed height variation in this small, flat garden, but also to remedy the problem of our naturally occurring, poor-draining clay soil," she says.

Stepping stones lead the way through the decorative pea gravel, which Rebecca uses as a water-conserving, weed-suppressing mulch that will also reflect the summer's heat back to the edibles. To soften the gravel and stones, she has added low-growing creeping thyme, dwarf grasses, and native salvias.

Adding food plants to the front yard can ruffle the feathers of lawn-loving neighbors, but when the garden is as ornamental as Rebecca's, it will become a point of pride for the community.

A chorus of diverse plants. While the berms set the stage, the garden headliners are the plants — artichokes with spiky silvery green foliage, compact but productive blueberry shrubs, and a trio of pineapple guava. Backup harmony is provided by carefully selected ornamentals — 'Kaleidoscope' abelia (an evergreen shrub with an ever-changing color show), the four-season oakleaf hydrangea, and the deep purply red foliage of 'Plum Passion' heavenly bamboo. Rebecca praises the performance of the three blueberry bushes. "In addition to offering tasty fruit in the summer, many varieties have beautiful hues of red, peach, and orange in their fall foliage, adding another level of interest to the border," she says. Plus in a mild climate many blueberries are semi-evergreen, making them ideal for long-lasting beauty.

A tidy appearance. When choosing edibles for a front-yard garden, Rebecca recommends giving a little more thought to appearances. "While the neighbors may appreciate the shared bounty of your garden, they won't appreciate an overgrown and messy-looking vegetable garden," she says. She recommends bypassing rambunctious sprawlers such as indeterminate tomatoes, zucchini, and pumpkin vines and instead planting well-mannered compact varieties of vegetables. If you must have tomatoes, choose varieties advertised for growing in containers, such as 'Micro Tom' or 'Patio.'

Drought-tolerant choices. Gardening in an arid region like California also requires seeking out drought-tolerant edibles. "While most edibles require ample amounts of water, there are some that can thrive on less, such as rosemary, thyme, sage, many varieties of citrus, pineapple guava, figs, and persimmons," says Rebecca. In warm climates, Rebecca recommends pineapple guava (*Feijoa sellowiana*) as a possible alternative for a small tree. "It's evergreen (perfect for screening!) but also thrives in both full sun or partial shade, making it perfect for many areas of the garden," she says. Other outstanding characteristics include its showy red-and-white flowers that are followed by "deliciously sweet fruit!"

Irreplaceable rosemary. Rebecca feels that no Californian garden would be complete without some rosemary plants. "They provide year-round beauty (flowering in late winter with blooms of blue or white) and are delicious in many common dishes," she notes, adding that with sizes ranging from low-growing, sprawling groundcovers to towering 5-foot specimens, there is a rosemary plant perfect for any spot in your garden.

BERM BASICS

A berm is essentially just a mound of earth with sloped sides built to add privacy, filter noise, separate different areas of a garden, screen undesirable views, create a windbreak, or provide additional planting areas. Taller than a raised bed, a berm is often 18 to 24 inches higher than the surrounding ground. In her plan, Rebecca uses a low berm to collect rainwater and provide visual interest to the garden. Though a large berm will require a significant amount of soil, the volume of soil needed can be reduced by using fill like branches, logs, brush, gravel, or stones as an inner layer of the berm. Generally, berms should be curved and made slightly asymmetrical for a more attractive and natural-looking shape that will blend better into the landscape.

Rebecca's Garden Plan

24' DEEP X 42' WIDE

For the front yard, Rebecca chooses compact plants that have a tidy appearance.

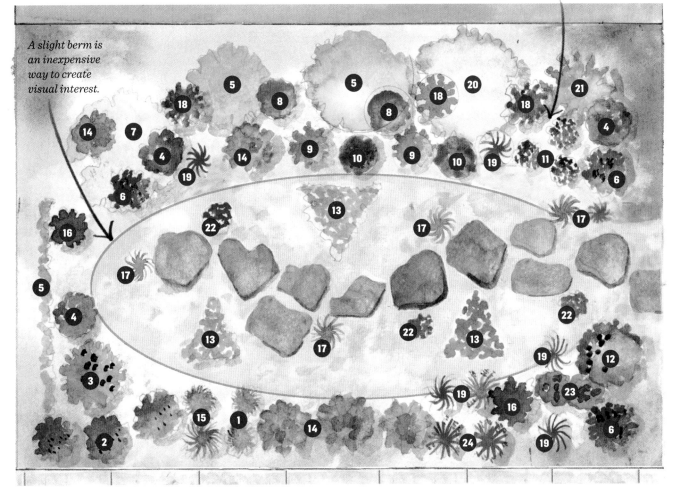

A slight berm is an inexpensive way to create visual interest.

Edibles

1. 'Honey Melon' dwarf pineapple sage (3)
2. 'Sunshine Blue' blueberries (3)
3. 'Wonderful' pomegranate (1)
4. Dwarf Meyer lemons (3)
5. Pineapple guavas (3, trained as standards)
6. 'Purpurascens' garden sage (3)
7. 'Morello' or 'Montmorency' sour cherry tree (1)
8. 'Gilt Edge' silverberries (2)
9. Artichokes (2)
10. 'O'Neal' blueberries (4)
11. Borage (3)
12. Dwarf Bearss lime tree (1)
13. Lemon or 'Lime' thyme (6)

Ornamentals

14. 'Howard McMinn' manzanitas (5)
15. Reed grasses (2)
16. 'Pink Splendor' mirror plants (3)
17. Berkeley sedges (4)
18. 'Snow Queen' or 'Alice' oakleaf hydrangeas (2)
19. 'Breeze' dwarf mat rush (lomandra, 7)
20. 'Bloodgood' Japanese maple
21. 'Newellii' cestrum
22. 'Nuevo Leon' autumn sage (3)
23. 'Matrona' sedum (2)
24. 'Hidcote' or 'Munstead' lavenders (3)

Edible Campus

With the global population surging past 7 billion, we're going to need to find new ways to feed ourselves. With that in mind, Professor Vikram Bhatt launched the Edible Campus garden at McGill University in 2007 to develop new ways to grow more food in urban places. The community-university partnership grows fruits, vegetables, and herbs in underused areas of the campus.

> Showcases how unused areas of schools, universities, and businesses can be put to use growing food

> Relies on homemade, self-watering planters and vertical structures

> Excess harvests can be donated to local food banks and shelters to support the community

The Edible Campus explores ways to increase food production in cities, particularly in spaces typically not used for plant growth —rooftops, balconies, and paved areas. "The garden serves as a model to showcase how anyone can produce their own vegetables, green their neighborhoods, and build healthy communities," says Reena Mistry, a research associate at McGill.

A true partnership. The Edible Campus is a "true community-university partnership." Alternatives and Santropol Roulant (local community action organizations) provided the impetus and necessary manpower needed to coordinate the garden — especially during the growing season when students are on holiday — and McGill University provided the growing space. Not only does the garden "green up" the university campus, but also it provides organic homegrown food to elderly and mobility-impaired residents of Montreal. "The garden is a product of a synergistic team and has ensured the establishment and continued success of the project," says Vikram.

Careful site selection. Before the sites for the Edible Campus garden were chosen, the McGill School of Architecture's Minimum Cost Housing Group, led by Vikram, carried out a detailed site survey to evaluate the available light and the shadows cast by the many buildings. The planting areas chosen after the site survey included a concrete terrace, plaza, and large stair wall. Within a short period of time the planted areas were transformed from sterile urban deserts into lush, high-producing jungles. "Although Montreal's growing season is very short, generally spanning mid-May to mid-October, the garden has annually produced more than 1 ton of crops since 2010," says Vikram.

Some gardens are focused on vertical crops, while others spotlight herbs, vegetable production, or berries. At the height of summer, vigorous pole beans scale the concrete stair wall while groups of containers around Burnside Hall spill over with tomatoes, cucumbers, peppers, celery, basil, eggplants, squash, salad greens, and many other crops. Clover

McGill's Garden Plan

Vining crops in containers cover a dull gray concrete stair wall with a lush green living tapestry.

Climbing plants are trained to go up archways that pedestrians can walk under.

MacDonald Stewart Library

Vertical Garden

Container Garden

Berry Patches

Vertical Garden

Burnside Hall

Raised Bed Garden

Kids' Garden

Raised Bed perennial garden

is commonly planted along the edges of the raised-bed gardens as a living mulch. This low-growing legume is able to withstand the gardening traffic, and it adds nitrogen to the soil, blocks weed growth, helps to retain soil moisture, and attracts bees.

At the start of the project, the Edible Campus occupied about 1,300 square feet for its container garden, but it has since grown dramatically. "The garden has expanded to over 2,150 square feet of raised beds, with 300 containers that grow about 30 types of vegetables (50 varieties) as well as an assortment of berries and fine herbs," says Reena. The growing containers follow the basic rules of green living — reduce, reuse, and recycle — as 98 percent of those containers are made from recycled materials or reused buckets or large plastic tubs that were customized with a bottom water reservoir to collect and release excess rain or irrigation water back to the crops.

Volunteer help. Much of the garden work is done by volunteers who are kept up-to-date through an e-mail list. The volunteer crew is made up of McGill University students and many residents of Montreal. "We have had a broad variety of people express interest in the project," says Vikram. There are five volunteers who work in two-hour shifts, pitching in twice a week to water, weed, and harvest the bounty growing between the university buildings. In spring they help to set up, fill, and plant the containers; in autumn, they gather and store the various pots for the winter. As for the food harvested from the edible campus, Vikram says that it is prepared in the kitchen of Santropol Roulant's Meals-on-Wheels service, where it is used to nourish and provide a connection to community members who may be isolated.

Vermicompost. Recycling the garden waste is an essential component of the Edible Campus and there is a worm composter nearby at Santropol Roulant. "The worm composter transforms 40 percent of the restaurant kitchen's organic wastes, and at the beginning of the season, the compost from the worm bins is mixed with the old soil, enriched with biomass, and aerated with perlite," says Reena. The containers are then planted with seedlings grown in the nearby greenhouse.

The success of the Edible Campus sends the message that — through the work of individuals and community organizations — food can be grown productively in urban spaces. Prof. Bhatt hopes that the edible garden at McGill University will inspire and encourage city and town dwellers to look differently at their urban surroundings, and to seek out underused or neglected areas where food can be grown and shared with the community.

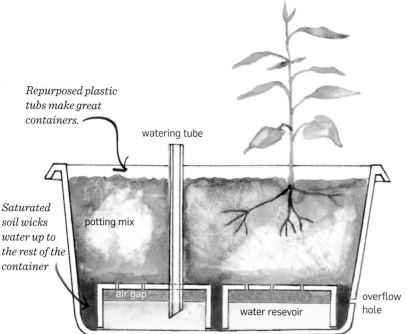

Repurposed plastic tubs make great containers.

watering tube

Saturated soil wicks water up to the rest of the container

potting mix

air gap

water resevoir

overflow hole

The containers in the Edible Campus are self-watering, meaning that they have a reservoir of water at the bottom from which the plants can draw when necessary.

McGill's Plants

CONTAINER GARDENS

- **Tomatoes:** 'Sapho', 'Green Zebra', 'Mountain Princess', 'Trust', 'Massada', 'Jaune Flamme', 'Totem', and 'Polbig'
- **Sweet peppers:** 'King of the North', 'Carmen', and 'Ace'
- **Hot peppers:** 'Early Jalapeño', 'Hungarian Hot Wax', and 'Ring of Fire'
- **Eggplants:** 'Black Beauty', 'Traviata', and 'Falcon'
- **Cucumbers:** 'Marketmore 76', 'Green Finger', 'Fanfare', and 'Diva'
- **Lettuce:** 'Jericho', 'Lovelock', 'Black Seeded Simpson', 'Green Star', and 'Spretnak'
- **Mesclun mix**
- **Arugula**
- **Bok choy:** 'Prize Choi' and 'Mei Quin Choy'
- **Celery:** 'Tango'
- **Parsley:** 'Giant Italian'
- **Basil:** 'Sweet Thai' and 'Aroma'
- **Leeks:** 'Runner' and 'King Richard'
- **Swiss chard:** 'Silverado', 'Ruby Red', and 'El Dorado'
- **Spinach:** 'Renegade'
- **Fennel:** Florence (bulb) and 'Orion'
- **Caraway**
- **Marigolds**
- **Nasturtiums**

RAISED-BED GARDEN

- **Kale:** 'Lacinato'
- **Swiss chard:** 'Silverado', 'Ruby Red', and 'El Dorado'
- **Kohlrabi:** 'Azur Star' and 'Korridor'
- **Turnips:** 'Purple Top White Globe' and 'Hakurei'
- **Beets:** 'Touchstone Gold', 'Red Ace', and 'Chioggia Guardsmark'
- **Radishes:** 'Celesta', 'Miyashige', and 'French Breakfast'
- **Peas:** 'Sugar Snap' and 'Sugar Ann'
- **Zucchini:** 'Dark Green'
- **Carrots:** 'Danvers Half Long', 'Purple Haze', and 'Yaya'
- **Garlic**
- **Onions**

RAISED-BED PERENNIAL GARDEN

- **Asparagus**
- **Tarragon**
- **Savory**
- **Thyme**
- **Sage**
- **Chives**
- **Caraway**
- **Sorrel**
- **Anise hyssop**
- **Lavender**
- **Fennel:** Florence (bulb) and 'Orion'
- **Oregano**
- **Mint**
- **Rosemary**
- **Basil:** 'Sweet Thai' and 'Aroma'
- **Dill:** 'Bouquet'
- **Cilantro:** 'Caribe'
- **Stevia**
- **Lemon verbena**
- **Strawberry**

VERTICAL GARDENS

- **Pole beans:** 'Kentucky Wonder' and 'Rattlesnake' (grown on twine)
- **Lettuce:** 'Jericho', 'Lovelock', 'Black Seeded Simpson', 'Green Star', and 'Spretnak'
- **Bok choy:** 'Prize Choi', 'Mei Quin Choy'
- **Celery:** 'Tango'
- **Parsley:** 'Giant Italian'
- **Basil:** 'Sweet Thai' and 'Aroma'

BERRY PATCHES

- **Blueberries**
- **Gooseberries**
- **Raspberries**
- **Currants**
- **Saskatoon berry**

KIDS' GARDEN

- **Pole beans**
- **Bok choy:** 'Prize Choi', 'Mei Quin Choy'
- **Celery:** 'Tango'
- **Parsley:** 'Giant Italian'
- **Basil:** 'Sweet Thai' and 'Aroma'
- **Marigold**

Backyard Beekeeper's Garden

I*t's a fact: bee populations are in decline,* and gardeners are noticing fewer and fewer bees each year. It's therefore more important than ever to take bees into consideration when planning and planting edible gardens. In his plan for a backyard beekeeper's garden, Kenny Point offers plenty of suggestions for enticing and supporting bee populations, and he details the various types of hives and shelters he uses in his own garden.

> Includes several types of beehives and houses, as well as a pond and a birdbath

> Diverse vegetables, berries, and fruits were selected for their bee forage qualities

> A kiwi vine trellis provides a shaded retreat for watching the bees work

Kenny's garden plan is modeled after his own property and includes many edible and ornamental plants, as well as shelters, water sources, and assorted elements that will support the various communities of birds, bees, and pollinators. "There are plants that flower and fruit at various times so that there is a flow of pollen and nectar throughout the seasons for bees and other pollinators," notes Kenny, adding that he favors native and heirloom selections rather than newly developed or hybrid varieties.

Protecting pollinators. Shelter for bees and other pollinators is also a very important part of Kenny's garden. His shelters range "from bee houses to hives, and even standing stalks or stems where insects can overwinter," he says. He especially enjoys the top-bar hives, which are horizontal structures, often supported on legs, with simple bars where the bees attach their comb. In particular, Kenny loves peeking in the windows located at the top of his top-bar hives. It allows him to see the inner workings of the colony without disrupting it.

The pond, located near the back patio, is used as a water source by the insect and pollinator populations in the backyard. The birdbath can also be used by bees and pollinators if a few stones are added to give them landing sites.

Feed for bees. To ensure happy bees, Kenny grows a wide variety of plants, focusing on those that produce nectar and pollen for honeybees. The food plants include fruit and nut trees and shrubs, as well as vegetables and herbs. On the back patio, tender figs and citrus fruits are grown in pots and brought indoors or sheltered for the winter. The fig trees spend the winter in an unheated area, like a garage, while the citrus plants are kept in a heated room. A blueberry hedge runs along the side of the house, providing a long season of tasty fruits — and even longer seasons of beautiful color — with little work. "Blueberries are easy to grow if you build and amend the soil to their liking," Kenny points out; the challenge is protecting the fruits and young shoots from wildlife.

Kenny provides more forage for his beloved bees and other pollinating insects by allowing clover and dandelions to grow in his lawn. The clover will also fix nitrogen, boosting soil fertility, and the early flowering dandelions will offer much-appreciated pollen to the bees in spring. Kenny encourages bug-munching birds to visit his garden by hanging bird houses and feeders throughout the property.

Kiwi trellis. Not one to ignore an opportunity, Kenny has built a T-bar style trellis near the patio to support food-bearing vines and offer shade to the sunny patio. The sturdy structure bears the weight of rampant kiwi (or grape) vines (pollinated by bees) while shielding the space from the hot summer sun. "The trellis adds to the ornamental appeal of the landscape" he says, noting that he chose to grow kiwi vines over grapes because he was looking for a more challenging and unusual crop.

Favorite edibles. Like most food gardeners, Kenny has a lot of favorite plants, yet his top edibles are garlic and kale. "Garlic is so easy to grow and has medicinal properties," he says, noting that gourmet varieties taste so much better than the garlic found in the supermarket. "Kale is another favorite because it is so nutritious, can be grown year-round, and is a very attractive plant." He allows some of his overwintered kale plants to flower each spring as a source of pollen for his bees.

Kenny also enjoys growing heirloom eggplants and gourmet mushrooms. "They're so unusual, mysterious, and beneficial," he says. When perusing his favorite seed catalogs looking for edibles to grow, Kenny finds that he usually comes back to the heritage varieties. "There are so many plants that I love and my focus is on heirloom varieties because they are so interesting, different, and come with a lot of history behind them," he says.

The joy of keeping bees. Kenny notes that he has found beekeeping to be a relatively low-maintenance task. "For the most part they do all the work and are pretty self-sufficient, so it is possible to keep bees and be somewhat hands-off in the process." To anyone interested in tending bees, he recommends that they pick up a good book and join a bee club, where they can find an experienced mentor. "They are fascinating creatures with incredible lessons to share and an amazing system of organization, communication, and social affairs," he adds.

Kenny also points out that the bees in his hives travel far beyond his own yard, benefiting the many gardens in the community, but because of this, they are susceptible to pesticides that may be applied on other properties. He stresses the importance of gardening organically to maintain the balance of nature.

KENNY'S BEEKEEPING TIPS

- **Variety is key.** A good mix of many different plants is important for a bee-friendly garden. He also recommends having a water source somewhere on the property.

- **Shelter is also critical.** Shelters can be bee houses for solitary bees, hives for honeybees, and even standing stalks or stems where some types of bees and other pollinating insects can lay eggs or overwinter. Place bee houses and hives in a sunny location sheltered from wind and near a water source.

- **Garden organically!** Kenny doesn't use any pesticides, not even organic ones, because they can damage bee populations. Instead, he relies on beneficial and predatory insects to control destructive bugs.

Kenny's Favorite Plants

HEIRLOOM VEGETABLES, FRUITS, AND FLOWERS

- **Tomatoes:** 'Amazon Chocolate', 'Black Krim', 'Pineapple', and 'Green Zebra'
- **Tomatillos:** 'Purple Keepers Modern Landrace' and 'Plaza Latina Giant Green'
- **Peppers:** 'Red Marconi' sweet; 'Fish', and 'Habanero' hot
- **Eggplants:** 'Rosa Bianca', 'Thai Long Green', and 'Listanda de Gandia'
- **Alliums:** 'Music' and 'Siberian' garlic; 'Gray' shallots; potato onions (multiplier onion similar to shallots); 'Bleu de Solaize' leeks
- **Artichokes:** 'Green Globe' and 'Imperial Star'
- **Asparagus:** 'Purple Passion'
- **Strawberries:** Red alpine, white alpine, and various everbearing

- **Squash:** 'Yellow Scallop' and 'Trombocino' summer squash
- **Watermelons:** 'Sugar Baby'
- **Edible flowers:** 'Alaska' nasturtiums, 'Flashback Mix' calendulas, borage, chives, daylilies, and garland (edible) chrysanthemum
- **Root crops:** 'Hollow Crown' parsnips, 'Lutz Green Leaf' beets, burdock (gobo), fingerling potatoes, and salsify
- **Salad crops:** 'Bright Lights' Swiss chard, Malabar spinach, 'Red Giant' mustard, arugula, and leaf celery
- **Thornless blackberries**
- **Ginger**
- **Cardoon**

OTHER BEE-FRIENDLY PLANTS

- **Berries:** Juneberries, filberts, and 'Black Lace' elderberries
- **Dwarf apple trees:** 'Pomme Gris', 'Yellow Newton Pippen', and 'Ashmeads Kernel' (include at least two different varieties for pollination)
- **Ornamental fruiting shrubs:** Red and black currants, aronias, and gooseberries

- **Highbush blueberries:** 'Bluegold', 'Reka', 'Duke', and 'Elliott'
- **Kiwi vines:** 'Hardy Meader' (male), 'Arbor-eat-um', 'Meyers Cordifolia', and 'Ananasnaya' ('Anna') on trellis

Composting Area

Solitary bee house

Locust tree

Kenny's Garden Plan

Locate your hives where they are sheltered from the wind but receive plenty of sunshine.

Evergreens

Tool Shed

Mushroom Logs

...erries

Top-bar Beehives

Langstroth Beehives

Sugar Maple

Trellis

Pond

Container Garden

...eirloom garden

Rain barrels

Highbush blueberries

HOUSE

Birdbath

Herbs

Dwarf Apple Trees

ornamental edibles

Native perennial plants

Allow dandelions to grow on your lawn to give your bees some extra pollen.

Best-Tasting Tomatoes

Tomatoes are the most popular garden crop in North America, with seed catalogs offering hundreds of varieties in a diverse range of fruit sizes, colors, and shapes. So how on earth do you decide which ones to grow in your garden? Just ask the Tomato Man, also known as Craig LeHoullier, who shares a descriptive list of his all-around favorite tomatoes.

> ❯ Highlights some of the most delicious heirloom varieties available, including 'Cherokee Purple'

> ❯ Plants are grown in pots and staked to reduce maintenance and improve yield

> ❯ Also includes eggplants, peppers, and herbs

Homegrown, vine-ripened tomatoes are one of the true joys of summer. Avid gardeners start their own plants from seed in early spring, babying their seedlings until they're ready to be moved into the garden after the last frost. Soon star-shaped yellow flowers appear, quickly followed by fruits that come in every color, size, and shape imaginable. "Tomatoes are, in a way, the perfect crop," says Craig. "Because they taste best when picked at the peak of ripeness, the flavors and textures will generally be superior to anything purchased."

Why heirlooms? Craig is a fan of heirloom varieties, and his garden plan includes many of his favorites. (Craig's view is that an heirloom variety is one that's been grown for at least 60 years and is open-pollinated, which means that you can save the seeds for future harvests.) Many heirloom tomatoes have histories as rich as their flavors, and some tomato lovers like to choose their varieties based on these stories. "With heirlooms, there is such fascination with the histories of many varieties, plus there is the amazing range of colors, sizes, flavors, shapes, and textures, which allow for very creative uses," says Craig.

Tomatoes are not a difficult crop to grow. For the best-tasting tomatoes, adequate sunlight is essential, so begin by picking an area with well-draining, rich soil and at least 8 hours of sunlight. Craig suggests that gardeners with less direct sun focus

focus on smaller-fruited varieties. He also advises leaving 3 feet between plants and 4 feet between rows to allow for adequate air circulation and optimum sunlight. People without garden space and those with soil quality or plant disease problems can grow tomatoes successfully in large containers.

Growing up. Craig recommends that tomato plants be grown vertically. "It allows you to fit more varieties into the garden, harvest a higher percentage of unblemished fruit, makes it easier to spot insect and disease issues early, and allows you to pick without stepping on and injuring the low plant parts," he says. "But, perhaps most importantly, growing vertically means less contact with the soil, which can vastly improve the health of the plant." If tomato plants are allowed to sprawl on the soil, they run a much greater risk of infection from disease pathogens.

To support the heavy, vigorous vines of indeterminate tomato plants, Craig advises 6-foot-tall cages made from concrete reinforcing wire and held steady by a sturdy stake. "Caging is much lower-maintenance than staking and pruning and provides a very high yield with no apparent drop-off in fruit size or quality," he says. Plus the rampant foliage of caged plants provides cover for the ripening fruit, preventing sunscald and also ensuring plenty of photosynthesis for the best flavor. Determinate tomatoes can also become quite large, but not overly tall, so for these Craig favors the 3- to 4-foot-tall wire cages available at garden centers. "The cone cages are actually perfect for them," he says. "You can also allow them to sprawl on the ground as long as the soil is mulched to prevent soil-borne tomato diseases."

Serving up the harvest. As Craig's massive tomato harvest starts to roll in, he and his wife, Susan, get to work turning their bounty into fresh salsa, roasted tomato sauce, gazpacho, and tomato bisque. "For those tomatoes we hold most dear, we just slice a variety of colors and flavors on a plate and add a drizzle of olive oil, some black pepper, and shredded basil leaves," he says. This allows the distinctive flavor of each variety to shine.

DETERMINATE VS. INDETERMINATE TOMATOES

Determinate tomatoes, also called bush tomatoes, grow to an easily managed height, produce flower clusters at the ends of their branches, and stop growing. Most of their fruit ripens over a very concentrated time span, which is ideal if you wish to can tomatoes or make a big batch of tomato sauce. The growth of determinate tomatoes is easier to control than indeterminate types, so they are usually supported with wire tomato cages and short stakes. Craig notes that 'Roma' is perhaps the most widely grown determinate tomato.

Indeterminate tomatoes, known as vining tomatoes, are vigorous plants that continue to grow and produce fruit throughout the growing season, only stopping when Jack Frost arrives in autumn or disease claims them. They produce their flower clusters on lateral shoots and can reach over 7 feet in height, so they require sturdy support in the form of tall, cylindrical cages or wooden stakes. The vast majority of non-hybrid tomatoes are indeterminate.

Craig's Favorite Tomatoes

'Cherokee Purple'. This heirloom is said to have been grown by the Cherokee Indians, but it was nearly lost through time. Craig received some seeds in the mail and was able to name and reintroduce it to the world in 1990. 'Cherokee Purple' is considered to be one of the best-tasting heirloom tomatoes in cultivation. The plants produce large purple fruits with reliable productivity and a superb, full flavor.

'Stump of the World' (or 'Mortgage Lifter'). 'Stump of the World' produces 1-pound reddish pink fruits. According to Craig, it boasts better productivity than 'Brandywine' but

has the same superb flavor that is often described as "rich," "complex," and "incredible." 'Mortgage Lifter', an even larger pink tomato, is a worthy substitute with a colorful history.

'Red Brandywine' (or 'Druzba'). A favorite among tomato lovers, 'Red Brandywine' bears medium-sized, deep red fruits that Craig recommends for those who like the smooth, typical red tomato. "The flavor is nicely balanced, and the plants offer great production," he adds. 'Druzba', from Bulgaria, is its equal in flavor and production.

'Speckled Roman'. This super-productive large, striped paste tomato is very attractive and makes great sauce, and Craig says that it's equally fantastic in salads. The fruits

grow between 4 and 6 inches long and have attractive orange-red skins with irregular golden stripes.

'Cherokee Green' (or 'Aunt Ruby's German Green'). A cousin of the revered 'Cherokee Purple', this unusual variety sports large green tomatoes — yes, they remain green when fully ripe! — with a blush of amber. It's considered to be one of the best-tasting green tomatoes. "Equally delicious, 'Aunt Ruby's German Green' has clear, rather than amber skin, making the optimum picking time a bit of a challenge," says Craig.

'Sungold' hybrid cherry. One of the most popular cherry tomatoes in cultivation — and the lone hybrid on Craig's list — 'Sungold' bears a heavy crop of orange  cherry-sized fruits with an intense sweetness that bursts in the mouth. "It's unmatched," says Craig. "It has a unique sweet flavor, and the plants are very prolific." Pick the small fruits as soon as they're ripe to avoid splitting. "Try to eat just one. I dare you," he says with a laugh.

'Cherokee Chocolate'. Craig calls this open-pollinated variety "a must-grow tomato." The fruits are large and brown and possess all the qualities of 'Cherokee Purple' but in a different-colored package. "This tomato was the result of a skin color mutation of 'Cherokee Purple' that I found in my garden in 1995," he recalls, adding that a flesh color mutation of 'Cherokee Chocolate' in 1997 led to 'Cherokee Green' (opposite page). "This family of tomatoes has great and unpredictable genes!"

'Lillian's Yellow Heirloom'. This heirloom is prized by tomato lovers for its large, meaty yellow fruits. The glowing goldfinch-colored tomatoes are juicy and sweet, nearly seedless,

and it has become a staple in Craig's garden. "It always makes my top-five list for flavor," he says, noting that his wife, Susan, may relish this tomato most of all.

'Opalka'. Hailing from Poland, this heirloom paste tomato is a must for creative chefs, says Craig. "'Opalka' bears fruits twice the size and ten times the flavor of the standard Roma varieties," he declares. The 5-inch-long tomatoes are meaty, sweet, and have few seeds.

'Lucky Cross' and 'Little Lucky'. This was Craig's first tomato "creation" from an accidental cross that involved the legendary 'Brandywine'. The medium to large bicolored fruits, growing on a potato leaf plant (leaves have smooth edges), have a flavor that ranks among the best of the open-pollinated varieties. Each tomato is a vibrant golden yellow, splashed with red. Craig also developed a smaller, rounded tomato with equal favor and

the same lovely mix of yellow and red, which he calls 'Little Lucky'.

'Yellow Brandywine' and 'Kellogg's Breakfast'. According to Craig, the large orange fruits of the potato leaf variety 'Yellow Brandywine' help fill out the color range of his mostly heirloom garden plan. "This is a pumpkin orange–colored tomato with attitude!" he says. "It has a nice tart bite, which is rare for yellow or orange types." For the same vibrant sunny color, but a sweeter taste treat, Craig says that 'Kellogg's Breakfast' can't be beat.

'Black Cherry'. Described by Craig as a "cherry-sized bite of 'Cherokee Purple'," the vigorous plants literally drip with 1-inch, claret-colored fruits. "It's a tomato-producing machine," says Craig.

Appendix

Resources

Gardening Supplies

aHa! Modern Living
877-704-3404
www.ahamodernliving.com

AgroHaitai, Ltd.
519-647-2280
www.agrohaitai.com

Baker Creek Heirloom Seed Co.
417-924-8917
www.rareseeds.com

Clinger Clips
info@clingerclip.com

http://clingerclip.com

Down to Earth Distributors, Inc.
800-234-5932
www.down-to-earth.com

Gardeners Supply Company
888-833-1412
www.gardeners.com

Hang-A-Pot
Hanging Gardens
sales@hangapot.com

www.hangapot.com

Kitazawa Seed Company
510-595-1188
www.kitazawaseed.com

Merrifield Garden Center
877-560-6222
www.merrifieldgardencenter.com

Plants on Walls
770-406-6330
www.plantsonwalls.com

Seed Savers Exchange
563-382-5990
www.seedsavers.org

Tainong Seeds, Inc.
760-598-2348
www.tainongseeds.com

Urbio Vertical Garden
www.myurbio.com

Wattelez
flowall@orange.fr

http://en.flowall.com
Producer of Flowall products

Plant List

Note: Edible ornamentals such as calendulas and sunflowers appear in both lists.

EDIBLES (includes edible ornamentals, herbs, and hops)

Common Name	Latin Name
almond	*Prunus dulcis*
amaranth	*Amaranthus* species; usually *A. hypochondriacus* or *A. cruentus* for seeds
amaranth, vegetable grown for leaves	*Amaranthus tricolor*
angelica	*Angelica archangelica*
anise hyssop	*Agastache foeniculum*
apple	*Malus* species
apricot	*Prunus armeniaca*
aronia	*Aronia* species
artichoke	*Cynara scolymus*
arugula, cultivated	*Eruca sativa*
arugula, wild or rustic	*Diplotaxis tenuifolia*, formerly classified as *Eruca sylvatica*
asparagus	*Asparagus officinalis*
barley	*Hordeum vulgare*
basil	*Ocimum basilicum*
basil, African blue perennial	*Ocimum kilimandscharicum × basilicum* 'Dark Opal'
basil, bush	*Ocimum minimum*
basil, holy	*Ocimum tenuifolium*
basil, lemon	*Ocimum × citriodorum*
basil, purple	*O. basilicum purpurascens*
basil, Thai	*O. basilicum* 'Horapha'
bay	*Laurus nobilis*
beans, bush	*Phaseolis vulgaris*
beans, borlotti (a type of dry bean)	*Phaseolis vulgaris*
beans, cannellini (a type of dry bean)	*Phaseolis vulgaris*
beans, fava	*Vicia faba*
beans, garbanzo	*Cicer arietinum*

Common Name	Latin Name
bean, hyacinth	*Lablab purpurea,* synonym *Dolichos lablab*
beans, lima	*Phaseolis lunatus*
beans, pole	*Phaseolis vulgaris*
beans, romano or flat-pod	*Phaseolis vulgaris*
beans, scarlet runner	*Phaseolis coccineus*
beans, yard-long	*Phaseolis unguiculata*
bee balm	*Monarda* species and cultivars
beets	*Beta vularis*
bitter melon	*Momordica charantia*
blackberry	*Rubus* species
blueberry, highbush	*Vaccinium corymbosum*
borage	*Borago officinalis*
bottle gourd	*Lagenaria siceraria*
broccoli	*Brassica oleracea* Italica Group
broccoli raab	*Brassica rapa* Ruvo Group
Brussels sprouts	*Brassica oleracea* Gemmifera Group
burdock/gobo	*Arctium lappa*
cabbage	*Brassica oleracea* Capitata Group
cabbage, Chinese, including Napatype cabbages	*Brassica rapa* Pekinensis Group
calendula	*Calendula officinalis*
Canada wild ginger	*Asarum canadense*
caraway	*Carum carvi*
cardoon	*Cynara cardunculus*
carrots	*Daucus carota* var. *sativus*
cauliflower	*Brassica oleracea* Botrytis Group
celeriac	*Apium graveolens* var. *rapaceum*

Common Name	Latin Name	Common Name	Latin Name
celery	*Apium graveolens*	garlic, elephant	*Allium ampeloprasum*
chamomile	*Matricaria recutita*	garlic chives (Chinese chives)	*Allium tuberosum*
cherry, Nanking/bush	*Prunus tomentosa*	ginger	*Zingiber officinale*
cherry, sweet	*Prunus avium*	goji berry	*Lycium barbarum*
cherry, sour	*Prunus cerasus*	gooseberry	*Ribes hirtellum, R. uva-crispa,* and *R. uva-crispa*
chervil	*Anthriscus cerefolium*		
chestnut	*Castanea dentata*	grape	*Vitis* species
chives	*Allium schoenoprasum*	grape, purple-leaved	*Vitis vinifera* 'Purpurea'
chrysanthemum, garland (tong ho, shungiku)	*Glebionis coronaria,* synonym *Chrysanthemum coronarium*	groundnut	*Apios americana*
		hairy bittercress	*Cardamine hirsuta*
cilantro	*Coriandrum sativum*	honeyberry/Haskap berry	*Lonicera caerulea* var. *edulis*
claytonia/miner's lettuce	*Claytonia perfoliata*	hops	*Humulus lupulus*
collards	*Brassica oleracea* Acephala Group	horseradish	*Armoracia rusticana*
cornelian cherries	*Cornus mas*	husk cherry/ground cherry	*Physalis prinosa*
crab apple	*Malus* species	Jerusalem artichoke	*Helianthus tuberosus*
cress, garden	*Lepidum sativum*	jicama	*Pachyrhizus erosus*
cucumber	*Cucumis sativus*	johnny jump ups	*Viola tricolor*
currant, red	*Ribes rubrum, R. sativum,* and *R. petraeum*	jostaberry	*Ribes × culverwellii*
		juniper	*Juniperus* species
currant, black	*Ribes nigrum*	kale	*Brassica oleracea* Acephala Group
dandelion	*Taraxacum officinale*	kale, Portugese (couve tronchuda cabbage, sea kale)	*Brassica oleracea* Acephala Group
daylily	*Hemerocallis* species and hybrids		
daylily, orange	*Hemerocallis fulva*	kiwi, hardy	*Actinidia arguta*
dill	*Anethum graveolens*	kiwi, fuzzy	*Actinidia deliciosa*
eggplant	*Solanum melongena*	kohlrabi	*Brassica oleracea* Gongylodes Group
elderberry	*Sambucus nigra, S. canadensis*	land cress (upland cress, American cress)	*Barbarea verna*
endive	*Cichorium endivia*		
epazote	*Chenopodium ambrosiodes*	leek	*Allium porrum*
fennel	*Foeniculum vulgare*	lemon	*Citrus limon*
fig	*Ficus carica*	lemon balm	*Melissa officinalis*
filbert	*Corylus avellana*	lemongrass	*Cymbopogon citratus*
flax	*Linum usitatissimum*	lemon verbena	*Aloysia citrodora*
flowering quince	*Chaenomeles japonica*	lettuce	*Lactuca sativa*
gai lan (Chinese broccoli)	*Brassica oleracea* Alboglabra Group	lime, Bearss	*Citrus × latifolia*
garlic	*Allium sativum*		

Edibles (continued)

Common Name	Latin Name
lovage	*Levisticum officinale*
luffa gourd	*Luffa cylindrica* and *Luffa acutangula*
mache (lamb's lettuce, corn salad)	*Valerianella locusta*
marigold, Signet	*Tagetes tenuifolia*
marjoram	*Origanum majorana*
marjoram, golden	*Origanum vulgare* 'Aureum'
mayapple	*Podophyllum peltatum*
melons	*Cucumis melo*
mibuna	*Brassica rapa* Japonica Group
milkweed, common	*Asclepias syriaca*
mint, Corsican	*Mentha requienii*
mint, ginger	*Mentha × gracilis* 'Variegata'
mint, 'Mojito'	*Mentha × villosa*
mint, peppermint	*Mentha × piperita*
mint, spearmint	*Mentha spicata*
mizuna	*Brassica rapa* Japonica Group
mulberry	*Morus* species
mulberry, black	*Morus nigra*
mustard greens	*Brassica juncea, B. rapa*
nasturtium	*Tropaeolum majus*
nettles	*Urtica dioica*
okra	*Abelmoschus esculentus*
olive	*Olea europaea*
onion	*Allium cepa*
orange	*Citrus sinensis*
oregano, common	*Origanum vulgare*
oregano, dwarf	*Origanum vulgare* 'Compactum'
oregano, golden	*Origanum vulgare* 'Aureum'
oregano, Greek	*Origanum vulgare* ssp. *hirtum*
oregano, Italian	*Origanum onites*
pak choi/bok choy	*Brassica rapa* Chinensis Group
parsley	*Petroselinum crispum*
parsnip	*Pastinaca sativa*
pawpaw	*Asimina triloba*
peach	*Prunus dulcis*
peanut	*Arachis hypogaea*

Common Name	Latin Name
pear	*Pyrus communis*
pear, Asian	*Pyrus pyrifolia* and other species
peas	*Pisum sativum*
peas, snap	*Pisum sativum* var. *macrocarpon*
peas, snow	*Pisum sativum* var. *macrocarpon*
pepper, sweet	*Capsicum annuum*
pepper, hot or chili	*Capsicum annuum*
persimmon	*Diospyros virginiana* and *Diospyros kaki*
pineapple guava	*Acca sellowiana*
plums, Japanese or Asian	cultivars of *Prunus salicina*
plums, European	cultivars of *Prunus domestica*
pomegranate	*Punica granatum*
poppy, breadseed	*Papaver somniferum*
potato	*Solanum tuberosum*
pumpkin	*Cucurbita* species
purslane	*Portulaca oleracea*
quince	*Cydonia oblonga*
quinoa	*Chenopodium quinoa*
radish	*Raphanus sativus*
radish, daikon	*Raphanus sativus* var. *longipinnatus*
rampion	*Campanula rapunculus*
ramps	*Allium tricoccum*
raspberry	*Rubus idaeus*
raspberry, black	*Rubus occidentalis*
rhubarb	*Rheum rhabarbarum*
rose, rugosa	*Rosa rugosa*
rosemary	*Rosmarinus officinalis*
rutabaga	*Brassica napus*
savory, common or summer	*Satureja hortensis*
scallions/green or spring onions/ bunching onions	*A. fistulosum*
scorzonera	*Scorzonera hispanica*
sea buckthorn	*Hippophae rhamnoides*
sedum	*Sedum* species and cultivars
serviceberry	*Amelanchier* species

Common Name	Latin Name	Common Name	Latin Name
shallot	*Allium cepa*	sumac, Tiger Eyes	*Rhus typhina* 'Bailtiger'
shiso	*Perilla frutescens*	sunflower	*Helianthus annuus*
skirret	*Sium sisarum*	sweet cicely	*Myrrhis odorata*
sorrel, French or garden	*Rumex scutatus*	sweet corn	*Zea mays*
		sweet potato	*Ipomoea batatas*
sorrel, red-veined	*Rumex sanguineus*	Swiss chard	*Beta vulgaris* Cicla Group
soybean/edamame	*Glycine max*	tarragon	*Artemisia dracunculus*
spicebush	*Lindera benzoin*	tatsoi	*Brassica rapa* Narinosa Group
spinach	*Spinacia oleracea*	thyme, common or English	*Thymus vulgaris*
spinach, Malabar	*Basella rubra*		
spinach, New Zealand	*Tetragonia tetragonioides*	thyme, golden	*Thymus* 'Aureus'
		thyme, lemon	*Thymus × citriodorus*
squash, acorn	*Cucurbita pepo*	thyme, silver	*Thymus* 'Argenteus'
squash, butternut	*Cucurbita moschata*	tomatillos	*Physalis ixocarpa*
squash, kabocha (Japanese pumpkin)	*Cucurbita maxima*	tomato	*Lycopersicum esculentum, Solanum lycopersicum*
squash, spaghetti	*Cucurbita pepo*	Turkish rocket	*Bunias orientalis*
squash, summer	*Cucurbita pepo*	turnip	*Brassica rapa*
squash, winter	*Cucurbita maxima, C. moschata*	watercress	*Nasturtium officinale*
squash, zucchini	*Cucurbita pepo*	watermelon	*Citrullus lanatus*
stevia	*Stevia rebaudiana*	wheat	*Triticum* species
strawberry	*Fragaria × ananassa*	wild ginger	*Asarum canadense*
strawberry, alpine	*Fragaria vesca*	winter melon (wax gourd)	*Benincasa hisbida*
strawberry guava	*Psidium littoral*	yacon	*Smallanthus sonchifolius*

ORNAMENTALS

Common Name	Latin Name	Common Name	Latin Name
abelia	*Abelia × grandiflora*	autumn sage	*Salvia greggii* 'Nuevo Leon'
African daisy	*Osteospermum ecklonis*	bamboo, golden	*Phyllostachys aurea*
alstroemeria, Fabiana Princess Lilies	*Alstroemeria ×* 'Zaprifabi'	bee balm	*Monarda* species and cultivars
		Berkeley sedge	*Carex tumulicola*
astilbe	*Astilbe* species and cultivars	boxwood	*Buxus* species and hybrids
Australian fuschia	*Correa* species and cultivars	butterfly weed	*Asclepias tuberosa*

Ornamentals (continued)

Common Name	Latin Name
butterfly bush	*Buddleja davidii*
calendula	*Calendula officinalis*
California poppy	*Eschscholzia californica*
calla lily	*Zantedeschia aethiopica*
cardinal flower	*Lobelia cardinals*
Carolina cherry laurel	*Prunus caroliniana*
catmint	*Nepeta* species
celosia	*Celosia* species and cultivars
cestrum	*Cestrum* species and cultivars
cleome	*Cleome hassleriana*
comfrey, Russian	*Symphytum × uplandicum*
cordyline	*Cordyline* 'Cardinal'
cosmos	*Cosmos bipinnatus*
crab apple	*Malus* species; some have edible fruits
cranesbill, 'Biokovo'	*Geranium × cantabrigiense* 'Biokovo'
cranesbill, 'Espresso'	*Geranium maculatum* 'Espresso'
crape myrtle	*Lagerstroemia indica*
creeping Jenny (yellow loosestrife)	*Lysimachia nummularia* 'Aurea'
crinum lily	*Crinum bulbispermum*
crocosmia	*Crocosmia × crocosmiiflora*
dahlia	*Dahlia* species and hybrids
dittany of Crete	*Origanum dictamnus*
dwarf mat rush (lomandra)	*Lomandra longifolia*
echeveria	*Echeveria* species
ferns	many species; *Blechnum gibbum* 'Silver Lady'
feverfew	*Tanacetum parthenium*
flowering quince (technically edible but usually ornamental)	*Chaenomeles × superba*
gardenia	*Gardenia jasminoides*
germander	*Teucrium chamaedrys*
ginkgo	*Ginkgo biloba*
goldenrod	*Solidago* species

Common Name	Latin Name
grape, purple-leaved	*Vitis vinifera* 'Purpurea'
grass, blue fescue	*Festuca glauca*
grass, dwarf fountain	*Pennisetum alopecuroides*
grass, Japanese forest	*Hakonechloa macra*
grass, red fescue	*Festuca rubra*
heavenly bamboo	*Nandina domestica*
hellebore, Corsican	*Helleborus argutifolius*
heucheras	*Heuchera* hybrids
holly	*Ilex* species
honeysuckle, Early Dutch	*Lonicera periclymenum* 'Belgica'
honeysuckle, Late Dutch	*Lonicera periclymenum* 'Serotina'
hopseed bush	*Dodonaea viscosa*
hostas	*Hostas*
hydrangea	*Hydrangea arborescens* 'Annabelle', *H. macrophylla* 'Blushing Bride', *H. paniculata* 'Limelight', *H. paniculata* 'Little Lamb'
hydrangea, oakleaf	*Hydrangea quercifolia*
iris	*Iris* species
island alum root	*Heuchera maxima*
Japanese maple	*Acer palmatum*
lamb's ears	*Stachys byzantina*
larkspur	*Consolida ambigua*
lavender, English	*Lavandula angustifolia*
lavender, French	*Lavandula intermedia* or *L. dentata*
lavender, Spanish	*Lavandula stoechas*
liriope	*Liriope* species
lily, oriental	*Lilium* hybrids
lobelia, annual	*Lobelia erinus*
locust, black	*Robinia pseudoacacia*
manzanita	*Arctostaphylos densiflora*
marigold	*Tagetes patula* hybrid
marigold, signet	*Tagetes tenuifolia*
meadowsweet	*Filipendula ulmaria*
mecardonia	*Mecardonia caespitosa* and hybrid

Common Name	Latin Name
million bells, 'Superbells Blackberry Punch'	*Calibrachoa* hybrid
mirror plant	*Coprosma repens*
mock orange	*Philadelphus* species and hybrids
mountain ash	*Sorbus* species
nasturtium	*Tropaeolum majus*
oak	*Quercus* species
oregano, ornamental	*Origanum* 'Kent Beauty', *O.* 'Norton Gold', *O.* 'Showy Pink'
pansy	*Viola × wittrockiana*
penstemon	*Penstemon digitalis* 'Husker Red', *P. heterophyllus* 'Margarita BOP'
peony	*Paeonia* species and hybrids
petunia	*Petunia × hybrida*
phlox	*Phlox* species and hybrids
pineapple sage	*Salvia elegans*
purple coneflower	*Echinacea purpurea*
reedgrass	*Calamagrostis* species
rhaphiolepis	Indian hawthorn, *Rhaphiolepis indica*
rhododendron	*Rhododendron* species and hybrids
rose, Harrison's yellow	*Rosa × harisonii*
rose, hedgehog	*Rosa rugosa* var. *alba*
rose, Nootka	*Rosa nutkana*
rose, red leaf	*Rosa glaua*, synonym *R.rubrifolia*
rose, rugosa	*Rosa rugosa*
salpiglossis	*Salpiglossis sinuata*
salvia	*Salvia* species and hybrids
santolina	*Santolina chamaecyparissus*
geranium, apple	*Pelargonium odoratissumum*
geranium, peppermint	*Pelargonium tomentosum*
geranium, rose	*Pelargonium graveolens*
schizanthus, 'Angel Wings'	*Schizanthus × wisetonenensis* Angel Wings Group
sedum/stonecrop	*Sedum* 'Matrona', *Sedum telephium* 'Lajos' ('Autumn Charm')
silverberry, 'Gilt Edge'	*Elaeagnus × ebbingei* 'Gilt Edge'

Common Name	Latin Name
Solomon's seal	*Polygonatum biflorum*
snapdragon	*Antirrhinum majus*
stock	*Matthiola incana*
strawflowers	*Xerochrysum bracteatum*, synonym *Bracteantha bracteata*
sumac, Tiger Eyes	*Rhus typhina* 'Bailtiger'
sunflower	*Helianthus annuus* and cultivars
sunset hyssop	*Agastache rupestris*
sweet alyssum	*Lobularia maritima*
sweet peas	*Lathyrus odoratus*
sweet potato vine	*Ipomoea batatas*
turtlehead	*Chelone lyonii*
tuberous begonia	*Begonia × tuberhybrida*
valerian	*Valeriana officinalis*
veronica	*Veronica* hybrid 'Whitewater'
viburnum, American cranberrybush	*Viburnum trilobum*
white bower vine	*Pandorea jasminoides*
witch hazel	*Hamamelis virginiana* and hybrids
yarrow	*Achillea millefolium*
yew	*Taxus baccata* and hybrids
zinnia	*Zinnia elegans*, *Z. marylandica* 'Pinwheel', *Z. hybrida* 'Profusion White'

GREEN MANURE CROPS

Common Name	Latin Name
annual ryegrass	*Lolium multiflorum*
buckwheat	*Fagopyrum esculentum*
clover, white Dutch	*Trifolium repens*
cowpeas	*Vigna unguiculata*
oats	*Avena sativa*
rye	*Hordeum vulgare*
vetch mix	*Vicia villosa* and other species
winter rye	*Secale cereale*

Index

Page numbers in *italic* indicate illustrations;
those in **bold** indicate charts.

wheat, 92, 227
wildflowers, 48
Wildlife-Friendly Garden, 96–99
window boxes, 53, 55, *55*
Windy City Harvest, 52
winter rye, 89
winter savory, 183
Winter Vegetables, Fall &, 211–13
witch hazel, 33

Y

yacons, 123
yarrow, 35, 170, 206, 207, 220, 223
Year-Round Front-Yard Garden,
    228–231
yew (*Taxus*), 39
        hedge, 35

Z

Zachos, Ellen, 12, 201–3
Zammit, Paul, 12, 21–24
zinnia, 33, 35, 36, 153, 154, 195, 220
zucchini, 33, 45, 68, 95, 98, 107, 119,
    123, 133, 136, 159, 170, 177, 179,
    195, 235

Other Storey Titles You Will Enjoy

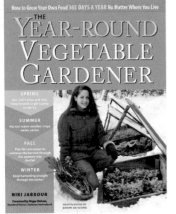

ALSO BY NIKI JABBOUR

The Year-Round Vegetable Gardener

How to grow your own food 365 days a year, no matter where you live!

256 pages. Paper. ISBN 978-1-60342-568-1.
Hardcover. ISBN 978-1-60342-992-4

The Vegetable Gardener's Bible, 2nd edition by Edward C. Smith

The 10th anniversary edition of the vegetable gardening classic, with expanded coverage and additional vegetables, fruits, and herbs.

352 pages. Paper. ISBN 978-1-60342-475-2.
Hardcover. ISBN 978-1-60342-476-9.

The Vegetable Gardener's Container Bible by Edward C. Smith

Detailed, illustrated advice on how to choose the right plants for a small-space container garden and care for them throughout the season.

264 pages. Paper. ISBN 978-1-60342-975-7.
Hardcover. ISBN 978-1-60342-976-4.

Vertical Vegetables & Fruit by Rhonda Massingham Hart

Grow your food up, with tepees, trellis, stacking pots, multilevel raised beds and more.

176 pages. Paper. ISBN 978-1-60342-998-6.

Week-by-Week Vegetable Gardener's Handbook
by Ron Kujawski & Jennifer Kujawski

Detailed, customizable to-do lists to break down gardening into simple, manageable tasks.

200 pages. Paper with partially concealed wire-o. ISBN 978-1-60342-694-7.

These and other books from Storey Publishing are available wherever quality books are sold or by calling 1-800-441-5700.
Visit us at *www.storey.com* or sign up for our newsletter at *www.storey.com/signup.*